Rethinking Public Relations

Why is PR so popular, yet so disparaged?

Why can PR people not produce for themselves what they are employed to produce for others – good reputations?

PR is a £2.3 billion UK industry with up to 50,000 jobs, a poor reputation, yet a pervasive influence on politics and markets.

Historically, it has been mostly weak propaganda and market boosterism, yet it escapes sustained academic scrutiny.

PR needs reform because it will not go away, and because it continues to grow. It must become reasoned persuasion. Until that happens through voicing more competitive group intermediation and through internal reform, it stands convicted as charged: contributing to communicative inequality in liberal market democracies.

Kevin Moloney has worked in PR for over 20 years, for public and private organisations, as well as being self-employed. He has taught one of the first UK PR degrees at Bournemouth University for the last decade, where he is Principal Lecturer in Communications.

Routledge Advances in Management and Business Studies

Rethinking Public Relations

The spin and the substance

Kevin Moloney

London and New York

First published 2000
by Routledge
11 New Fetter Lane, London EC4P 4EE

Simultaneously published in the USA and Canada
by Routledge
29 West 35th Street, New York, NY 10001

Routledge is an imprint of the Taylor & Francis Group

Typeset in Baskerville by Wearset, Boldon, Tyne and Wear
Printed and bound in Great Britain by Biddles Ltd, Guildford and King's Lynn

British Library Cataloguing in Publication Data
A catalogue record for this book is available from the British Library

Library of Congress Cataloging in Publication Data
Moloney, Kevin, 1943–
    Rethinking public relations : the spin and the substance / Kevin Moloney.
       p. cm.
    Includes bibliographical references.
     1. Public relations. I. Title.

HD59.M62 2000
659.2—dc21   99-086064

ISBN 0–415–21759–8

To Muriel, Rachael and Paul

Few truths have ever won their way against the resistance of established ideas save by being overstated.

Isaiah Berlin

Contents

Acknowledgements

Acknowledgements are due to those who stimulated the questions which have called forth the responses in this book. PR people in the UK come first, because I know from long years of experience the joys and sorrows of the job. What they do and what I did is the first cause of this book. Those experiences created the motivation to set out the benefits and costs of PR, and to strike the balance between them. My judgement is often critical of PR, but it does not deny PR or seek to bury it. It argues, instead, for a clearer understanding of its utility to liberal, democratic, market-orientated states such as the UK, and urges the reform of PR practice in the interests of a more equitable society.

Second, there are acknowledgements to the ten cohorts of students at Bournemouth University who have asked many, many questions about why they came to the south coast of England. This author knows that if you do not teach, you do not fully understand.

Third, there are the many teaching and working colleagues who have sparked a thought, amended another, who have said yes, no and maybe to arguments. These colleagues are full-time at Bournemouth University, are associated with it as part-time teachers, examiners or advisers, come from 16 UK campuses gathered under the umbrella of the PR Educators' Forum, or gave information on behalf of their organisations.

In particular, thanks to Valerie Cowley, Phil MacGregor, Danny Moss, Paul Noble, Richard Reader, Tom Watson, Jon White and Christine Daymon who read drafts, to Karen Ephram who was research assistant, and to Prof. Stephen Letza who made financial support possible.

Errors of fact and lapses of style are, of course, mine alone, as are all opinions.

Kevin Moloney
Bournemouth University
January 2000

Abbreviations

Public relations is referred to as 'PR' because that is by far the most common referent in use. For ease of reading, it is varied to 'public relations' here and there. The Institute of Public Relations is the 'IPR' while the equivalent US representative body, the Public Relations Society of America is 'PRSA'. 'PRCA' is the Public Relations Consultants' Association and 'APPC' is the Association of Professional Political Consultants. The 'ASA' is the Advertising Standards Association.

1 'It's a PR job'

The argument in overview

Public relations is done today in the UK by more interests, causes and people than ever before; yet it suffers from a low reputation. This is an extraordinary irony: that PR has to endure the fate that it seeks to avoid for those in whose name it works. Say 'PR'[1] and not far away from mind and mouth are concerns about the manipulation of opinion, the promotion of the rich and powerful, the one-sided presentation of fact and figure. Why is this? Because PR is a propaganda tool?[2] Because it is a hidden persuader? Because it undermines elected representatives and neutral civil servants? Because it sells fresh fruit and pension policies? Because it is puffery and not worth respect? Who holds these opinions? How do PR people react? Are there benefits to PR? Does it matter that PR is held in low opinion? If it does matter, what can be done?

These are the issues explored in this book, and they coalesce into a proposition: PR is a noticeable and widespread activity in contemporary UK society but, despite this pervasiveness, it attracts low levels of reputation. Why? It could be that this asymmetry of prominence to reputation is eccentric, small change in the currency of our daily, social relations, and not worth a second look. This would not be the case, however, if the low esteem were the consequence of legitimate concerns which affect the quality of our public lives.

This book seeks answers to these questions. **Chapter 2** looks at the pervasiveness of PR and its low reputation. PR is now an industry, when it was once an adjunct to advertising and marketing. It was once done by a group of people called 'the gin and tonic brigade', recruited from the louche end of the metropolitan middle classes; now school-leavers want a degree in it. It is an activity which is now openly embraced by the Monarchy with the appointment of a Communications Secretary to the Queen. It has its clique of leading practitioners in the House of Lords. It is an instinctive reaction of all modern governments and, very publicly, the reaction of New Labour. Indeed, at times one cannot see the policies and actions of the government because of the fluttering around it of public relations people. The Church of England has a spin doctor: the Dean of Westminster Abbey had one in the public tussle with the Master of Choristers he sacked; and Oxford

University flourishes with one. There is hardly an organised group of people in the land, from the local tennis club to ICI, which does not seek 'effective communications', does not issue 'press releases', 'lobby' or have amongst its members a 'public relations officer', an 'information officer', or a 'campaigns co-ordinator' – all in order to improve their 'image', 'reputation' and 'corporate social responsibility'. Even retired South American dictators, waiting out legal arguments over prosecution for crimes against humanity, have PR advisers.[3]

PR employs at least 25,000 people, probably nearer 50,000, and has a £2.3 billion budget in the UK. For those who pay the bills, PR is a worthwhile activity which delivers value for money. It delivers desired results for Shell and Greenpeace, for insiders and outsiders, for the efficient and dignifed parts of our political system, and for voluntary and leisure interests. Viewed as management, PR has developed from an optional extra to a mainstream function which communicates strategic business messages. Viewed as campaigning, PR provides the techniques for pressure and cause groups to influence public policy. Viewed as entertainment, it even has its own television shows in *Absolutely Fabulous* and *Spin City*.

Yet this prominence as an activity of the elite, as a significant provider of jobs, as a high profile business tool, as a crusading aid for pressure groups, or as a harmless puff for our favourite local club does not bring PR social prestige, high status or good opinion. PR people and their trade journals often write in two alternating styles about their business, but never at the same time: 'PR is coming of age' and 'It still has some way to go'. PR does not attract the acclaim of, say, tourism or marketing, other activities which have grown mightily over the last 40 years and whose status has prospered. Comparisons will be made with advertising, and the role of journalism as a denigrator of PR will be explored. PR has a drag anchor; it is summed up in the colloquial phrase 'It's a PR job'. The implication is of something not being what it appears, a victory of presentation over content, a small workaday kind of deceit, producing small doses of distrust.

A small dose of deceit?

If the deceit is 'workaday'and its production is by lowly PR, why should the reader continue? The answer lies in the pervasiveness of PR in contemporary UK society, and in the concerns this pervasive activity generates when it touches on important public aspects of UK life. **Chapter 3** asks whether the pervasiveness of PR is symptomatic of wider and deeper trends, and what these trends are. Indeed, PR flourishes so fruitfully today that it has been called the 'profession of the decade'. Why does its jargon slip so easily off our tongues? Some commentators, employing medieval descriptors of power and influence, have called it the Fifth Estate.[4]

From this perspective, PR is certainly a highly organised service industry, but its pervasiveness also finds another, more localised, individual expression. This is in PR as a 'cottage industry' done by the amateurs, say, in the local tennis club, and in PR as the 'personal kit' of the fame-addicted celebrity or of the aggrieved individual fighting for a cause. This pervasiveness also suggests an answer to the question of where in society PR can be characterised as taking place. Its principal social location is the construct known as civil society, that area of public life bounded by indi-viduals and the family on one side and by government on the other, and characterised by all manner of voluntary associations, including business ones. The relations between civil society and goverrment, and the presen-tational activities of government are the other two locations.

PR is public behaviour of 'display-for-attention-and-advantage'. It is an act of self-representation seeking advantage from the significant other(s). Sometimes this display is not on view to a large public, since the significant other is a private person or private body, or it is hidden behind official secrecy. Sometimes the display is made very public in the media but without its PR source being revealed, raising questions of access to powerful institutions and of manipulation of readers, listeners and viewers. PR is, however, often publicly and privately in denial that it seeks self-advantage. It does not shriek from the page or brochure like the paid advertisement. It sees itself as saying 'true' or 'real' things and as represent-ing 'important' activity. Sometimes, it says that it is 'educational'. It claims – even insists – that it should be displayed, noticed and given advantage because of these qualities. It often wraps up self-interest in the terms of a wider interest. It may be that PR's display-for-attention-and-advantage is a particular expression of a larger social environment, for it is clear that PR's form of display has similarities with advertising and marketing. Indeed, what links these operationally different displays together is the concept of promotion – the behaviour of self-interested exchange. Germaine Greer, among others, has identified the marketing mentality as the dominant cul-tural expression of the millenium: PR is its cousin, more invisible than mar-keting, promoting ideas and institutions as well as goods and services.[5]

The most important period for the growth of PR in the UK is the forty years since 1960, and the most important phenomenon of that period in generating PR has been an accelerated pluralism.[6] This has taken two forms. The first is the acclerated pluralism of values and behaviours of the population of the UK. This *civic pluralism* has been linked with various social movements (e.g. environmentalism, consumerism) and with a greater propensity to join voluntary associations. These groups – large and small, loosely organised, national and local, dedicated to a social cause or lifestyle, proclaiming new ideologies, hobbies, leisures – have invariably promoted themselves through PR, not least because it is accessible and low-cost promotion. This pluralism has been accelerated in that more groups, representing more differing values and behaviours, have spoken out than previously.

The second form that accelerated pluralism has taken is in markets and business – *commercial pluralism*. Since the late 1970s, the ruling ideas about the UK economy have shifted to favour markets and business, with competition favoured over co-operation, individualism over community, private over public. PR has been used to promote this new emphasis at two levels. The first is at the ideological level of acting as a transmission belt[7] to spread these ideas from political parties, think tanks, business peak organisations and elite individuals into society generally. Second, at the operational level of gaining market share for the producers of goods and services, PR has serviced marketing. This push for markets has opened up powerful growth opportunities for the PR industry, with an estimated 70% of its jobs in that area. This commercial pluralism has accelerated in comparison to the previous period before the mid-1970s, in that business values have been more accepted by more people, whether willingly or not, in the UK.

The connection of PR with accelerated pluralism is offered as the specific cause of its growth. There is, however, a less proximate cause, one working since the start of the twentieth century, and one which is a major cultural signifier of this century: systems of mass communications. Mass persuasive communications have developed in response to two factors: the rise of manufacturing industry and its need for mass consumer markets, and the rise of representative government and its need for votes in elections of universal franchise.

Persuasive mass communications encourage the spread of pluralism, and they are the subject of a cocktail of contemporary changes in technology, working practices and values. These changes favour PR, in the sense that the media has become more dependent on PR as a supplier of editorial and programming material – to such an extent that one can talk of the PR-isation of the media (see **Chapter 4**). A very visible sign of this is the rise of celebrity news.

Chapter 4 also notes that commercial pluralism has created media businesses and more media marketing to readers, listeners and viewers, with the aim of keeping them as consumers. The rise of civic pluralism has encouraged more media outlets (professional and amateur, if that distinction still holds) ready to report new values and behaviours. Both these developments benefit PR. With more space to fill, fewer newsroom workers rely more on increasing amounts of PR material. This reliance threatens journalism, that is to say, work based on autonomy of judgement about facts and opinion. It encourages a new employment category, media staff who mould news, 'infotainment', lifestyle and celebrity copy to maximise audiences in target populations. This transformation from journalist to media staffer is eased by the status of the PR industry as the modern media's most important supplier. Pressure and cause groups also use PR attitudes and techniques widely to propagate their views, as do employers who treat PR as an internal media system for manipulative communications to employees.

These changes, above all accelerated pluralism, affect the quality of public debate in UK civil society and lead to a souring of pluralism, to a grumble culture. They trigger the question: 'Have we become an argument culture?' Have those more numerous, self-interested voices of difference and defiance, amplified by PR, developed a public atmosphere of unrelenting contention and verbal aggression which favours disagreement and conflict? This is a negative interpretation of the consequences of the increased struggle for advantage in civil society caused by more pluralism. A positive one is that sharpened debate, whetted by PR, identifies strengths and weaknesses more quickly, and hastens the negotiation stage of public debate. We are clearly now a more adversarial society, where wrangling in the political and commercial marketplaces leaves after it a residue which some citizens and consumers call truth. The connections to civic and commercial pluralism, to the contemporary media, and to the self-interested but bitter tone of much public debate show up the network of links PR has with the liberal, democratic, market-based, capitalist society which constitutes the contemporary UK. But this embedding of PR in the political economy raises real concerns. The next chapters explore which interests have gained most from this exchange, and at what cost to others.

Benefits and costs

Chapters 5 and **6** are extended critiques of PR following discussion of definitions and benefits. PR is famously hard to tie down: one tally is 472 definitions. Indeed, 'Why try?' is one response to this terminological inexactitude, for PR is so noticeable, widespread and pervasive that there is no need to define it. But ubiquity cannot hide the need for more precision; PR cannot take credit for social benefits nor accept debits for social harms unless it is identified.

What sort of activity exactly is it that writes press releases, deals with journalists, lobbies ministers, writes brochures, organises competitions, roadshows and exhibitions, does internal communications, manages issues and worries about reputation? What is it which produces small doses of distrust and which travels under many job titles? What is PR? To those who dislike it, it is an insidious manipulation or cheating propaganda in favour of what the insult thrower does not like. To those who accept it, it is the legitimate promotion of the interests of an organisation or a cause. PR people often weary of these questions of definition, grunting back with comments such as 'navel gazing' and 'let's get on with it'. But it is worth persisting with the questions to see what parts of PR, if any, are deserving. A charity carrying out community relations resents its work sharing the same label as media relations for celebrities or lobbying for favourable tax changes.

To those who do it, it is difficult to know where it stops and when it strays into marketing, advertising and politics. To those who study it, PR is notoriously difficult to define. As a concept, it can be defined as communications management by an organisation with its publics. As a practice, it is mostly dealing with the media – a definition which probably matches most lay people's understanding of it. The most durable UK definition concerns an organisation having 'goodwill' and 'mutual understanding' between itself and those it affects. This has lasted probably because it reflects an organisation-centred view, and most PR has traditionally been done for organisations.

Another definitional approach is to look at the effects of PR on society; this is the principal perspective followed here. Such an approach illuminates PR as a category of persuasive communications done through the mass media or through private lobbying by groups to advance their material or ideological interests. It has historically been done mostly by business and government, but in today's climate of accelerated pluralism the inventory of users extends to voluntary organisatons, to cause, pressure and interest groups, and to individuals seeking celebrity status or redress of grievances. It is an accessible and low-cost set of techniques. PR is always persuasive, communicative behaviour designed to win a margin of benefit in a pluralistic competition for advantage. Because of its low reputation, however, there is a flight from the term 'public relations', so that it is often difficult to see exactly where it is done. As regards practitioners, it is done by both specialist and non-specialist staff in organisations and groups, and by individuals in their own interests. PR has many benefits for those who produce it (PR people and their employers) and those who consume it (media audiences, consumers, policy-makers); these benefits are the subject matter of nearly every book written about the subject. As regards business and capitalist values, PR is an established technique for spreading them throughout the political economy. As regards markets, PR is the principal flow by volume of information about consumer choice in retail markets. As regards politics, PR provides a flow of information about policies and politicians which keeps government, the political class and the electorate in contact. It is appropriate, in a party-competitive, elected system of government, that the political class has actively and continuously to persuade voters. As regards pressure, cause and interest groups, PR in its lobbying form is an effective form of communication linking them into policy networks and communities, and into the public policy decision-making process. As regards the media, PR is a major supplier of low-cost, subsidised material, much of which reflects important developments in UK society. Finally for individuals, PR is a means to celebrity status and to redressing grievances. PR is not going to disappear from UK society: it is, as a set of attitudes and techniques, organically linked to it.

There are costs, however, arising from PR which amount to serious matters for citizens and consumers. These coalesce into two sets of concerns. The first is that historically PR has mostly been communications in favour of business interests and of government. It has been one-way communications, done without respect for or consent from other interests in UK society. It has often hidden the source of its messages, or projected them with the authority of the state. It has employed more emotion than reason in its persuasion. It has been and still is principally manipulative communications, becoming at its worst weak propaganda. Historically PR has been used by business and government as a means of social control; what stands out from an analysis of that approach is that mass involvement in politics and business does not hinder a thriving political economy, but that monopolistic, persuasive mass communications does. The strengthening of value and group pluralism reduces the manipulative consequences of PR by promoting more adversarial public debate. There is, furthermore, plenty of scope for the reform of PR practice to reduce the manipulative intent of its messages.[8]

Chapter 5 reviews the academic literature on American PR which is highly critical of its propagandistic use by business and government; Chapter 6 concentrates on the UK experience, especially its historical aspects, and on how PR writers cope with PR as propaganda.

The second set of concerns about PR revolve around its impacts on markets, politics and the mass media. UK citizens and consumers see these impacts as a threat to a cherished British ideal, that of equal and proportionate access to these three public institutions, institutions which strongly influence the quality of their public and private lives. Is PR the friend or foe of competitive markets, accountable politicians and senior civil servants, and an independent media? **Chapter 7** starts by setting these concerns in context and then analyses the links between marketing, markets and PR, a topic which has received little previous critical attention. The focus here is principally on PR as persuasive communications in the hands of the producers of goods and services – marketing PR (MPR). This is PR as the organiser of competitions for the top three reasons for buying a holiday and as the author of the supermarket brochure on low calorie, healthy eating.

Markets, politics and media

There is a growing use of PR by marketeers at a time when they believe that advertising alone is not persuasive enough, when the consumer is better educated, is seen as 'active' and 'ethical', and is considered to be 'compassionate'. Under certain circumstances, these flows of MPR are beneficial to consumers in providing market knowledge for informed choice. They also help producers build up marketplace values such as high profile awareness, brand identity and good reputation. The persuasive communications from market observers (market PR as opposed to marketing PR) such as regulators, pressure groups and government bodies is also tracked in its relation to PR, as is the question of 'information abuse' by PR people in the City.

One response to concern over marketing and market PR is that the rule *caveat emptor* applies. The reaction might be: 'So what – people will do anything to sell, we know that' and 'Who cares about PR if it shifts volume and meets targets'. Or, in the case of PR from regulators and market critics, the reaction might be: 'Scare talk from nanny: I'll continue consuming.' There is much in this *laissez faire* attitude which is appropriate to the operation of free markets, but if one or more of four conditions of communications deficit for consumers operate, they make such a response inadequate. There is less competition when these conditions apply. The first condition is that information about goods and services contained in marketing public relations (MPR) does not flow across markets or impact on consumers equally because not all producers are equally active. Second, some producers use an information subsidy to produce more MPR than other producers. (The argument focuses on retail markets but most of it can be applied to business-to-business markets.) Third, all consumers are equally persuaded by equal amounts of MPR. Fourth, there is hidden sourcing of MPR: unless its self-interested origin is declared, consumers think that the information is independently sourced editorial or is educational. If some or all of these conditions hold, then MPR amounts to a communications deficit for consumers in the marketplace. It creates an imperfect competition of information. Where they do not hold, MPR as an information flow strengthens markets towards what economists called perfect competition.

Another concern about markets and PR lies in the sheer volume of persuasive communications in UK society: the continuous pumping of promotional material at citizens and consumers. That MPR is adding to the volume raises aesthetic questions since MPR thereby increases the marketisation of public spaces in UK life. Where are the public places where we can avoid the sales message?

Chapter 8 turns to the concerns raised by the involvement of PR in politics. PR as lobbying is the most serious example: it raises acute concerns about access by powerful interests to elected governments – concerns so acute that they were a contribution to the end of Conservative government in 1997. Lobbying raises questions of invisible influence on government: how does the citizen know, and should the citizen know who is lobbying ministers, special advisers and civil servants? In the UK the word 'lobbying' is now inextricably associated with 'sleaze', 'cash-for-questions' and 'cash-for-access'.

Is this association just a fashionable prejudice against lobbying? After all, today's lobbying is in direct line of constitutional descent from the Magna Carta rights to petition and to seek redress. Many reactions to lobbying are based on observers' estimations of the organisation or the cause being lobbied for, rather than on the lobbying process itself. For example, a train operating company wants to buy new rolling stock, the investment costs of which will only be recouped after the operating franchise has expired. In these circumstances the company can hardly avoid 'talking' to the rail regulator and government. If, however, you are a competing train operating company or you do not like private railways, these 'talks' are seen as 'propaganda'. A charity 'talks' to government about legislation banning the use and export of landmines. If, however, one works in the defence industries, these talks could be described as 'pious meddling'. This illustrates the point that PR is an instrumental activity serving a principle or principal, and that if the message or its source is disliked, it will often be 'shot' in its role as messenger.

Lobbying in liberal, market-orientated societies cannot be stopped, but it needs to be reformed to prevent an undermining of electoral politics. Reform should focus first on politicians and senior civil servants, and only then should attention turn to lobbyists. PR in politics, however, has become more than lobbying. It also involves the introduction of mind-sets and techniques taken from commercial PR and used by political parties and government as spin doctoring and as political marketing. The balance of advantage has swung too far in favour of spin doctors – slightly ridiculous public figures – in their relationship with journalists. The balance reflects the ascendancy of a party or a government in public opinion; spin doctors will lose influence as their party or government falls in public approval.

The visibility of PR activity is a critical question when its links with the mass media are analysed. PR is a large-scale source of material for the media, but that source is invisible to readers, listeners and viewers for much of the time. A significant proportion of news and features which fills the media originates with PR people, and is given to journalists in a ready-for-use form. **Chapter 9** argues that this is a concern because it undermines audiences' trust in the media. A high level of trust in the mass media is an important component of an effective, liberal, representative democracy. In making their judgements about public life, citizens (and consumers) need to know that the information they receive from an institution calling itelf 'free' and 'independent' is characterised by reasoned argument, factual accuracy and known sourcing. The relative autonomy of the mass media is an important civic quality for UK society. The connections between government, political parties, business and all other vested interests, on the one hand, and the mass media, on the other, should be known. The chapter also looks at the decline in the number of journalists, and the influence this has had on editorial attitudes to PR material. Hard-pressed journalists with an increasing amount of space to fill have come to regard PR material as subsidised journalism, at hand to help them meet production targets. The PR industry is today the most important supplier to the media. This fact, and the diffusion of PR values more generally in society, justify a concern about the 'PR-isation' of the media and of journalism.

Reputational matters

Chapter 10 examines more closely the charge of low reputation against PR. That it is made at all is an irony of Titanic size. Before exploring that incongruity, it is worthwhile looking at the impatient reaction by senior PR people to the charge of low reputation: 'We don't navel gaze; we get on with the job.' This is understandable as the reaction of confident professionals under pressure in a growing business. Furthermore, it is a tried and trusted defence, for it has had to be used since the appearance of modern PR in the last quarter of the nineteenth century in America. PR has always had a bad reputation with the public and its professional competitors, such as journalists and advertisers. Thus, in the sense of low reputation not hindering a burgeoning activity, the irony does not matter.

To the observer, the irony over the reputation of PR is richly incongruous in several ways: so much so that, if irony is allowed to be so, it is paradoxical as well. It may be that low reputation has not stopped growth but has slowed it. In that, there is the consolation of job security for those who have to put up with awkward questions. Moreover, the impatience of the busy PR person may not lie in the anger of denial, but in something else – that PR seeks other outcomes for its principals which cannot be said out loud.

Reputation is an elusive phenomenon when considered in connection with institutions and groups of people. How distinct is it from the terms 'image', 'identity', 'perception'? Is it a corporate vanity? A reputation is held by others – are these holders all as significant as each other? How is it measured and how does it relate to other judgements which may be competitive with it, such as success and survival? Reputation is defined, in the first instance, as social prestige attached to an organisation, cause or person in the perception of others. The assumption is that more social prestige is better than smaller amounts or negative amounts. However, it is not clear that the assumption holds true in all circumstances, and it is this variability which causes problems for PR – problems brought upon itself because of its devotion to better reputation as an overriding outcome. Organisations and causes may have to – may choose to – behave in ways which achieve other goals at the price of loss in reputation. PR finds this prioritisation difficult to deal with, not least from the viewpoint of corporate social responsibility and ethics. In associating their work so much with reputation, PR people are shooting themselves in the foot.

Reputation becomes a more involved issue when it is argued that all who work for an organisation or group are responsible for its reputation. This transforms PR into a state of mind, as well as a staff function. On that score, PR is done by all. More complications emerge when it is asked who is the object of the reputational questions: the employing organisations and groups, their values and activities or the PR people employed. There is also the issue of the distribution amongst the public and professional groups of the low reputation of PR. Does it matter if the general public or competing professional groups do not like PR? Does their opinion matter if the PR paymasters are satisfied?

Chapter 10 goes on to explore what it is like to work in PR and how working in a buoyant industry encourages denial of or indifference to the reputational question. There has been massive expansion of PR work in the UK. PR people feel that they are in a growth area. It is popular with the young: ten-to-one ratios of applications to admissions to study it, London agencies measure applications in the hundreds, if not thousands. PR feels, to those who do it, in tune with the times: markets, lifestyle choices, speaking out and having your say, not putting up with what you do not want. Moreover, they see that PR is colonising journalism and other marketing communications such as sponsorship, cause-related marketing and direct mail.

It is estimated that today up to 50,000 people work in PR in the UK, up from 4,000 at the beginning of the 1960s. A small number are high-profile – lobbyists, spin doctors, celebrity PR agents – and most of these do not seek the attention they receive. For some, PR has an explicit social role. If they work in business, it is to bring social harmony; to be an organisational ombudsman, working 'the two-way street' between an organisation and the public; to be the corporate conscience, encouraging corporate citizenship. Most PR people, however, work in the low-profile world of marketing, promotional and campaigning departments of businesses, public sector and voluntary sector bodies. They want attention to their messages and not to themselves. The typical mind-set of people doing PR as a career or as a volunteer is invariably similar to that of the suitor: great enthusiasm, boundless energy and stratagems for impressing the object of desire. You want to tell the good things that you (your company or cause) are: the good things that you do. You are upset if your object of desire (the media, the decision-makers) does not notice or does not reciprocate: you are shattered if there is rejection. As in love, so in PR: it is the rejection which is so incomprehensible.

Characterised this way, PR people have great difficulty in accepting that they could be perceived in a suspicious and negative way, or, most hurtfully of all, as propagandists. In fact, they resort to psychological denial by working each day as an island of time and by making new beginnings, new campaigns. In this way, they remain the constant suitor, wanting to persuade, never tiring of it. Women make up at least half the UK workforce and a big majority of the student body. They face career questions about 'technician' or 'managerial' status which, to the extent that there is a real distinction, will discriminate against them. PR women may also face, on average, the under-payment differential endured by the female UK workforce. While they do, they will note the irony that their majority in PR will increase its reputation.

Higher education has a stake in the prosperity of PR. With up to 3,000 students on PR courses, it trains – and hopefully educates – much of the next generation. Sixteen institutions offer the subject on a stand-alone basis or as the major component of other degrees, with some fifty staff. In a mass marketised higher education system, it has been a 'nice little earner'. For its teachers, it has presented the problems and opportunities of starting up a new discipline. They (we) have taken the intellectual framework of the American PR academics Grunig and Hunt, and imported them wholesale to UK campuses. The Grunigian paradigm is a felicitiously flexible one: it allows PR to be taught as the practice of communicative virtue, while not denying that it has a past as the practice of communicative supremacy. This flexibility allows students and teachers to feel a comfortable association with an awkward past but hopeful future; it thus allows the *teaching* of PR but does not dissolve the residual hard questions which *teaching and researching* about PR pose.

One of those hard questions is about ethics and PR, a combination of words rarely formed on the PR lip. Even authors on the topic (Seib and Fitzpatrick 1995) talk of an oxymoron. But ethical PR will force its way onto the practical and academic agendas because of two factors outside the PR industry: more concern with business ethics, and more state and voluntary regulation. There is also one internal factor: if PR people want professional status in the sense that doctors, lawyers and architects have it, they will have to face ethical questions about truthfulness, contribution to the public good, codes of behaviour.

An alternative?

It is likely that the trends in society (value and group pluralism, the strengthening of consumer markets and capitalism, the rise of consumer and cause campaigning, regulatory government) which have increased PR in the UK over the last forty years will continue. For most PR people, this signifies more of a good thing. They would share the view of one of their own (Michie 1998, p. 316) that 'the vast majority of PR activity has always been at worst innocuous and at best a force for enlightenment'. **Chapter 11** rejects such a bland, self-serving, unsupported view. It notes that most professional and academic justifications for PR are wanting: they focus too much on institutional needs; they implicitly align PR with business or government; and they are fixated by idealised values such as mutual understanding and goodwill. There is often an institutional and ideological imperialism infused through much PR, as well as a covertness which implies dominant/subordinate social relationships (seen in its effects on markets, politics and the mass media). This imperialism and covertness generates its low reputation amongst those on the receiving end of much PR.

The practice of PR in the UK does raise substantial concerns. Too much of it still originates from the most powerful social actors, mainly big business and government. Too much is manipulation or propaganda – one-way communications with little respect for the autonomy of the receivers of the message. Too much PR is 'laundered' as editorial material through the media, giving it a gloss of accurate fact and independent opinion.

These are serious matters, because they have a detrimental influence on the effectiveness of free markets, the amount of public space in the UK free from commercial messages, the integrity of elected, representative politics, and the standing of a media which calls itself 'free', 'independent' and 'objective'. After balancing the positive and negative consequences of PR, there remains a strong residue of concern, which could be reduced by reforming its practice.

A number of possible changes are identified. They derive from a reconceptualisation of PR to be considered by those producing and consuming it. This rethinking is based on empirical descriptions of PR in UK markets, politics and media (see Chapters 4, 5, 6, 7 and 8). But it has an idealistic consequence for those wanting a more equitable UK society. PR is the promotion, through the persuasive use of data, words, visuals and behaviour, of government, organised interests, social movements and causes in society (and sometimes of individuals). This makes PR, *as a matter of observation*, an instrumental activity in interest intermediation and group competition. It is the communicative aspect of the struggle for advantage among interests, and can be conceptualised as happening in a social space characterised as the 'persuasive sphere'. This should be seen as the successor to the public sphere concept, now redundant because it could not cope with the fact of modern mass communications. PR can also be employed by individuals to advance their personal interests. *As a matter of value*, this reconceptualisation also invites the less powerful and the isolated in society to consider using PR. In this idealistic form, the rethink advocated here seeks to encourage greater use of PR as an effective activity for organisations, causes and individuals challenging the dominant, the orthodox and the conventional.

Such a reconceptualisation in this non-empirical form, however, has to defend itself against charges that it confuses appearance and reality: namely, that PR of itself has no social power, and it is the social power of the user which confers potency on PR. This is a major critique against arguments for reform. Ameliorating social effects does not abolish social causes. Up to now, most PR is communication from powerful social actors advancing their interests. Reforming the communications does not weaken the interests. There are three responses to this critique. The first is that, although powerful interests produce more PR than less powerful ones, it does not follow that a great quantity of PR is the same as more effective PR, where effectiveness means being more persuasive among intended publics. This mis-match between volume and effectiveness applies particularly to the cognitive and conceptual content of PR messages. These ideas may have high social resonance and be quickly accepted, even though they come from small, resource-poor groups. An example is PR for the ordination of women when it was first broached.

Second, when the PR messages of business and/or government are challenged in a highly pluralistic competition of values, ideas and groups, the contingencies of actual public debate make outcomes favouring the powerful uncertain. The highly contested response to the bio-tech companies promoting genetically modified food is a case in point.

Third, the more that PR is based on accurate data and reasoned argument, the more the social power of its originator is discounted by an informed, sceptical public opinion. The case for fair trade as opposed to free trade, for example, is not weakened by the low financial resources of its PR orginators, world development groups. The conclusion drawn from these responses is that where PR is reasoned persuasion communicated through full competition among interests and groups, it is likely that the acceptance of their messages will depend on their cogency for their publics, rather than the resources of their senders. Such a PR is a societally beneficial PR and is promoted by both the persuasive sphere in which the competition of interests speaks and by reforms to the internal architecture of PR.

The author does not believe that there ever was a golden age for PR, or that there ever will be one. Indeed, golden ages are suggestive of a romantic and idealised approach to social relations which, rather, should be based on an equitable distribution of material and non-material resources throughout society, moderated by an ethically inspired politics. There is a more modest and practical hope, however, that the drag anchor of low reputation which keeps PR mired at the bottom of league tables will be cut away and its reputation rise a little.

But if better reputation comes about, it will not only be because PR can be made the 'common or garden' tool of any organisation, group, cause or individual in the ways set out above. PR seeks to increase awareness: it is time now for those at which it is aimed to be more aware of it. PR seeks advantage for its principals. It is now right that PR becomes 'democratised' and 'individualised', in the sense that the public as citizens and consumers come to see it as an activity which is directed at – if not against – them, which they can evaluate and discount if it is not in their interests, and which they themselves can also use to defend and advance personal interests and common causes.

The argument of this book starts with the asymmetry of PR's high salience and its low reputation. The conclusion is that a reformed PR will reduce some of the asymmetry. It will do it through the release of PR from its over-association with powerful interests and causes; its adoption by less powerful ones; through increased awareness of it or resort to it by individual consumers and citizens; through its adoption of reasoned persuasion; through politicians reforming their behaviour so as to be above suspicion when lobbying and being lobbied; through journalists declaring their use of it; through media literacy and civic education; through internal and external regulation. As a result, PR's reputation may increase, but that matters less than that PR should be recognised by all for what it is, and that it should be done in the future by the many to bring about fairer access to important public goods.

The political economy as context

A distinguishing characteristic of this book is that it approaches its topic (mostly) from the outside and examines it from the vantage point of a wider context. The context chosen is that of the political economy, that large part of the UK's public life where political and economic ideas, behaviour and decision-making intermingle. This is the most fitting approach for the evaluation of an activity which is *both* a portable set of attitudes and techniques carried by individuals to their various tasks, *and* a structured industry, bought in to service the promotional needs of its principals. Given this individualised and industrial nature of PR, it must be looked at in the many settings in which it is used: in markets, in politics, in the media, in the public, private and voluntary sectors, and for ambitious and aggrieved individuals. This ubiquity of usage does not make PR a free floating set of attitudes and techniques, unconnected with the particular content and shape of ruling ideas, social forces and institutions which make up the UK's political economy today. PR is connected to its wider context because it advances the purposes of its users and gives them benefits which other forms of promotion could not.

So far the term political economy has been used as the societal address – where politics and economics mix – at which PR can be found. But the address needs writing out in full for it illuminates a feature of PR. The term has been revived in the UK in the last 20 or so years as a counter to a claim that the economy is an independent sphere of social activity which dissolves the political or banishes it to other spheres (Caporaso & Levine 1992). Such claims cannot convincingly be made for the economy: the economic affects people's ideas, values and attitudes as much as their pockets. Consider unemployment and inflation in the UK in the last 30 years. Markets organise exchange and allocation more efficiently than central planning, but the exchange and allocation can involve child labour. PR is used for the promotion of ideas, values and attitudes held by competing, if not conflicting, interests in UK society, and the site for that contestation is sometimes the economy and sometimes the political system. A political economy perspective allows for an inclusive approach which can handle the multiple, sometimes separate and sometimes related sites where it is done.

It is necessary to define further the political economy approach taken here. Not only is that approach over-arching, it is also based on a presupposition about power in society. Societal power – the transformative capacity of individuals and insitutions to make their preferences prevail – is the constitutive matter which realises the different forms of allocation known as economics and politics. This presupposition admits that the concepts of perfect markets and perfect democracy construct an equality of relationships for their social actors by banishing power through the agency of equal exchange. Perfect markets and perfect democracy, however, do not exist in practice. What do exist are imperfect markets and imperfect democracy, made imperfect by unequal concentrations of material and ideological resources. The inequalities are more or less power. Hence the political economy posited here as the context for evaluating PR comprises systems of unequal power relations in UK society.

Finally, there arises the question of the relationship of the political economy to a related concept – civil society. To classical economists, the latter is the former in that it is the area of society where relations between people are made through voluntary contracts and where government does not intervene. This definition squeezes out politics in any sense which involves the state. The principal use of the term in UK literature seems to be consistent with this classical interpretation and it will be used in this text as a sub-set of the political economy. Civil society is that part of the system of economic and political power relations where the state is absent or where it is weak as an agent. In this way, all PR remains located in the political economy: where PR does not involve government and is about markets and/or voluntary associations, it is done, more precisely, in civil society.[9]

2 The PR industry from top to bottom

It is hard to avoid noticing public relations these days: it is a pervasive activity in our society. The Establishment and the political class have taken to it with enthusiasm. The Queen has taken on a Communications Secretary as part of the modernisation of the Monarchy at an estimated total salary of £190,000 (*The Independent on Sunday*, 21.6.98, p. 1), and the BBC reports that Simon Lewis will be the third most senior official at Buckingham Palace. His brief is 'to devise a PR strategy for the Queen and the other Royals' (*PR Week*, 3.7.98, p. 28), which puts PR right at the centre of the Establishment. 'PR to the Queen – by Appointment' is an entry which adds weight to a CV and which puts PR under constant media watch. It seems in tune with the times that Prince Edward and his wife Sophie Rhys-Jones both run their own businesses – he as a TV producer and she as a PR person.

The Church of England is urged by the Archdeacon of Northolt (*PR Week*, 3.4.98, p. 7) to appoint 'a spin doctor', and the director of communications of its ruling body, the General Synod, wants to appoint 'lead bishops' to be public 'spokesmen on issues like marriage and homosexuality'.[1] The Dean of Westminster Abbey appoints a public relations consultant when he sacks the Master of Choristers and before a retired Scottish judge delivers his judgement on the affair (*The Independent on Sunday*, 6.9.98, p. 13). Clerical dissidents also use PR: the first Catholic woman priest sees it as a duty to be media friendly and two weeks after her ordination had given 61 interviews, including one to the *Zulu Times*.[2] Oxford University advertises for a head of press and public relations, 'a newly established post aimed at extending and developing the University's public profile and demonstrating, through pro-active strategies with the media, its pre-eminence as a world class institution at the forefront of research' (*The Times Higher Education Supplement*, 30.7.98). Freemasons in Somerset have a public relations officer 'to win over public opinion' (*Western Daily Mail*, 3.9.98, p. 12). The House of Lords has four ennobled PR peers following the 19 June 1989 Summer Honours List – Ladies Glenys Thornton and Mary Goudie, Lords Tim Bell and Timothy Clement-Jones. *The Observer* (21.6.98, p. 19) comments: 'We have a

Government obsessed with media manipulation, so there are honours ...
for spin doctoring'.[3] Maybe, but it is nothing new, because the four join
two PR men already with ermine on their collars – Lords Chadlington and
McNally, both of Shandwick, one of the largest PR companies in the
world. With this social endorsement, perhaps *The Spectator* (10.1.98, p. 8)
is right to proclaim that 'PR is the profession of the decade'. *Granta*, the
watchdog magazine for good writing, declares that 'spin' and 'soundbite'
are 'key words for our era'. PR even has its own popular TV sitcoms –
Absolutely Fabulous and *Spin City*. Can one be more noticed than that?

Perhaps it is more accurate to write of the saturation of UK society with
PR activity. Ewen (1996) found that state already existing in the US when
he started tracing the intellectual history of corporate PR there: 'Living in
a society in which nearly every moment of human attention is exposed to
the game plan of spin doctors, image managers, pitchmen, communications consultants, public information officers and public relations specialists, the boundaries of my inquiry appeared seamless ...' (p. 19).

One of the most noticeable features of the New Labour Government is
its presentational skills and media management. It has removed ten
departmental PR chiefs inherited from its predecessor (*The Observer*,
28.6.98, p. 18). It is criticised for 'spinning' its policies, and condemned
for spending between two and three times the amount of its predecessor
on special advisers, most of them apparently public relations experts.
Indeed, New Labour is, to its enemies, above all a hollow creation of
image-makers, with no spine of substance. Peter Mandelson and Alastair
Campbell are widely held to have helped Tony Blair become Prime Minister through management of the news, by controlling sources, controlling
timing and briefing unattributably – classic PR work. The management
continues in government, sometimes against its own supporters: so much
so that one sacked minister, Frank Field, talks (*The Daily Telegraph*, 4.8.98,
p. 2) of the 'cancer' of spin doctors. Two journalists[4] write books declaring
that, while in opposition, Mandelson manipulated news, portrayed New
Labour in the best possible light, and rewarded and punished journalists
who wrote favourably or otherwise about Tony Blair. Campbell is not
elected nor an established civil servant, yet the Prime Minister's Press
Secretary is described in *The Times* editorial of 24.6.98 as 'the iron hand in
New Labour's velvet glove'. Francis Maude, the shadow Chancellor of the
exchequer, resorts to a jibe against PR when he condemns the Government's three year public expenditure plans announced in June 1998 as a
headline grabbing exercise – before he fails the plans as bad economics.
The Times reports (19.6.98, p. 10) on William Hague's first year as Leader
of The Opposition with the view that 'a more serious and substantive
image had been courted'. The Prime Minister presents 'state of the
nation' reports and 'annual reports to the nation' about manifesto
promises. Paddy Ashdown, leader of the Liberal Democrats, says on BBC
television news at 1 p.m. (30.7.98) that 'It is bad that this is a PR matter',

and later on BBC radio news at 5 p.m. that 'It's a bad thing that this is a PR exercise'. The Prime Minister replies with 'It is not about PR or style'.

The tabloid and broadsheet papers report and photograph for their front pages the lifestyle of celebrities, who are famous for being famous through deals struck with the media by their PR consultants. The public relations industry has firms and individuals specialising in 'celebrity PR': Freud Communications, the MacLaurin Group, Aurelia Cecil, Mark Borkowski and Liz Brewer, for example. But first in this field is the ubiquitous, plainspeaking personage of Max Clifford, famous for engineering the human and animal circumstances which led to *The Sun* headline 'Freddie Starr ate my hamster' (13.3.86). Fun and frothy their work may be, but these promoters and protectors of the gliterati carry negotiating clout. It was Matthew Freud, not libel lawyers, who got a front page apology in the *Mail on Sunday* (31.5.98) for his client actress, Brooke Shields, for false allegations about a drugs-related incident at Nice Airport a week before. Even broadsheets have space for celebrity PR. *The Times* (8.8.98, p. 17) reports on the tensions facing David Beckham as he returns to the football pitch after his World Cup foul and completes it with advice from three of the PR 'industry's sharpest brains' on how to behave publicly.

Less glitzy circumstances surround Louise Woodward, the au pair convicted of child killing in Boston, USA. She returns to England on 18 May 1998 in a first class airplane seat (it is not clear whether she paid for it or was 'bumped up' by BA); holds a press conference at Heathrow airport throughout which her MP 'minded her'; tells the press that she has not sold her story to the press and, indeed, has done an interview for the BBC *Panorama* programme for which she was not paid; returns to her Cheshire home; goes inside to be re-united with her sister; and comes out again after ten minutes '... in denim jacket, jeans and trainers to smile for a few pictures with her parents, Sue and Gary' (*The Guardian*, 19.6.98, p. 2). There is a support group in her home village in Cheshire. There are ribbons on trees. Two days before Louise's return (17.6.98), the *Daily Mail* carries a report (p. 6) on the actions of the dead child's parents: the headline is 'Parents in a PR war'. The nannies' agency which employed Woodward is reported (*The Observer*, 21.6.98, p. 4) to have 'lobbied successfully' against American legislation which would have required more babycare training for young au pairs. And if you do not want to do PR for a business or a cause, PR has been personalised and customised for the individual as part of the self-improvement culture – 'Be your own spin doctor'[5] is now at the airport bookshop.

The spread of PR jargon into everyday language is also noticeable. It has penetrated journalese, which has adopted the verb 'to spin' in its house style: 'President Clinton attempted to put a positive spin on his latest political failure ...' is how *The Times* (19.6.98, p. 21) described another day's political manoeuvring in Washington. The verb to 'unspin' has been heard on BBC Radio 4.

If the public relations industry is a noticeable activity, it is also a wide-spread one. Thirty years ago, we would not have talked of an 'industry': that word connotated high physical production volumes, large customer and employee numbers, usually in mineral extraction, transport or manu-facturing. Then, it was still a novelty to hear services described as indus-tries. Now, the Department of Trade and Industry commissions reports on PR (in 1994 from management consultants BDO Stoy Hayward) and finds that 'the UK PR sector is one of the most highly developed in Europe'. In 1963, there were an estimated 4,000 PRs (four-fifths of them in London), 300 PR companies and a £50 million expenditure by the industry.[6] In 1967, there were 766 PR companies and in-house departments in the UK, and 9,200 in 1997.[7] In the early 1990s, the industry's turnover in the UK was estimated at £1 billion and its workforce to be 48,000 – 28,000 more than in advertising.

The latest 1998 figures on turnover are £2.3 billion[8] and it is a reason-able assumption that the number of people employed is now over 50,000.[9] The revenue of the Public Relations Consultants' Association (PRCA) has grown from £33 million to £220 million between 1984 and 1996 – an increase of 567%.[10] Membership is up from 110 to 136. *PR Week* reports, in its 1998 contact book, that some 1,000 suppliers support the PR industry with 60 categories of products and services.

But the employment figures underestimate the actual number of people doing PR; the figures appear to measure only explicit job titles and persons who self-declare. For example, government PR people never pub-licly use the term, calling themselves instead public information officers. There is also, as detailed below, a flight from the term 'public relations' by many businesses and by some PR agencies because of the negative conno-tations. Moreover, the methodologies for counting are not clear. Looked at as a set of persuasive communications techniques, PR is done by an uncounted but much larger group of people in honorary, voluntary and paid posts in the public, private and voluntary sectors – several multiples perhaps of 50,000.

Consider these jobs described in *The Guardian* Society section (29.7.98, p. 2). Lindsay Keenan 'has been employed to campaign against the genetic manipulation of food crops for 15 months' by Green City, a Glasgow-based wholefood co-op: 'My work consists of lobbying the British and European Parliaments and supplying information and co-ordinating the group's campaigning efforts.' Ron Bailey 'has been employed as a road traffic reduction campaigner for four years' and:

> I organise large numbers of people to lobby on the road traffic reduc-tion issue. I get them to write and provide them with arguments to counter the MPs' objections. I encourage members of the public to get involved in the campaign. A lot of my work is deliberately focused on trying to reach middle-England – organisations such as the

Women's Institute. I travel around the country speaking about the importance of road traffic reduction. This year's tour took in 60 towns.

The PR departments of Monsanto, the AA and the Road Haulage Association would recognise this work.

People do PR and they need training: the education system has noticed. Since the late 1980s, it has been taught at higher education level in colleges and universities.[11] There are few, if any, estimates of what proportion of business studies courses in further education colleges have an identifiable and separate PR curriculum, but in higher education the subject is taught at diploma, bachelor and masters degree level at 16 campuses, mostly 'new' universities. Higher education has got the message that public relations is a popular job destination for school-leavers, and therefore likely to generate students in large numbers and so attract funding. A PR degree has been offered at Bournemouth University for nine years and applications have been consistently 10 to each place: this ratio is not uncommon at other campuses. If universities and colleges have noticed the size of the PR industry, so have students. A 1995 MORI survey reported that PR was final year students' third most popular career choice after journalism and teaching (*The Independent* tabloid section, 14.4.96, p. 13; *The Times* 2.10.98, p. 49).

Part of the response of the PR industry to more attention and greater impact is increased sophistication in its practice. *The Times* reports (19.6.98, p. 45) that City of London public relations agencies have profiles and 'amenability' ratings on financial journalists by which to gauge whom to introduce to their company clients. The in-tray of anyone working in PR today flows over with training courses for public affairs, issues management, crisis management and communications, audience management, media relations, lobby management, and PR support services. These workshops are expensive (e.g. £417.13 for a day in 1997, and £1056.33 for two days) and have compressed urgent titles such as 'placing a value on corporate personality', 'what price reputation' and 'mobilising internal communication to drive change'.

The public relations of public relations

Yet while it thrives, PR does not enjoy a high reputation with the general public and with some professional groups. Reputation is the social prestige or dislike which a person, institution, job or activity attracts. High reputation is the attraction of large 'quantities' of prestige. The ranking by prestige of Balliol College, Bath, Birmingham, Bradford, Brighton, Bristol and Bournemouth Universities, for example, can be established by either gossip or surveys.

There is, however, an irony here. The public relations of public relations is in a poor state; PR is generating low opinion about itself. Compare this state of affairs with other activities. The parallel would be if observers of an activity criticised it for not bringing about the outcome it existed to make come about. It would be as if medicine did not increase health, teaching reduced knowledge, or gardening meant fewer flowers. This point is sharper when we remember that the IPR's definition of public relations focuses on reputation and its management. Its *1998 Handbook* (p. 2) starts with definitions: 'Public relations is ... about reputation – the result of what you do, what you say and what others say about you. Public relations practice ... is the discipline which looks after reputation.' That more PR should lead to less of the benefit it promotes being available to itself is a rich irony.

The abbreviation 'PR' has entered everyday language, as has some of its jargon (campaign, press release, image, spinning, spin doctor, sound-bite, on message, off message, prebuttal, rapid rebuttal, minder, positioning, relaunch) – but rarely with positive connotations. It is a fairly safe bet that the proverbial Martian would see that government, institutions, most of the rich, powerful and famous, an increasing number of charities and pressure groups 'do PR', yet the public and many professionals use the term as a mocking colloquial reference. The phrase 'a PR job' describes words or actions about which there is a perceived or actual gap between presentation and reality, a gap which is either actively disguised or not owned up to. An example comes from the mouth of the public affairs director of Camelot, the national lottery organisers, on their appointment (*The Guardian*, 24.7.98, p. 7) of a new staff member to develop corporate citizenship and social responsibility policies: 'It is not just a PR exercise.'

The public immediately understands the former Prime Minister John Major's labelling as 'a PR stunt' the Opposition's position over differing attitudes to corporal punishment (BBC TV *News at Six*, 29.10.96). Major can use this phraseology because he knows that the term PR generally carries a negative charge with the general public. People in the boardroom are also dubious about it even though they are the biggest single users of PR. A 1997 MORI poll of the favourability ratings by business leaders towards support services gave it a rating of 28%, below law and advertising at 45%, accountancy at 60% and telecommunications at the most favourable point of 83%.[12] Perhaps the examples above are from people who are professional disparagers, but in some mouths the phrase has a painful edge. Doreen Lawrence, the mother of the murdered teenager Stephen Lawrence, rejected the admissions of racism in the London police by their Commissioner Sir Paul Condon as 'That is a PR job' (*The Guardian*, 2.10.98, p. 1).

'PR' is what 'spin doctors' do, and people are wary. It is not clear, for example, that the attempt by President Clinton's aides to get Monica Lewinsky a job in the PR department of Revlon after their affair ended is a positive endorsement (*The Guardian* supplement Clinton Crisis, 12.9.98,

p. 4).[13] Max Clifford, who is the *bête noir* of the UK public relations establishment, is in tune with popular language when he told *The Independent* (magazine section, 26.10.96, p. 30) about his Favourite Hypocrisy: 'I stand up and say that an important part of public relations is lies and deceit. We all know that but they won't ever admit it. It gives me tremendous pleasure to hear PRs say they don't lie.' Max Clifford is right about PR people not admitting to lying; but they are aware of their low reputation.[14] Stephen Farish, the group editor of *PR Week*, the industry's trade magazine, writes in the commemorative publication *Managing Communication in a Changing World* (London) to celebrate 50 years of the IPR in 1998:

> Part of the problem is that public relations which is all about the 'management of reputation', according to the IPR definition, itself has a reputation which is right off the end of the Ratner scale. In fact, you would be hard pushed to find an industry which is as gleefully vilified as the noble profession of public relations – otherwise known as 'the latrine of parasitic misinformation' as it was dubbed by the Guardian.
>
> (p. 58)

Doubt about publicly associating themselves with the term also spreads to the more buttoned-up PR professionals. *PR Week* reports (23.2.96) that the large agency Burson Marstellar had dropped the term in favour of 'perception management'. It later notes (26.4.96, supplement) that 'the term "PR" is giving public relations a bad name'. When Peter Hehir, a leading PR entrepreneur, said that the term was 'unhelpful', he was voicing a common view among senior businesspeople; there is anecdotal evidence of a flight from the term 'PR' towards substitutes, which usually include 'communications'. *PR Week* also reported that other refugees from the term were Mistral who preferred 'communicator', Greenlines who talked of their 'integrated communications service', and Propellor Marketing Communications who said that their name was a considered one. Later, the magazine wrote (7.6.98, p. 7) about 'anecdotal experience of consultants and in-house practitioners in the UK ... [that] communications is on the up but "public relations" is consistently undervalued as a management asset, and seen instead as a downstream "packaging" function'.

Lord McAlpine has updated Machievelli's *The Prince*[15] as a handbook for success in business. He sees the value of PR, but calls those who practice it 'twitchers of image' who use half-truths and convenient words. His advice to employers is never tell PR people more than they need to know. Indeed, the term 'Machiavellian marketing' has been coined to describe what PR people call public affairs and government relations.[16] In general, London lobbying firms, do not use the term PR to describe their work, estimated to be worth £70 million in 1998, with about a fifth coming from privatised companies (*The Independent*, 14.7.98, p. 1). Some lobbyists publicly distance themselves from 'PR', and most prefer in their literature descriptors such as 'public affairs' and 'government relations'.[17] Hesitation over titles extends to the academy. Two UK journals which invite PR lecturers to submit articles do not include the term in their titles, and there is some anecdotal evidence that they are not keen on the editorial use of the term, promoting instead the terms corporate and marketing communications. This bias away from the words 'public relations' is summed up in the order of the title and sub-title of one textbook widely used in the UK: *Strategic Communications Management: Making Public Relations Work.*[18]

The lecturers who teach PR know about the low status of their subject: when asked if it had a low reputation with the general public, 78% of respondents in a survey of the PR Educators' Forum answered 'yes'. There was a small majority in the same survey who thought PR had a bad reputation with managers and employers. Respondents also felt looked down upon by their peers in traditional disciplines outside of business studies.[19] These latter academics largely ignore PR as a social phenonemon worthy of study but when they do take notice of it, they are invariably critical. Typical is Webster who, in his review of 'the information society', sees PR as a pollutant of disinterested, rational and transparent debate in society.[20]

PR's reputation is also insecure overseas. A Spanish student with an MA in PR from a British university reports that her friends were not impressed: in that country, PRs are seen as nightclub hostesses. British PR teachers working in China report a TV soap opera entitled 'Mrs Public Relations' about, again, hostesses – but this time in hotels. In the USA, the slang for a public relations person is 'flack', and there is little admiration in the term. In 1970, the novelist Kurt Vonnegut wrote that '... public relations men and slick writers are equally vile in that they both buggered truth for money'. Olasky (1987), a PR man turned teacher, wrote for public relations people 'who want to understand why corporate public relations is sinking deeper into ethical and political quicksand'. He wrote for the conservative, libertarian right; from the neo-marxist left, Gandy (1982) argued that public relations people used an 'information subsidy' to reduce the cost to politicians and public officials of access to information favourable to their employers, the large corporations.

The low status of PR is not a new phenomenon. It was noticed by Pimlott (1951) in the America of the 1940s, the land which Noam Chomsky declares invented public relations.[21] Pimlott was a British observer of the American scene in the early post-war period up to 1950 and he remarks then that 'the fact is public relations practitioners have never enjoyed good public relations'. He notes that the American 'father' of PR, Ivy Lee, who was an adviser to the Rockafeller business empire, was known as 'Poison Ivy'. More generally, public opinion saw PR as a technique favouring the rich. The PR man is a 'plutogogue' who identifies with 'unworthy' causes, who is thought to use dishonest techniques, and who makes claims which are 'eyewash'.

Advantages for funders and producers

A rebalancing of the argument, however, is needed at this stage. Whatever the strength of the case against, PR in the UK is a prosperous activity, with 50,000 people turning over £2.3 billion and with a surplus of job seekers. Those are the dimensions of its visible head in terms of job titles and self-declaration; its invisible tail is much larger. It is a pervasive activity done by business, non-business and anti-business groups, by all points of the political compass, and by material and ideological interests. They use it – as a discrete organisational activity and as a state of mind – because they judge that it will advance their interests. How is that? These are questions for the supply side of PR, about value to its funders and to its producers. (See Chapter 7 for benefits to PR consumers as well as producers.) Two ways to assess value are to inspect what claims trainers make and to look at outcome statements by funders and producers.

Most PR trainers claim favourable outcomes in two areas: influence on public policy-making processes and on news management. A London company's claims, for example, for its one day seminar on 'public affairs campaigns' in 1994 is typical:

> For an increasing number of businesses, and other organisations, the threats from government legislation and regulatory action are especially acute. There is a need to anticipate and address the social and legislative changes, the curbs and regulations – the issues – which bulk large in today's business environment … The development of effective public affairs campaigns is not merely a defensive matter either – such programmes can provide opportunities for competitive advantage … The whole range of marketing, PR, research, legal, intelligence and lobbying activities are needed to design and implement a successful public affairs campaign to counter these threats.
>
> (A Hawksmere flyer for 12.12.94 seminar)

Another conference reminds attenders that 'over a £100m is wasted on ineffective lobbying' and that lobbying 'is an accepted part of the democratic process and one which businesses, trade associations, public bodies and other organisations all have to learn to use to their advantage – if only for fear of being wrong-footed by other groups or organisations with contrary interests' (Hawskmere flyer for 2.10.95 event). A two-day seminar has sessions on 'how to get "good news" stories in the press', 'how to get press coverage for un-newsworthy products', and 'how to handle a hostile press interview' (Meet The Press flyer of 27/28.4.98). Another two-day seminar urges PRs to find out 'how to get maximum positive editorial coverage in the press and on radio/TV' (Meet The Press flyer of 16/17.11.1998). Yet another trainer was offering a one-day 'summer school' on media intelligence and analysis. The benefits claimed included:

- compare your media profile with the competition's
- tell you if your audiences are getting the messages (or not)
- tell you which publications are gunning for you
- identify the important journalists you are not getting through to
- find out if the factory fire last year had a detrimental effect on your image
- generate hard evidence for a libel case.
         (Infopress Communications flyer for 20.8.98 summer school)

Trainers also look for growth areas: 'Ethnic media in the UK' is the title of a day seminar on 'PR and marketing to ethnically diverse communities' which, it is claimed, 'account for 20% of spending in the UK' (Hawksmere flyer of 10.11.98). Another area is employee communications: 'Your people as brand evangelists' is the title of a one-day conference (*PR Week* flyer for 21.1.99 event).

Again, the focus is on public policy-making and public perceptions, with fewer claims for marketing advantage. For example, both Shell and Greenpeace were active PR campaigners during the Brent Spar affair in 1995. Here is what Shell said of Greenpeace's PR and of its own in a briefing brochure:

> From April 30 ... the pressure group waged an expensive, all-out publicity campaign. They used powerful modern global communications technology to speed images and messages – many of them inaccurate and exaggerated – around the world.

About itself, Shell's UK Media Relations Manager said:

> 'Our strategy was to counter allegations with facts, to explain the technical, regulatory and scientific case to all who would listen, and to keep on saying it at every opportunity until – as it did happen – people became more convinced.' ... During the Brent Spar affair, the [media relations] team organised three major news conferences, handled some 1,800 media enquiries ... issued about 40 separate news releases, hundreds of fact sheets, charts, drawings, photographs and sections of our own video footage and arranged more than 100 radio and TV appearances for senior Shell spokesmen.

Trade unions see value in PR, and many have press offices and communications staff. Here is the TUC 'relaunching' itself in 1994: 'Promoting trade unionism and making the TUC count in the public affairs world is at the heart of the TUC's relaunch. To meet this challenge the TUC will undertake regular campaigning and public relations initiatives on a systematic basis, both nationally and regionally, aimed at the media and Parliament' (*Campaigning for change: a new era for the TUC*, 1994, p. 11).

The use of PR is not confined to the search for advantage in marketplaces and work places; it is found widely in the voluntary and public sectors and amongst 'good causes'. The Carers National Association felt compelled to defend publicly the effectiveness of lobbying at the time of the Drapergate affair in July 1998, when a political aide to a senior Labour politician was accused of offering access in order to gain clients for a lobbying firm. They wrote to *The Guardian* (13.7.98, p. 17) that:

> The media has failed to distinguish between the activities of many charities and user groups who engage in lobbying to influence policy and those lobbyists and commercial companies who, for a fee, act for more powerful interests in our society. Groups lobbying on behalf of disabled people and their carers ... have experienced greater political access since this government was elected.

Ashworth Hospital Authority, a high security psychiatric prison, advertised for a communications director (*PR Week*, 24.7.98, p. 24) because 'it is currently going through a period of high-profile and dynamic change and needs to hire a communications director to plan, manage and execute a pro-active communications strategy to influence the long-term public perceptions of the hospital and mental health issues in general'. *The Independent* reports that 'Second World War widows have always deserved a better deal, but they only won the day with the help of an intensive advertising and PR campaign'. The Army is looking for a sports PR consultant 'who will actively promote Army sport, the Army's sports personalities and the "sport in the community" initiative for the Millennium' (*The Guardian*, 8.8.98, p. 23). PR also provides value at a more down-to-earth-level usually treated marginally by the mainstream PR literature: marketing support. The managing director of a well-known shoe brand explains why 'PR is the only marketing tool being used to launch the new range' (*PR Week*, 7.1.93, p. 16): 'The market we are going to will respond better to somebody writing about the product because it's good, than they will to us using advertising to tell them it's good.'

Comparisons with advertising and journalism

If these alleged outcomes and advantages are real, why does PR provoke more criticism than advertising? Peter Mandelson is known to his critics as 'Prince of Darkness', but no such soubriquet attached to Philip Gould, the Labour Party's former advertising specialist and current pollster. Gould had been associated with the communications side of the Labour

Party since 1985, when Mandelson was appointed the Party's director of campaigns and communications. He set up the Shadow Communications Agency, an informal grouping of advertising specialists ready to run election ad campaigns for the party; he advised the 1992 Clinton election campaign on how to avoid the sort of presentational mistakes made by Labour earlier that year in the UK general election; and concentrated up to his resignation on polling for New Labour. He was as much a party apparatchik as Mandelson, but not as much decried. Advertising as an industry[22] is larger than PR and has been critiqued by Vance Packard in *The Hidden Persuaders* [23] – a description more fitting to PR people than to those who persuade off the page in an eye-catching mixture of visuals and words. Yet economic prominence and critical attention have not brought advertising into such low regard.

One explanation is that advertising is an older established industry which has in the past been subject to obloquy – witness *The Hidden Persuaders*. Grant notes (1994, pp. 28, 31–34) in her review of inter-war UK domestic propaganda that its reputation was low and below that of the press.[24] If there is a maturation process for the status of new forms of work and it matches the cycle of diffusion for an innovation, growing acceptance and reputation awaits PR. But it is taking a long time to arrive; in 1948 Goldman was writing (p. 23) that it 'has so far failed of complete acceptance as a profession'. He noted that because of 'cultural lag', surgeons took more than a century to avoid 'the barber's tag'. On that timetable, PR is coming up to its century.

Another argument is that advertising does not attract low regard precisely because it is so visible. It is very obviously display-for-notice-and-advantage, where the display is a 'shriek' from the page.[25] It is easy to imagine a PR person smiling at the compliment that their work was subtle: PR often seeks to 'whisper' from the deep background. To an ad person, the compliment is not so clear. The issue of visibility (here in relation to advertising) is a more major concern about PR, and extends to marketing (Chapter 7) and political lobbying (Chapter 8). More generally, in terms of work prospects and budgets, PR saw itself in the UK as the junior partner to advertising until the later 1980s. It was advertising agencies which had PR sections and not the other way around: these advertising agencies were called 'full service'. Advertising budgets were invariably in £millions, while PR mostly worked for less than £100,000. Now, with the integration of commercial communications, it is more difficult to measure performances but the evidence is that PR is gaining ground.

The role of the media in the creation of the parlous public reputation of PR needs significant evaluation. Some PR people believe that it is the determining factor. It is not a new role for West (1963) reports the existence of a Society for the Discouragement of Public Relations, but it is a persistent role. This has happened at a time when satellite, cable and digital television is finishing off the former BBC and ITV duopoly, and when 219 local and three national (Classic, Virgin and Talk) radio stations are competing with the BBC's 38 local and five national stations (*The Times*, 11.9.98, p. 42).[26] The relationship between PRs and journalists centres on both sides trying to match their mutual dependencies[27] in the supply and demand of information. The matching can be perceived in various ways but they reduce to the title of one survey:[28] 'a partnership or a marriage of convenience?' The survey shows that, on average, editors believe that a quarter of all media coverage is based on PR-sourced material, while PRs believe that the sourcing is 40%. Some PR people blame journalists as their most dangerous bad-mouthers because of their control over the content and tone of public debate. They also note that, like the police, journalists are everywhere; moreover journalists do not deal with advertising agents.

To the lay observer, the PR/journalist relationship would seem to be an unproblematic one of information supply and demand. To those inside the relationship, it is otherwise. Journalists and PRs are often in a state of war – or at least in a state of armed neutrality. Their relationship is often expressed as a 'love-hate' one with strong potential to become 'hate-hate' (see Chapter 9). Journalists do not like PR people because they see them as a block, a barrier to facts, figures and people to which the media want access for a 'good' story. The story is usually showing up the fact, figure or person involved in a critical light. PR people tend to offer the less critical fact, figure or person to the journalist for inspection or interview. Journalists complain that this behaviour leads to a blander story than the one which they could get if the PR person was not guarding the gateway to information.

On the other side, the PR person feels that the journalist is usually seeking out the critical view of the organisation, cause or person which it is the PR person's job to represent. It is irritating to be always asked negative questions of an organisation or person one likes or believes in, or which pays one's wages and/or which one fears. The constant stress on the negative grates on the soul of the PR person after a while, but the balance of power in the PR/media relationship does not normally allow this to be shown – another source of negative feeling for the PR person. The supply and demand for information determines the balance, and it is usually the case that there are fewer journalists 'buying' than sources 'selling' it. The outcome on both sides[29] is at best formal politeness: minimum information given away by both sides and a search for more amenable sources or journalists.

Other structural, less personal factors also work their way in to upset the balance. There is the journalist's perception that his/her paper or station carries too many 'puffs' (favourable, unresearched news items) on behalf of advertisers, powerful interests or the editor's cronies. Some journalists go so far as to talk about the 'courtier media'. Second, there is the perception of a dumbing down of content and journalistic standards in the broadsheet press and terrestrial TV. Third, it is believed that PR people are better paid and have an easier professional life than journalists. To these perceptions can be added cuts in journalists' staffing levels[30] occurring at the same time as the growth in media outlets over the last twenty years, culminating in a feeling among journalists that they are being colonised by PR values and behaviour. In these cirumstances, journalists are likely to be critical of PR and they are in the best position to voice their feelings: they control the words read and heard by their audiences – audiences which PRs want to influence.

It is the (usually private) contention of PR people that journalists continuously bad mouth them out of spite, fear or envy, and that they are the prime builders of their low reputation. An example of a mildly derogatory reference is *The Guardian* (8.8.98, p. 21) with: 'Few senior business figures now doubt that they must take ethical issues seriously. In most cases, that is more than a public relations stance.' A coruscatingly dismissive piece of anti-PR journalism shows how powerful negative feelings can be generated. The *Financial Times* carried the headline (29/30.11.97, Weekend FT, p. iv) 'The pioneer of today's spin-doctors'. It argued that 'Goebbels was a master manipulator' who 'pioneered the techniques of "news management" and public relations'.

Summary

This chapter has argued that PR is an activity which is remarkably noticeable and widespread in our society today – so much so that it is an icon of our times. In volume of activity, it has become a nationally dispersed industry; in social reach, it is done by the Establishment and by the local tennis club; in diversity of goal, it is done by government, global corporation, social campaigner, charity and would-be celebrity. Its funders and producers spend £2.3 billion on it and employ 50,000 people. For them, there are beneficial outcomes and operational advantages allegedly on offer. But despite this pervasiveness, the PR of PR is bad, and through tense relationships with journalists, the low reputation is reported widely. All these factors combine into an unusual asymmetry – a voluntary, legal, universally practised activity devoted to raising the reputation of what it represents, yet generating disquiet about itself. This is the starting point for the next chapter. Is this pervasive activity with low reputation linked to other trends in UK society?

3 Profession of the decade

Part one: Why so pervasive?

The *Spectator* magazine writes of PR as the 'profession of the decade'. Michie (1998) declares that the UK is 'in the midst of a PR explosion'. Indeed, so fitted to contemporary Britain is PR that three authors give it the title of 'fifth estate', adding it after the fourth estate of a free press to the traditional sites of power in the realm.[1] If the PR person is an iconic figure for contemporary UK society, what are the reasons? Michie (pp. 314–15) offered two interconnected reasons: 'individuals, companies and organisations of all kinds have become acutely aware of the need to raise their profile in the news media if they are to exist in the minds of their target audiences' at a time when 'we are also caught up in an equally spectacular multiplication of available media channels'; and 'PR-consciousness is dramatically rising' and so are the business opportunities created for market-making by such 'consciousness'. In this context, note that Matthew Freud sold his celebrity PR agency for £10 million in 1994.[2] The journalist Lynn Barber, who specialises in interviewing the famous, has observed that the power of celebrity PR vis-à-vis the media has increased over the last decade.[3] The combined circulation of the celebrity news magazines *Hello!* and *OK* is 850,000 in the UK.

This chapter and the next ask whether the pervasiveness of PR in contemporary UK society – the result of it being a noticeable and widespread activity – is symptomatic of wider and deeper trends. Ewen's (1996) description of the USA as a PR 'saturated' society has validity for the UK citizen and consumer. Its sense of excess mirrors Moore's (1996, p. 7) image of PR producing 'walls of sound' in society. He notes the similarity between Jonathan Swift's description of straining to be heard in eighteenth-century England and modern communications: 'Whoever hath an ambition to be heard in a crowd must press, and squeeze, and thrust, and climb with indefatigable pains, till he has exalted himself to a certain degree of altitude above them.'

PR is not a free-floating, spontaneous activity – one which is noticeable, widespread, pervasive *and* unconnected to other social phenomena. To put PR into the category 'industry' implies that it is the outcome of a supply and demand interaction. For example, it is implausible to argue that the UK lobbying sector of the PR industry grew from the mid-1980s onwards just because PR people sold it well to business: it is intuitively more likely that it grew as a supply-side response to changed relationships between government and industry, and that business bought PR services as a favourable agent of change. Greenpeace in its campaign against Shell over the Brent Spar oil platform was 'supplied' with favourable public opinion, as are groups against blood sports and genetically modified food. Equally, it is implausible that Matthew Freud could sell his client and media contacts list without there being a market for celebrity news. Editors judge that the appearance of PR man Max Clifford on television and front pages fulfils an editorial need.[4]

Apart from its industrial structure in the service of business and voluntary groups, PR can also be conceptualised as a set of portable attitudes and techniques available to individuals. In this regard, PR is expressive behaviour by a person seeking a personal, favoured outcome. Anyone can publicly adopt those attitudes and techniques, either in their own or a local interest. This is not PR as a collectively organised, professionally done and paid for function, either integral to an organisation or servicing it from outside; it is not PR as an industry. This is PR as 'personal kit' and as a 'cottage industry'; as a set of techniques and attitudes which the individual or small group can deploy in the media, in lobbying and in consumer relations to secure advantage. This is the PR of an author promoting a book; of a person entangled with the civil or criminal judicial system;[5] of a congregation seeking to expel their priest; of a dissatisfied consumer publicly complaining about bad pensions advice; of a community group protesting against a new road scheme; of a band of hobbyists promoting their model train exhibition in the church hall; of a protester making a public point with or without pressure group help.[6]

This categorisation of PR into the industrial, the 'cottage industry' and the 'personal kit' forms allows its instrumental nature to be identified. You do not do PR for its own sake. It is instrumental activity, display-for-notice-and-advantage, and done to influence favourably the significant 'other', and done by the large company, by the national pressure group, by the individual, by the local community group. Edmund Burke would recognise in the tens of thousands of these groups around the country the contemporary equivalent of his 'small platoons' and 'sub-divisions' of society, in which feelings of commitment and of service are generated between members, in which 'public affections' germinated and in which today's community feeling – and its predecessor 'public spiritedness' – come alive in shared effort.[7]

But why is the PR producer and consumer readier now to resort to and respond to PR than in an earlier period? Does PR by Shell, by Outrage, by government, by the local tennis club, by a celebrity, by an aggrieved individual connect with specific society-wide economic, political and cultural trends in the UK today? What is the nature of these connections? But first, it is revealing to look at what some PR people have said about them.

Insiders' views

PR people write about this connectivity and see it as mutually beneficial for PR and UK society. The Institute of Public Relations (IPR) celebrated its 50th anniversary on 10 February 1998 and published *Managing Communication in a Changing World* for the event. In it, two social phenomena were identified by Graham Lancaster (the co-founder of Biss Lancaster, a marketing public relations agency, in 1978) as influences on PR in the last 20 years: the decline in social deference and the growth of consumer capitalism. He traces the influence of these changes (pp. 46–7) on PR and then via PR back into society:

> It was from these fertile grounds – the loss of trust and deference in institutions and the insatiable demand for technical and style guidance – that the modern PR industry grew into the robust and powerful business it is today. By re-earning trust for our great companies, brands and institutions – raising their favourability ratings. And by using third party endorsement and data-driven campaigns to achieve what PR does so much better than advertising – anticipating and then filling the vacuum of consumer uncertainty in purchase.... Raising trust in corporations and helping informed customer choice. Pretty important issues in any successful democracy.

Simon Lewis, now the Queen's Communications Secretary but then working for British Gas, wrote in the same booklet about 'the developing trends which will challenge the public relations industry and the IPR in the twenty-first century' (pp. 31–3). His analysis extrapolated seven external factors. They are: more media outlets, more influential single-issue pressure groups, greater responsiveness by companies to stakeholders, more communication by companies, globalisation, mounting environmental concerns, and young people with more responsibility earlier in life. He also noted three influential factors internal to the industry: legal, accountancy and management firms trespassing on PR territory, more debate about the regulation of PR, and the continued growth of PR.[8]

PR and accelerated pluralism

The rest of this chapter and the next explore the cluster of specific connections between PR and its host society (connections with business, markets, pressure and cause groups, media, celebrity and a soured atmosphere of public debate); they can all be related to a more general significant change in UK society – its increased pluralism. This change has taken two forms.

Since the 1960s, the UK has witnessed great, observable changes in personal behaviour by its citizens and in collective behaviour by voluntary groups. The personal behavioural changes derive principally from altered values regarding sex, gender, lifestyle, the environment, race, consumption and religion. The collective behavioural changes derive from the need to establish enough social acceptance and tolerance for these changed personal behaviours to be practised by individuals, free from the harassment of prevailing dominant social forces. These two kinds of changes have given individuals a choice of personal behaviours, and of collective action in groups[9] to promote and defend those choices. This increased pluralism of values and groups has been associated with social movements (e.g. feminism, environmentalism, consumerism, multi-ethnicity, sexual equality) and it is open to question which of the two changes described above is the more influential in the growth of modern social movements. The latter are, however, distinguished by 'contentious collective action' which, argues Tarrow (1994), is created by judging opportunistically which political circumstances will successfully sustain 'contention by convention' (e.g. sit-ins, media events, petitions, demonstrations, networking).

The argument here is not that changes in observable, personal behaviours and in the development of groups freely joined by individuals are phenomena new to the period studied. For example, wealthy women in the eighteenth century asserted 'rights' modern women would acclaim today and, in religion, unitarians held ideas about the workings of the universe closely associated with the 'laws' of modern science. Voluntary associations have a long history in the UK; in the modern period they date back to the political clubs of the late eighteenth century and to Chartism in the early nineteenth century. They continued throughout the Victorian period with the growth of the trade unions, co-operative and hobby/leisure movements. Nor is the argument that they did not use techniques which we today would label as PR. There is ample evidence that they did use PR. (See Wring (1998)[10] for insights into the use of PR by the political left in 1930s, and Black (1973) for the major involvement of the National Union of Local Government Officers in the 1948 foundation of the IPR.)

Since the 1960s, the trend to more pluralism of publicly expressed values and behaviours and to more voluntary associations has accelerated.[11] But what is the connection of this accelerated pluralism with PR? The key link lies in the need of individuals for new personal values and behaviours to be accepted or at least tolerated by society. One cannot be gay in an open way if homosexuality is illegal; one cannot be a sovereign consumer without the labelling of genetically modified food; one cannot be an informed citizen if advice to ministers is secret. PR is display-for-notice-and-advantage. It is a set of techniques amenable for the promotion of values, done by an industry, done by an individual alone or by voluntary groups, and available in paid professional form or in 'personal kit' and 'cottage industry' forms. This shift in UK society to more expression by individuals of different personal values via voluntary, often local, groups is identified here as value pluralism and group pluralism of a civic kind. Brought together they will be called civic pluralism.

In addition to this kind of pluralism, a commercial variant of pluralism has come to the fore in the UK in approximately the same period. From the middle of the 1970s, it was noticeable that the climate of ideas about markets and business was shifting away from the collective and the planned towards the singular and the autonomous. This altered paradigm for the UK political economy has resulted in business and pro-market interests predominating over their ideological and material competitors. Collectivism and corporatism have faded, whether temporarily or not. Now, the mainstream political parties vie to be more business-friendly. They do so because of a broader shift in ruling ideas in favour of many business values. In this shift, competition is proclaimed over monopoly; consumers are flattered rather than producers cared for; markets have grown up where the plan once regulated; private wealth is privileged over public goods. As a result, there is now in the UK a pronounced commercial pluralism. This is the condition where market and business values, ideas and practices in the pursuit of monetary advantage prevail, despite substantial challenge from non-business or anti-business groups. Without it, accelerated pluralism would not affect the lives of the population of the UK. Tens of millions are affected by personal and civic value changes: all are affected by market and business changes.

Overall, the increased emphases on different values and differing personal behaviours, on voluntary associations for their promotion and defence, and on the marketable and the profitable have combined to create a sustained pressure for change in private and public life. PR is principally concerned with public life; the pressure for change in that domain can be characterised as more obvious, more variegated and less monolithic than in the period between World War II and the 1960s. The outcome is a more competitive, argumentative and commercialised public domain: one reached through the dual agencies of increased individual expression and group representation, and of more powerful businesses and markets.[12] It is an outcome which encourages promotional activity generally, and which encourages PR in particular as an appropriate means to secure advantage for individuals, pressure and cause groups and for the suppliers of goods and services, both publicly and privately owned.

The promotional mind-set

Against the background of this generalised acceptance of the promotional mind-set, PR has prospered and become a set of attitudes and techniques accepted in work and non-work behaviour. It is clear that the increased resort to PR since the 1960s involves both the business and public sectors, who were early, major users of PR, and newer users in non-business and anti-business groups. In addition, late adopters, such as aggrieved and ambitious individuals have taken to PR, noting its perceived efficiency in the struggle for advantage and its low cost. Increased PR activity since the 1960s is at root connected with the communicative aspects of the rise and dominance of the neo-liberal paradigm in the UK, which has been an incubating environment for more civic and more commercial pluralism. Pluralism is a competitive condition in which the 'one' has to compete for survival amongst the 'many'. PR is an accessible set of promotional attitudes and techniques for survival in this competition.

Before looking more closely at accelerated pluralism and PR, it is helpful to clarify parts of the surrounding context. Is accelerated pluralism the same as neo-liberalism? Apart from any coincidental identity, they are separate: the former is a societal process and the latter a philosophy. The neo-liberal welcomes pluralism as an agent for the expression of individualism and free association, but also notes that is a process of interest intermediation rather than a set of values regarding the individual and the state. Thus pluralism facilitates the expression of values and behaviours which are inimical to neo-liberalism. For example, environmentalism and consumerism have flourished during the period of accelerated pluralism, but they are viewed with suspicion by the neo-liberal as imposed, external costs on markets. Put another way, pluralism allows power to countervail power, without regard to consistency with neo-liberal values.

The second contextual point is that PR is a public activity. The previous description of civic (value, group) pluralism and commercial (markets and business) pluralism emphasises public as opposed to private behaviour. The focus is on the public aspects of private matters, for PR does not operate in the private domain of individuals where intimacies are found, even though analogous processes of display, persuasion, influence and power exist there. PR is *public* relations: public communicative relations of display-for-notice-and-advantage aimed at the distinct public 'other'. These relations are observable, at least, to the subjects and objects of the display and to third parties, whether in small numbers or in masses. In the private domain, the distinction between subject and object is blurred by the intensity and proximity of relationships. This is the difference between influencing a life partner, a parent or a child as opposed to a legislator, a trade association or an employer. PR, therefore, deals indirectly with private matters and only in a public way. It is involved with private domain matters (e.g. sex, religion, individual abuse) when they are in the public domain for one or more of three reasons: commercialisation (e.g. sex as a market activity), conceptual and ideological dispute (e.g. marriage versus divorce), or regulation (e.g. children, parents and adoption).[13]

The third contextual point is that it is important to identify the social location where PR – this public activity available to individuals, to small voluntary groups and to big business alike – is done when it does not involve government directly or immediately. It is mostly done in civil society, where this is understood as the zone of social action, bounded by government on one side in terms of social power and influence, and by the individual and family on the other side, and is extended to include markets. Civil society is a term made to bear many meanings (e.g. civilised as opposed to uneducated society, the site of ideological production in capitalist society, the liberal alternative to totalitarian society), as discussed by Kumar (1993). He indicates that the majority British and American usage is to locate civil society as an area of social activity separate from government, where there is freedom of association, and excluding the private life of individuals and of family. This is the meaning adopted in this book and is identified as the social site for most PR (see Chapter 1).

In summary, PR in the UK since the 1960s is an attitudinal and communicative consequence of societal change – accelerated pluralism – through which it is structurally connected to its host society. The connections are worth looking at in more detail for what they say about PR.

More groups, more PR

The accelerated pluralism, which has been identified as the structural cause of the increase in PR, has a pressure and cause group basis; it either challenges business interests (e.g. the campaign to end live animal exports) or promotes public goods (e.g. the campaign for more open government). So far, non-business groups have been discussed quite narrowly in terms of examples of voluntary associations of individuals with new and challenging values. It is time to place these non-business groups in the context of the UK political economy: how they interact with the political decision-making process.

Grant (1995) has shown how these groups have grown in membership since the 1960s: a well-known example is the Royal Society for the Protection of Birds which, with 1,001,200 members in 1998, has more members than the three main political parties. It is hard to estimate the total number of these assorted voluntary groups which represent interests and causes nationally and locally and which are promotional to greater and lesser degrees. In the environmental field, James and Moloney (1995) note that the 1990 *Directory for the Environment* listed 1,500 entries; the 1993 *Environmental Yearbook* 2,750. Their literature review reveals 'guestimates' that membership doubled between 1960 and 1970, and again from then to 1980. A 1992 figure gave membership at 5.8 million people. It is harder still to estimate the number of groups in the anti-roads movement, when activists form loose, temporary alliances to combat particular schemes and then re-group elsewhere.

The UK's most famous tunneller since prisoners of war escaped from German stalags is Swampy; he was digging away at both Newbury by-pass and Manchester airport in 1997/8 with the support of other full-time activists and local suppporters. Swampy and his colleagues are expert at PR techniques as their mastery of media relations shows, an expertise confirmed by appearances on national TV panel shows. Indeed, sometimes the clash of interests over roads is described in language natural to PR people and journalists – as a 'PR battle' won by 'eco warriors'.[14] The ease with media relations on the part of these 'outsider' groups – those not on the consultative lists of government departments – is a reminder that the political agenda and status of groups and organisations is a determinant of their PR style. ICI, an 'insider' organisation, is more likely to lobby Whitehall privately and avoid the media when it seeks to influence public policy.[15] But the boundaries of PR as a polite activity are moving: proactive 'planning lobbyists' are working for property developers, and 'professional resistance' all the way up to Parliament is the tactic of some middle-class protest groups.[16]

A similar PR style to Swampy (but with elements of the insider approach) has been described by Bryant (1996), a former Tory councillor turned roads activist, in the attempt to stop the bulldozing of Twyford Down to clear the way for the Winchester by-pass. That PR campaign was characterised by close relations with national journalists, lobbying politicians at Westminster and Brussels, middle-class spokespeople and media-friendly statements and events for the local media; the building of local support groups, and a loose alliance with Friends of the Earth at the national level. Nationally established groups have PR departments and practices that would sit easily in business headquarters: press officers, campaign teams, liaison with marketing and advertising people, parliamentary officers. For example, Stonewall, the pressure group for lesbian and gay equality, sent a direct mail shot to members after the death from bullying of a schoolboy, with 'the good news ... that Government officials have promised to listen to Stonewall's recommendations'.

These examples of relatively well organised high-profile groups can be represented as one end of a continuum of group PR. At the other end are the resource-poor groups, such as the 700 voluntary groups in the London borough of Tower Hamlets.[17] Eight per cent of them lobby local councillors, community relations officers, and people on public bodies with regeneration funds. They do not talk about 'doing PR'; rather they advocate their case, they talk persuasively. It is estimated that another ten per cent do PR as would be recognised by industry professionals, using annual reports, executive briefings, media appearances, and public speaking.[18] Resource-poor groups like those in Tower Hamlets are represented locally in councils for voluntary services and these, in turn, are represented nationally by the National Association of Councils for Voluntary Services.

This body brings together 250 local councils in towns, cities and rural areas. These are doing media relations in their localities, sending out newsletters and lobbying to advance their interests with local government and businesses, while at the national level they are trained in communications.[19] It is claimed each of these 250 local councils represents, on average, 100 single interest groups, many of them doing PR. Another national body, the National Council for Voluntary Organisations, which represents many nationally organised voluntary bodies, says on its website that it 'is a highly effective lobbying organisation and represents ... views ... to government, the Charity Commission, the EU and other bodies'. The council and two-thirds of its 1,000 constituent bodies use PR techniques such as lobbying, media relations, staged events, conference and exhibition presentations.[20] Charity fundraisers also use many PR techniques; donations have dropped by a third since the introduction of the National Lottery. Although these PR people may say 'public relations' in private, they prefer 'campaigning' or 'communication' in public.

In terms of functions, large pressure group PR and business PR differ most noticeably in the fund-raising and membership liaison functions in groups, mirrored by sponsorship and community relation functions in businesses. But there remain more similarities than differences. A national charity with 500 employees, 8,000 members and 95,000 'volunteers' wants a PR manager 'to embrace the challenge of raising our profile within a rapidly changing environment'. The tasks and the militaristic tone of the advertisement wording could have come from the recruitment section of human resource management in a plc.[21] The spread of the marketing culture in UK society has 'marketised' attitudes and practices in voluntary sector bodies. PR is a natural beneficiary.

This great river of promotional material from pressure and cause groups is the communicative expression of civic pluralism (of both values and groups) which is a major influence on the public policy decision-making process.[22] It is both the symbolic aspect of the proactive struggle to assert new ideas, values and behaviours in civic society (e.g. anti-racism, sexual equality) and the symbolic aspect of the reactive struggle against dominant interests (e.g. opposition to pollution by industry, to the live export of animals, to monopoly practice in markets).

More business, more PR

It is a commonplace among PR people that PR is stronger to the west of the UK and that towards the east, it is weaker. This is because the neo-liberal paradigm in general, and commercial pluralism in particular, are more dominant in the USA. Modern public relations developed in the fourth quarter of the nineteenth century as marketing communications in the USA for land-selling companies and railways as the West was settled. It was also used defensively by business interests when they were defending monopolies, breaking strikes, explaining railway crashes in the 'trust busting' and 'muckraker' era. It was later used by press agents working for the new studios in Hollywood. The history of PR in America was almost exclusively associated with business until 1916, when its techniques were used by the official Committee on Public Information (known as the Creel committee) to gain suppport for American entry into World War I. It developed significantly in the UK in the inter-war years with prestigious, large organisations such as Southern Railways, The Port of London Authority, the Empire Marketing Board, Shell, Imperial Airways employing PR people (see L'Etang 1998 and Chapter 6 of this book).

PR people in the UK today consider their practice to be nearer to the American than to that of mainland western Europe. In Eastern Europe, it was unknown as an activity outside of government before 1989 but since then it has grown as various forms of liberal democracy and markets have appeared. The American author Brady writing in the middle of World War II (1943, pp. 287–93) prefigured this navigational rule of thumb when he linked the direction of travel to political forms: 'Broadly speaking the importance of public relations ... decreases as one moves away from countries with long and deep-seated liberal, democratic, and parliamentary institutions.' It was 'almost non-existent' in Germany, Italy and Japan. His argument is that public relations is a technique used by dominant business and social groups in liberal capitalist democracies to ensure their dominance, while the same groups in other forms of society rely on feudalism and totalitarian government. He associated PR with liberal, market-orientated, capitalist societies and with Anglo-American societies in particular. Together with lawyers and the press, PR people are among the 'pliant agents of organised business' (Foreword, p. xv).[23] They 'sell the public' 'the enterprise system' with appeals to 'social harmony' and 'class collaboration' and the 'middle class' perspective on behalf of the 'big businessman' who 'educates' or 'leads' the general public for the 'community' good. This line of argument makes PR a 'manufacturer of consent' in favour of business interests, and is taken up by Carey (1995), Herman and Chomsky (1988) and Tedlow (1979).

What is the evidence in the contemporary UK to support the thesis that PR is a 'pliant' agency for promoting business interests? Historically, PR has been used by big business in the USA and the UK to promote and protect its interests; in the UK today that process continues (see Chapter 6). Business is the largest user, if not employer, of PR in the UK: the connection between the two is so close that it is assumed to be organic and natural. The peak organisations for business – big and small – lobby government privately and are heavily reported in the media when they go public. Individual businesses do the same when their interests are affected.[24] Business leaders and spokespeople are in the media with views on a gamut of issues – much more so than trade unionists. PR texts written by UK authors devote more space to PR as a business service than to alternative users in the public and voluntary sectors.[25]

In the 1960s, when government policy towards the political economy was corporatist, business and trade union representative bodies used PR as communicative support for price and incomes policy, industrial restructuring, investment and productivity increases, national planning,[26] and industrial relations reform. Since the middle of the 1970s, and the successful challenge of the ideas, attitudes and policies known as Thatcherism (the UK version of the neo-liberal paradigm) to the preceding dominant ideas and attitudes about the political economy, the intellectual and affective climate has become even more nurturing of closer links between PR and business. The pre-Thatcherite ideas and attitudes were collectivist, equalitarian, and hesitant or unenthusiastic towards markets and business. Thatcherism is more directly market- and business-friendly in its emphasis on the individual rather than the collective, its celebration of self-help, its promotion of enterprise, its praise of capitalism, and its denigration of planning and socialism. Policy continued into the later 1990s when the major elements of this paradigm were accepted by the new Labour government in 1997.

The 1979 election of Mrs Thatcher therefore witnessed the publication of previously unheard of messages from a UK government: persuasive communications to accept entrepreneurship and markets. PR benefited both from the new readiness of business to assert publicly the values of the 'enterprise society', and from the consequent larger flow of marketing communications into markets which were proclaimed to be invigorated by other supply-side reforms, such as price and social market deregulation, the reduction of trade union power and privatisation. For a while in the early 1980s, promoting markets and marketing was the defining management activity.

PR as a set of communications techniques and as an industry was put to 'pliant' and profitable service in the promotion of business in three distinct but interrelated ways. First, it was used to promote business as an important – if not the most important – interest in the UK political economy (through the media PR of business peak organisations and leaders). Second, it was used to promote the specific interests of business sectors and individual companies (through the lobbying PR of trade associations and single firms). Third, it promoted the goods and services produced by tens of thousands of businesses for sale in markets (through PR for markets). The rise in prominence of PR since the 1960s has one of its major sources in the various versions of market- and business-friendly policy tried, amended and abandoned by governments in the past four decades.

More markets, more PR

Freer markets are a fuller expression of pluralism in the commercial domain, and attempts were made in the 1970s, 80s and 90s to move UK markets towards more open entry and competition. It is clear that PR benefited from this policy drift. It is hard to estimate what percentage of PR jobs are devoted to marketing tasks, but a serviceable rule of thumb is 70%. Chapter 7 describes how PR is increasing its share of commercial communications budgets vis-à-vis advertising, and how the professional focus on integrated communications campaigns and the promotion of complex, marketing propositions, such as 'environmentally friendly', 'organic' and 'lifestyle' consumption, favours PR.

The PR entrepreneur Graham Lancaster, quoted earlier p. 33, stressed the contribution of PR to consumer markets. It is hard to demonstrate conclusively and empirically its rising contribution, but it is asserted as a matter of course in the relevant literature and is an unchallenged assumption in the conversation of PR and marketing people. These workplace assumptions reflect a wider social acceptance, particularly since the fall of the Iron Curtain in 1989, that markets are a better distributor of scarce resources than central planning.

PR for markets and for marketing is PR as persuasive communication in the hands of the producers of goods and services rather than of public policy decision-makers. It is a noticeable, widespread and pervasive form of PR. It is a near universal form of promotion of goods and services in the UK marketplace. This is PR as the promotion of genetically modified food and of the national lottery, as the organiser of competitions, say, for the top three reasons for buying a holiday, as the organising hand behind the radio road show or exhibition stand at the county show, as the author of the brochure on healthy eating picked up in the supermarket or the leaflets on financial services which fall out of the newspaper each Sunday. Where there are markets, there is promotion and, therefore, PR.

PR is in its most widespread, popular and pervasive form when it works for consumption. It is PR as popular culture aimed at the majority of UK citizens in their role as consumers. It links youth culture to consumption via sponsorships, testimonials of use, and events creation with pop stars and celebrities. It links families with consumption via lifestyle editorial. It is PR for goods and services at a time when marketeers argue that the consumer is more educated, aware and critical about society in general, more sensitive to environmental and ethical issues, and more ready to act on her beliefs. These marketeers point to social activism extending to markets. Examples are campaigns for fair trading with the developing world (e.g. FairTrade), for the 'pink pound', for the boycott of Shell petrol, especially in Germany, at the time of Brent Spar, and for the end to fur sales and to tobacco products (e.g. ASH).

Summary

Contemporary PR in the UK is both a professional, management activity done in bureaucracies, and a portable set of attitudes and techniques for individuals. It is a structured industry serving other industries, a 'cottage industry' done by voluntary bodies and social activists, and 'personal kit' for celebrities and aggrieved individuals. It has grown out of the accelerated civic (values and groups) pluralism and commercial (markets and business) pluralism of the last forty years of twentieth century Britain. The adoption by millions of UK citizens of new values and behaviours towards, for example, the environment, consumerism, gender roles, sexual behaviour, multi-ethnicity; their membership of tens of thousands of voluntary groups to promote and defend these changes; the expansion of markets and businesses as the core economic institutions – these are the constituent elements of the accelerated pluralism to which PR is connected as a communicative outcome.

PR is a low-cost distribution of public information using specific techniques of display-for-notice-and-advantage. Local and national voluntary bodies and pressure groups use it extensively, preferring to call it campaigning or communications. For businesses, PR is a specialist management function to defend and advance their interests in UK public policy-making and in markets, to increase the sale of goods and services. PR for business has always been active but it has flourished since the late 1970s. Its use has grown in UK markets since they became (generally) more competitive under the Thatcherite reforms. PR for goods and services is often linked to popular culture via celebrity endorsements and new lifestyle promotion.

4 Profession of the decade

Part two: Why so insistent? PR links to external and internal media and persuasion

Another area where accelerated pluralism creates more opportunities for PR is the media. This is especially valid when viewing the media as business and as the first destination of most PR activity. Michie (1998) has posited PR growth on the prior increase of 'available media channels'. Recent growth in the UK has been unprecedented and it is plausible to talk of the the media-isation of society. It is, moreover, possible to differentiate among types of media growth since the 1960s. There have been increases in media channels (e.g. the arrival of commercial radio), in technologies (e.g. cable and digital), in new forms (multimedia and computer-based) and in titles. PR is a major beneficiary of this mutlifaceted growth because most of its techniques are designed for media acceptance and editorial space has greatly multiplied. Commercial pluralism results in more opportunities for the media-as-business; civic pluralism generates more copy for these more numerous outlets. It is arguable that media owners and PR people[1] have been the major beneficiaries of media growth, while benefits for media staff and audiences are more problematic.

Labour Market Trends (November 1998) from the Office for National Statistics show that people employed in the media – TV, radio, film, and newspapers – have increased over the four-year period from June 1994 to June 1998 from 124,000 to154,000.[2] The current expansion began in 1967 with the first local radio station at BBC Leicester; by 1970 there were 20 such stations. Commercial (mainland legal) radio began in 1973 with Capital Radio and LBC. By 1996, there were 176 such stations operating by broadcasting: 28 by cable and 14 by satellite. The 1996 Broadcasting Act envisages up to 300 digital terrestrial and satellite channels (see Franklin 1998, pp. 18, 129, 141). Technical changes have influenced working practices inside the media to the great advantage of PR. These include the rise of ENG (electronic news gathering), the need for multi-skilled staff, the rise of freelances, the decline in staff positions, the decline in trade union recognition, the imposition of individual contracts, lower entry salaries, more media studies graduates, and less internal training. These changes result in fewer full-time journalists doing more by more means in less time. The use of PR material reduces the work pressures on modern journalists. The contemporary UK media, therefore, presents PR people with the attractive double prospect of more editorial space to occupy than ever before and of fewer gatekeepers to control entry.

These internal changes have paralleled the commercialisation of managements at the helm of media businesses quoted on the Stock Exhange, with the imperative to increase profits by means of a more marketised approach to media content. This priority is realised as celebrity as news, the 'dumbing down' of media contents, the rise of 'red top' and 'broadloid' newspapers,[3] the appearance of 'infotainment', and the 'focused' programme for 'targeted' audiences. Franklin (1997) has gathered all these changes together into the Newszak thesis that news is a product designed and promoted to gain market share for the media business, with an emphasis on entertaining, unchallenging, personal items.

For the PR industry, this amounts to a PR-isation of the media (see Chapter 9). The balance of power in the PR/journalist relationship is swinging in favour of PR. PR industry surveys,[4] independent research (see Chapter 2), and trade gossip all confirm the large amount of PR material getting into editorial pages with little, if any, independent checking[5] (Franklin, pp. 112–14). This is especially true about business, consumer goods and services, and lifestyle pages and programmes, as well as free newspapers and advertorial supplements. Little independent checking is also a feature of political news obtained from spin doctors, who are ready to berate journalists if they are critical and with whom journalists feel they have to 'keep in'. This lack of checking is partially the result of reduced media staffing levels; it also follows from the conscious or unconscious acceptance by editors and newsdesks of the Newszak concept. Indeed, the most trivial element of Newszak has called forth a whole new branch of the PR industry: celebrity PR (see below).

Some PR people have been concerned about this media expansion because of the difficulty in keeping track of titles and journalists, and creating tailored stories, features and ideas: they describe it as fragmentation, with an implied loss of control. To those who see PR as a flexible promotional tool to be used opportunistically, this fragmentation view is too negative. Instead, they see more channels for reaching their target publics and know that media staff are hard-pressed to fill editorial space. The growing demand for their material is just one sign of the balance of power tilting towards them.

Apart from having a more numerous and a more sympathetic media to supply material to, PR has developed its own forms of media in competition with the established ones, particularly in the magazine sector. PR has unpdated vanity publishing into its modern, corporate form – contract or customer publishing, where a business pays a publisher to produce and distribute a magazine devoted to its goods and services. The best known examples are British Airways' High Life, and the magazines of Sainsbury's, the AA, and Marks and Spencer. Since 1990, this sector has grown by 300%, has become an industry worth over £300 million, and with low cover prices has eaten into the sales of established bookstand magazines.[6]

The PR industry is the beneficiary of the expanded media in another way as well: PR as a personal service for the powerful, rich, famous or those just called a celebrity. It now provides a combined promotion and protection service working either with or against the media on behalf of elite individuals. The rich and powerful have for long had personal accountants, lawyers and fitness trainers; now they have personal spokespersons.[7]

Celebrity culture

A process of celebrity manufacture is going on. Witness, for example, the rise of the 'celebrity chef' and even the 'celebrity academic'.[8] Witness the rise of *Hello!* and *OK* magazines. Witness the many media appearances by Max Clifford – variously described as publicist, PR 'guru', or PR 'maestro' – as a kind of expert witness of the process. He is explicit about the manufacturing: 'Everything is about image – which is wonderful for me because image-making is my profession' and 'I have no problems creating false images for stars because they exist for amusement. They manipulate the media to put bums on seats or sell records.'[9] This manufacture – this lying – is not new, for it was seen at the time of the rise of the film industry at the turn of the twentieth century, and there have always been press agents at work to fill the show business columns of the tabloid press. Both celebrity manufacture and press agentry are propaganda in a relatively harmless form.

Celebrity manufacture has increased since the mid-1980s. Ekow Eshun writes:[10]

> There is, among the public today a greater awareness of the process of manufacture involved in creating a star. We know that they are not simply born. Instead ... they must seize their moment and spin it and spin it until the result is newspaper headlines, TV appearances and lucrative product endorsements. Thanks to the media's own obsession with spin, we are all less naïve about the collusion between event organisers, agents, paparazzi and stars that helps create a tabloid sensation.

This sounds like a *cri de cœur* shouted out in great liberal hope. It is a somewhat optimistic judgement about the mass media audience: it seems unlikely that many readers of *Hello!* and *OK* are bothered enough about media representations to want to enoy their magazines at two levels.

The souring of pluralism

Tannen (1998) has written about a souring of pluralism which she calls the argument culture. 'Our spirits are corroded by living in an atmosphere of unrelenting contention – an argument culture ... which urges us to approach the world – and the people in it – in an adversarial frame of mind' (p. 3). She draws a distinction between the positive of *making an argument* in public for a point of view and the negative of *having an argument*. Her argument-makers are the media, journalists, politicians, academics and e-mailers. She writes about US society, but the tone she ascribes to its politics and civil society, as bitter and corrosive arenas of negative and destructive argument for self interest can be heard sometimes in UK society today. If to complain is a first step in the making of an argument, there are signs that British consumers are moving in that direction: a survey found that over half of UK consumers had formally complained in the previous year.[11] PR is a megaphone for this tone and, indeed, Susskind and Field (1996, pp. 1–9) explicitly blame PR for its contribution to what they call an 'angry public'; the characterisation can be related to the argument culture in that social anger is a cause of argument and often leads to more. They argue that the public is angry because 'business and government leaders have covered up mistakes, concealed evidence of potential risks, made misleading statements, and often lied'.

PR benefits from the media's role in this putative 'argument culture' because the media's editorial need is invariably for the negative, the sensational and the polarised. The media has always thrived on public disputes and contests, and there is now more UK media. PR grows when the media want material or spokespeople for one side in dichotomous articles and interviews. It also benefits from media demand for celebrities who are often extreme in their behaviour and words, to the point of being salacious and offensive.

In a broader context, PR benefits, too, from a more competitive civil society where interests are in a sharper contest for advantage. Susskind and Field argue that US business and government leaders fuel this sharper – in their word, angry – contest, aided and abetted by conventional PR, which they explictly name. They write that these leaders 'attempt to blunt or undercut the public's concerns by dredging up countervailing "facts" or rebuttals from pseudo-independent experts and unscientific polls. They commit to nothing and admit to nothing.' This more competitive civil society can be seen in the UK today. The concept of 'public spiritedness', explicit in the 1950s, is not found on many lips today. The rise of business to its position as the most powerful and privileged interest in UK society, and its attempted justification of that prominence, leads to a PR contest between it and anti- and non-business interests. The business interest is challenged over its share of gross national product and income, and over the validity of business values, ideas and policies. Forty anti-capitalist groups combined in a 'carnival against capitalism' on 18 June 1998 to demonstrate in European cities against international trade and debt policies.

Even putting the contest over business to one side, civil society is still generally more competitive in the UK today than it was in the 1960s, and PR benefits from this larger competitive arena for the struggle of interests. The previous chapter described how social movements have grown in prominence in their challenge to established values and behaviours. For groups arising from these movements, PR is a key element in an organised and structured communicative challenge to the status quo. They run 'campaigns' and, if they are large and established, they have communications departments. The most frequently mentioned example is Greenpeace and its campaigns against Shell and against genetically modified food. As regards aggrieved individuals, PR is a set of attitudes and techniques by which they can state their case. They use the media and they lobby decision-makers with – or without – a PR professional to state their case. Examples are Louise Woodward, the *au pair* accused of child murder, and Geoffrey Boycott, the cricketer charged with violence against his mistress.

PR for pressure and cause groups and for individuals brings more voices to the argument culture. PR is the modern, mass mediated, voice of the many or the one, struggling to gain material and/or ideological advantage in a hostile or indifferent world. That PR voice is usually assertive in either a defensive or offensive way, often to a combative point. PR is always a voice, even when spoken in private, privileged channels. It is always persuasive by intent. It is display-for-notice-and-advantage. These pleadings for self-interested advantage do sour the debate surrounding the accelerated pluralism of values and of groups.

All these trends and forces propel UK society towards membership of the argument culture. But has the UK reached that state? That would be too strong a conclusion, since Tannen describes contemporary US society, but there is enough evidence to conclude that the UK represents a weak version of the argument culture. The UK is, so far, a 'grumble' culture and PR plays a role in sharpening the sense of dissatisfaction, disempowerment and dispossession which motivates the 'grumble'. Class and the social deference which it engenders, the lingering sense of public spiritedness, the underdevelopment of the PR industry in the UK compared with USA standards, the sense of social solidarity which may be growing among some citizens/consumers – all these are specific UK factors halting movement from the 'grumble' to the the full-blown, bitter opposition of 'argument' which Tannen condemns.

Media evidence for a UK grumble culture can be found in shows on UK television,[12] such as those of Gerry Springer, Winifred Ophrey, Robert Kilroy Silk and Vanessa Feltz – milder versions of the US radio 'shock jocks'. The simplifications of tabloid newspapers – a journalism more developed in the UK than the USA – reduce issues and events to new and often amusing forms of slang and of slogan. The whole Charles and Diana relationship after divorce can be read as one long public argument – domestic row made public soap opera – of six-years duration. The ritualised form of politics seen in the House of Commons is politics reduced to the opposition of two sides, highly adversarial and personal. Markets and businesses are openly combative in their search for marginal advantage, and their competitive instincts lead to aggressive statements about uniqueness and specialness, either through lobbying or more assertive advertising and marketing PR. The rise of 'outsider' groups with aggressive tactics for challenging conventional thinking and behaviour, such as Outrage, Earth First!, UK Alarm, Animal Liberation and Road Rage, add to a cacophony of clamouring interests and causes, shouting their self-interest in civic society – all willingly aided by the PR megaphone.

PR as a large-scale industry, as a 'cottage industry' and as 'personal kit' has brought the competition of interests into the open, into the public spaces of civil society. This does not mean, however, that there was no competition of interests before – just that it was often hidden and class-biased. In the UK, the Establishment was the network for handling the competition between privileged interests – privately. Miller (1987) argues that this decline of the most privileged network in UK society has led to more lobbying. A grumble/argument culture is not new: the media and PR today ensure that it is a public culture.

This allusion to a historical dimension shows a major weakness in Tannen's thesis. Her argument does not have a chronology (about the US) and it does not proffer any developmental pattern to her central idea of increasing verbal aggression.[13] Quantifying non-physical aggression expressed in society is impossible, but what can be described is the amount, distribution and quantity of reportage about it. PR in the UK has encouraged that type of reportage by viewing verbal aggression as a transmission channel for more of its messages. Another weakness in Tannen's presentation is that she reveals at the end (p. 276) that she does not want to put an end to argument but wants to diversify modes of dialogue.

Is a grumble culture dysfunctional for society? Is an argument culture? Tannen's call for diversification suggests that when there are several dialogic modes operating, they are functional. Many grumbles/arguments are opening positions in negotiations and are later traded as concessions. A grumble/argument culture has something of the *rite de passage* about it. PR people involved in bid battles for companies, or in employer–trade union talks, or in lobbying campaigns about legislation, note a general process where legal, political and communicative positions are traded over time as mutual concessions in the search for agreement. If there was only the grumble/argument culture, and if it did not lead to negotiation, arbitration or judicial modes of resolution, the general competition of interests would destabilise society.

PR has soured pluralism rather than dissolved it in the acid of argument. PR has been the sharpened voice speaking out for an interest, an idea or an individual. The Tannen thesis is only partially applicable to the UK. Another account of the phenomenon may be offered: that it is a PR and media age re-statement of J.S. Mills' metaphor: the clash of ideas has truth – or at least majority accepted opinion – as residue. Bitter, argumentative debate in civil society is still an acceptable price to pay for a higher level of conflict resolution between interests. Monologue leads to stasis via complacency; dialogue is progressive via uncomfortable adjustment: PR adds to the discomfort which encourages adjustment.

PR as internal media

The focus of this chapter so far has been on the mass media which PR supplies with subsidised material. PR itself, however, is a media system for communicating with employees of an organisation or group. As such, it is invariably the voice of the controlling dominant coalition and the communications are one-way (from top to bottom) or at best two-way asymmetrical (listening to employees so that the communications are honed to be more persuasive). Harrison (1995, p. 13) notes that the house journal form of internal PR goes back to the nineteenth century; Dickens mentions a magazine edited by cotton workers in New England in the 1840s; and Lever Brothers and the Manchester Co-operative Society published them over 100 years ago. Modern practice, however, begins in the USA in the 1930s, when many large American corporations responded to the growth in the unionisation of their workforces during the Great Depression. Marchand (1998) describes this process, noting in his case study of General Motors (p. 216): 'With many of the old programs of welfare capitalism in disarray and company unions increasingly ineffective in forestalling inroads by the COI and AFL, convincing internal propaganda seemed more essential than ever ... Employee magazines ... once again proliferated.' PR's internal role is as important now to employers as it was then, but the principal challenge to them comes not from trade unions but from increased commercial competition and, since the 1960s, from the accelerated pluralism, both civic and commercial, which has created a more uncertain ideological environment in which to trade. Indeed, businesses in intensely competitive markets see employees as ambassadors and evangelicals for their corporate brand as much as for their product brands. Besides businesses, more groups have turned to PR as a means of promoting both internal cohesion and a unified message via members to their external environment. Many charities and pressure groups run communications courses for their volunteers.

The predominance of one-way communications to employees is explicit in unitary organisations such as businesses, the military, religious orders and government departments, but is diluted in more pluralistic ones such as universities, knowledge-based businesses and voluntary sector bodies. The more bureaucratic the organisation, the more one-way and manipulative the communications. In them, senior management control access to favoured material and symbolic goods, and they discipline labour to be more productive in a prescribed way (Alvesson and Wilmott 1992). If ideology is claimed to be asymmetrical systems of beliefs and ideas designed to maintain unequal power distribution among people, internal PR is a fertile testing ground for verification. Titles of conference papers on internal PR are illustrative: 'Securing buy-in and commitment from your employees by developing a strong emotional connection with all your different audiences' (Walt Disney); 'Developing a completely new brand identity and securing buy-in throughout your whole organisaiton to the new values' (Leonia Bank, Finland); 'Harnessing the proactive power of internal communications to achieve the right organisational culture to drive your business forward' (Visa International).[14] *PR Week* writes about 'Playing the right cards to ensure staff loyalty' and 'It is important to get the management story out, to be in control of the story to your own people'.[15]

What sorts of internal communications is PR involved with? They are principally in the category of communications about employee attitudes and behaviours at work. Their intention is to persuade the workforce to be more motivated, committed, involved, productive, flexible, customer sensitive and ambassadorial. The contents deal with financial results, sales figures, sponsorships, corporate identities, new contracts, brand quality, customer service, employee awards, new postholders, incentives, flexible working, restructuring, take-overs, redundancies and redeployments. They are mostly communications mediated through internal newspapers, newsletters, posters, videos, business television,[16] conferences, e-mail, exhibitions, suggestion and productivity schemes, surveys, small group discussions, cascade briefings, open days and incentive travel. PR people become involved in contractual and industrial relations matters through personnel and human resource management departments, producing communications under their imprint rather than their own. But relations are not always smooth, as employee communications involves PR in one of its few internal 'turf' wars: is it PR or personnel who controls messages to employees? At other times, PR works directly to line management to improve quality and quantity on production lines. Preparing notes for cascade briefings is the nearest most internal PR people get to face-to-face communications. Communications of a functional, technical nature (e.g. changes to accounting or production procedures, as opposed to employee attitudes to these changes) only very rarely involve PR. They are line management work. Nor is PR involved as a function with the most informative- and meaning-rich category of internal communications – gossip, coffee and printer station networking.

PR people specialise in employee communications, either as employees or as agencies. The master task is to maximise the contribution of workers to organisational goals. PR writers put it typically as follows: Smythe, Dorward and Reback (1992, p. 106): 'Organisations which deliberately try to involve employees more and invest in improving their internal communication, find that staff tend to more innovative, more confident about new ideas and more ready to accept new ways of doing things'. Haywood (1990, p. 108): 'The objective of real employee communications must be to create understanding and support among employees to enable the company to operate more efficiently.' Gregory (1996, p. 18): 'People are an infinitely expandable resource.' Sperber and Lerbinger (1982, p. 139): 'The power of employee communications is that it ties individual members of an organisation together to accomplish a common purpose.' Examples of senior management (the dominant coalition) relinquishing control of internal PR are very rare and are usually found in the public sector: Harrison (1995, p. 119) quotes one at Sheffield Council, and there was the Open University's internal newspaper.[17]

Does PR employee communications influence employees? Presumably those who paid for it think that it does. Internal PR is currently more practised than it was 40 years ago, judged by job adverts, the number of specialist agencies and the amount of attention in the trade press. The type, however, seems to have changed. In the 1960s employee communications had similarites with the public information model of PR: it was in-house journalism, largely informative and hardly exhortatory. It often had the physical format of newspapers. This was the period when the British Association of Industrial Editors flourished. Since the 1980s, similarities are more with commercial communications: honed and shaped messages with a point of view asking for – insisting on – endorsement by employees. The underlying theme is 'change or leave'. The shift in communicative style is related to organisational and ideological changes in business, to the decline of Fordist manufacturing industries, to downsized bureaucracies, to the rise of privatised utilities seeking culture change, to smaller businesses in more competitive markets, to deregulated labour markets and weaker trade unions. The new internal PR has increased emotional content and become evangelical in tone. Employers are now told 'how might you use communication channels to convert your workforce'; companies need staff 'who act as internal and external evangelists for the business and its brand'; 'it's possible for employees to go further and actually live the brand'.[18] The Labour Party has a similar tone in its mailings to members as it moves from being a member-representative body to a member-servicing one: in a word, promotional.

A look at themes in organisational culture provides another perspective on the question of effectiveness. From the conventional PR perspective, senior management inside organisations resources employee communications to maintain the supremacy of its views and policies. Where organisational culture is unitary, employee communications are a memetic system for passing attitudes and behaviour on down to the workforce. Where the organisation is pluralist in culture, internal PR is one among several communication flows competing for influence: there is competition to the views of senior management. Other sources are trade unions, middle mangement and non-management employees, and professional and skill groups. (Martin (1992) measured this unitary–pluralist division as a typology of integration, differentiation and fragmentation.) The effect of differing organisational cultures on employees can be seen in workplaces with trade unions. The latter invariably have different views and policies – if not different values – from the senior management and use alternative communications. If their views about a workplace are reported in the external media, it is a sign of a highly pluralistic organisational culture. This unitary–pluralist typology complicates the question of effectiveness in that under it effectiveness now implies that internal PR meets communicative competition from formal and informal sub-cultural groups. This competition presents problems of evaluation for PR producers. For employees, however, who are the consumers of internal PR, questions of effectiveness revolve around attitudes to work and to amounts of personal autonomy in completing it. The prudent rule of *caveat emptor* applies as much here as with PR in markets, politics and the media.

In general, internal PR is an under-reported subject in the PR academic and operational literature. This may be because it is perceived as unproblematic: it has to be manipulative and propagandistic because work is organised as an imperative, one-way, top-down hierarchy; the communications style follows. What is written by PR people implicitly confirms this: their subject matter is greater effectiveness for PR producers, and their tone is one of instrumental rationality. Indeed, employee relations fit uneasily into the current paradigm associated with the American academics Grunig and Hunt (see Chapters 6 and 10) and the way that it is taught in the UK. The emphasis is on PR as the practice of virtue rather than the practice of supremacy, and it is seen as compromise and negotiation with other interests. Inside organisations, especially businesses, this emphasis limits 'the right to manage' and dilutes a universal commitment to shared purposes sought by senior management/ dominant coalitions The latter desire compliance, if not obedience, to their purposes, and their tolerance of other purposes is limited. Their dominance is entrenched in company law about the supremacy of shareholder interests, the law of personal employment contracts and in management's limited acceptance of trade unions and of other stakeholders. With such dominance given to them in law and practice, managements are unlikely to concede much control to what is often called the most important asset of organisations, people. The current practice in most workplaces favours internal PR as a top-down process, which is at odds with the current fashion among PR people to emphasise two-way communications.

If this mismatch is to be reduced in favour of communications as nego-tiation and compromise, it may be in the knowledge and creative indus-tries and in 'learning companies' that it will begin. Where intellectual exploration and creativity are applied by employees to work content, they will also apply the same forensic qualities to work structure. The concept of organisations as pluralist bodies is adapted to handle the heterodox, and it is in the academic literature about organisational culture and com-munications that the complexities and uncertainties of competitive internal communications are explored. Daymon (1998, 2000) argues that much thinking about internal PR is simplistic, biased and one-dimensional: organisational members as well as leaders influence commu-nications, and leaders influence with both what they do and what they say. Internal PR assumes that it influences, if it does not control, the thinking and behaviour of organisational members, since it views work as hier-archical and employees as passive. It is one of the few areas of operational communications where the 'magic bullet' theory of effects still holds sway: communicators powerfully influence their audiences. Internal PR will meet the limitations of these views head on when it has more work experience with knowledge industries, staffed by creative people.

PR theory and persuasion

In the knowledge industries, internal PR will also face the question of its relationship with persuasion. Employees in these industries are adept at dealing with the difficulties of data interpretation, the many-sidedness of opinion, and the give and take of argument. They are often well informed, evaluative and creative people. Internal PR will take on the same qualities, as it does in some universities. It will become what the current PR paradigm (associated mainly with the American academic Grunig; see Chapter 6 and Chapter 9) labels symmetrical or balanced, two-way communications and it will be characterised by compromise and negotiation. In so being, the paradigm explicitly but wrongly squeezes per-suasion out of what it calls 'excellent' or most effective PR practice, an ideal and minority-practised category. This raises questions about the descriptive power of the paradigm. Dozier and Ehling (1992, p. 175) write, for example, about 'waning interest in persuasion among public relations scholars ... Persuasion is less relevant than other processes (such as compromise) when a symmetrical model of public relations is prac-ticed'. The consequence is that the paradigm itself has an asymmetrical relationship to persuasion, associating it with PR which is not 'excellent'.

This unbalanced relationship is unsustainable. Why, for example, should PR's use of compromise or bargaining and negotiation as commu-nicative processes be treated differently from its use of persuasion? In what ways are they preferred processes? Indeed, are they separable processes? Do persuadors see themselves as using an inferior one? It is demonstrable that compromisers, bargainers, and negotiators use persuasion in, say, industrial relations, and that persuadors use compromise, bargaining and negotiation in say, retail selling. The paradigm makes the distinction that compromisers are problem solvers and persuadors are compliance gainers, but again the two processes inter-penetrate: problem solving needs compliance by the parties in the last resort and compliance needs a solution to align with in the last resort.

Both sets of process give the audiences and consumers of PR a choice of acceptance or rejection. The two sets, however, exist alongside non-voluntary communicative processess such as instructions, orders, edicts and imperatives which flow from force, superior social power, law and legislation. This distinction between voluntary and coercive communicative processes is significant for PR. Its communicative processes allow an acceptance or rejection by its audiences. The communicative processes of force, power, law and legislation communicate imperatives. PR is not an order, compulsion, injunction or statute, even when it is communicating about force, power, law or legislation. This important distinction is veiled by the compromise/persuasion dichotomy of the paradigm, and it may be that the dichotomy is an inadequate, mistaken attempt to locate the distinction. On this argument, it seems that persuasion is interpreted as reducing the automony of those being persuaded, and so is classified as coercive, while compromise, bargaining and negotiation respect it. This is rejected: persuasion is a communicative process responding to the autonomy of audiences as much as compromise. PR exists because there is autonomy in its audiences, its consumers. Persuasion enfolds compromise as a possible process outcome.

It is demonstrable that PR people in markets, in sponsorships, in corporate hospitality and in lobbying, for example, use processes of persuasion, compromise, bargaining and negotiation in search of compliance and problem solving. Because their audiences are autonomous, they cannot order or injunct. They can only persuade, negotiate and/or compromise to achieve their goals. It is evident that organisational managers cannot coerce employees to behave in a preferred way. They use persuasion and, to their distaste mostly, they sometimes have to compromise. Indeed for some managers, persuasion is part of the 'art' of management[19] and it happens inside a macro culture of self-interested exchange (the marketing culture) which is itself reliant for reproduction on persuasive mass communications.

The association of persuasion with PR which is not 'excellent' has led to a corrective amendment to the PR paradigm. It arises on the grounds that the exclusion of persuasion reduces the paradigm's credibility with PR people for many find that 'persuasion inherent in the asymmetrical models is not unethical or ineffective' (Grunig and Grunig 1992, p. 310). The amendment is called mixed motive PR, and is constructed so as to take in the most common PR practice: using persausive communication to get compliance by the public with preferred goals of attitude and behaviour; and where that fails, compromising the goals.[20] Mixed motive PR includes persuasion (and its antithesis propaganda) in what is called its 'craft PR' element, and includes compromise and negotiation in what is called its 'professional PR' element. With this amendment to its original construction, the Grunigian paradigm moves out of a conceptual cul de sac which seals up persuasion with ineffective, 'non-excellent' PR and so gives itself more classificatory and predictive power.

PR is a form of persuasive communications. What hostility to persuasion as a communicative process correctly identifies is that some forms of persuasion are corrosive of humanistic, liberal, democratic values, and that these abusive forms have been used by PR in its degraded forms of communicative manipulation and propaganda (see Chapters 5 and 6). With that correction, Miller's (1989) position on persuasion and PR is preferred: 'Two "Ps" in a Pod'. His working assumption that both seek symbolic control over environments is accepted here, as are two of his refinements. PR is a sub-set of persuasiveness, one that deals with the collectivities of publics and clienteles. Second, that the control sought by PR is through symbolic transactions, but that effective persuasion often requires coercive force. As regards the first point, the following comment is needed. It is argued here that PR is always persuasive for as a communications sub-set, it shares in the inherent persuasiveness of all social communications (see Chapter 7). As regards the second, it is a basic judgement that most PR has been and is coercive because it has become manipulative and propagandistic, and that PR as coercion can be avoided only when it is conditioned by reason and source visibility at least. This may lead to the operational quandary for the working PR person that reformed PR which is not coercive may be ineffective.

Summary

The rise of commercial pluralism has led to more media businesses and more media marketing by them aimed at readers, listeners and viewers. The rise of civic pluralism has encouraged more media outlets to report the new values and behaviours expressed in contemporary UK society. This has benefited PR in a number of ways. Utilising the new technologies, the media-as-business has invested in new delivery channels and titles, and this has increased the editorial space to be filled. Media staff working practices have increased reliance on PR material. The values of a more commercialised media, seeking market share for profit, have emphasised news and programmes as tailored products, designed to appeal to the targeted audiences. Celebrity news is such a product. It is a category of PR built around undistinguished public personalities shaped by news values, and it has risen to a higher prominence in the 1990s as a marketised media attempts to fill more space to attract more users.

The modern media is now more suceptible to the products of its most important supplier, the PR industry. Outside this commercialised media, the newsletters, magazines and, increasingly, websites of pressure and cause groups use PR attitudes and techniques to spread their views. The dominant coalitions which control organisations and groups do the same by the creation of PR for employee and membership relations. This PR is an internal media system designed to manipulate employees' and members' behaviour in line with managerial objectives. The dominant coalitions are expressing in communications, as they do in other work functions, the 'right to manage'.

Accelerated pluralism has soured the tone of the public debate about values and ideas. PR has played its part in this souring as it is communicative behaviour by groups, organisations and businesses in their competitive struggle for advantage. Where competition is intense, PR messages are sharpened in tone and content. This souring, however, is tolerable if it resolves more conflicts in society. UK public debate is more a grumble culture than an argument culture. It is more accurate to say that PR is contributing to what Wernick (1991, ch. 8) has called promotional culture: 'promotion' is any communicative act with 'the function of advancing some kind of self-advantaging exchange' (p. 181). PR sits well inside the promotional culture of 'self-advantaging exchange', yet the current paradigm of PR thinking has had difficulty in associating persuasion with 'good' PR. This has been resolved by amending the paradigm to include a category revealingly called 'mixed motive' PR. The next two chapters take up the theme of self-advantage (or self-interest) and look at the relationships between PR, manipulation and propaganda in the US and UK contexts. But the first task is to examine the benefits and costs of PR, and to define it.

5 The balance sheet

One response to PR today is to regard it as selling with a modern name:[1] an activity which is certainly pervasive – but in the sense that that very quality makes citizens and consumers aware of it and so neutralises any harmful effects. Thus they can be forearmed before the salesman, the politician, the vested interest. *Caveat emptor* (buyer beware) – the argument would go – always has been and always will be alone sufficient defence against those with something to sell. In a market economy allied to a competitive, representative political system, reported on by media, most of which is commercially owned, we expect salespeople, politicians and journalists to be 'tricky' – selective with data, biased in argument and coaxing in manner. Jensen (1997) has called people who present only half a case 'hemispheric communicators': 'they are an important informational engine for society and let people know of those things that would otherwise not be known' (p. 68). We expect them to be persuasive.[2] If salespeople did not sell, if politicians did not canvass voters and the media did not seek the largest audiences, UK society could not function, the argument would assert.

This response makes PR a matter of workaday persuasion against which our social acculturation has given us innoculation. Cialdini (1993) makes this point in the introduction to his study of 'compliance professionals', such as salespeople, advertisers, PR people and fund-raisers (his examples), with the question: 'Just what are the factors that cause one person to say yes to another person?' He writes (p. xii): 'Of course, the compliance professionals aren't the only ones who know about and use these principles to help them get their own way. We all employ them and fall victim to them, to some degree, in our daily interactions with neighbors, friends, lovers and offspring.'[3] Thus PR as an industry, as a set of attitudes and techniques does not merit much concern: the response could be 'we consumers of PR are as bad (well, almost) as the producers of PR'.

This book takes the opposite view. The concerns raised by PR are twofold. The first set involves PR as communications in favour of dominant groups in political economies like the UK: it has been, may still be, but the hope is that it will not be. They are about PR's linkage to the underlying structure of power relationships in the UK political economy. The second set flows from that linkage, but in a more localised and focused way. It is about the effects of PR on three important institutions: the marketplace, politics, and the media. These concerns taken together make the pervasiveness of PR as an industry and as a set of attitudes in contemporary UK society a topic worth investigation, analysis and, ultimately, reform.

An anatomy of PR

To begin, how are we to identify more closely the subject of investigation? So far, PR has been presented as a known phenomenon, concisely defined but not discursively dissected. This lack is a consequence of the argument that PR is a widespread, noticeable, and pervasive activity, and so familiar that dissection is unnecessary. Another reason is hesitation before what is almost a mass production business: there are, famously, 472-plus existing definitions claimed by some to be in circulation: there is little marginal utility in offering yet another.[4] Finally, PR people themselves play fast and loose with what is PR, including and excluding purposes and techniques to suit their business pitches and their sense of status. For example, for those who see PR as strategic advice to top management, media relations is something they certainly do not do; for those who have to combine the bizarre in people, location and theme into an 'event', internal communications to an industrial workforce would be a foreign work experience; for some who lobby Westminster and Whitehall, to be called a PR person is cause for consulting one's libel lawyers. Definition by personal customising is at its most refined when the definer declares herself to be in 'communications', when the sign on the door says she is in PR. Is there an explanation for this definitional fuzziness?

The most durable, formal definition in the UK is that of the Institute of Public Relations (IPR) which settled in the 1950s on 'the planned and sustained effort to establish and maintain goodwill and mutual understanding between an organisation and its publics'. To this, the Institute added in 1993 that 'Public relations is about reputation – the result of what you do, what you say and what others say about you'. The relationship between the two definitions is problematic: are they inconsistent with each other? Do they carry equal weight? Why are there two? Consistency is not the strongest feature of representational and trade bodies and, in having two definitions, the IPR may have been trying to achieve several ends: appearing 'modern', catching new emphases in PR work, placating internal factions. Challenging the IPR's definition(s) in terms of contemporary usage is that of the influential American PR academics, Grunig and Hunt (1984), whose thinking has had a disproportionate influence on UK PR teachers (see Chapters 4, 6 and 10): PR is the management of communications between an organisation and its publics.

This definition is popular in the UK because it resonates with most PR practice: a management activity to advance organisational interests. Signitzer[5] has described this as the 'organisation theory approach', and notes that definitions can be placed in two other categories: the marketing approach and the societal approach. Most formal and working definitions used in the UK fall into the first category, the organisational, by a very large margin; then into the second; with few, if any, in the third. Signitizer associates the societal category with the question: 'What is the contribution of public relations to the function (functioning) of societies ...?' This book is an attempt to develop an answer to that question.

A societal approach to defining PR includes the following elements. PR is mostly a category of persuasive mass communications done by interests in the political economy to advance themselves materially and ideologically through markets and public policy-making. Historically, PR has been used in the UK principally by business and government. The exception to the mass communications mode is the private lobbying of government in which persuasion is applied behind closed doors. The producers of PR are always persuasive by intention towards the consumers of PR and, often, manipulative. PR is done by government, public bodies, monarchy, churches, businesses, voluntary organisations, cause, pressure and interest groups and individuals seeking celebrity status and redress of grievances. It seeks to enhance the reputation of its users and manage issues for them. It is associated with liberal, democratic, capitalist, market-orientated economies and is a communicative consequence of them. It is often difficult to identify because it is given alternative work titles. Indeed, at the turn of the millennium, there is in the UK a flight from the term 'PR' (Moloney 1997, pp. 3–6) and it may well be that the term 'public relations' will fall into disuse, with the term 'communications' being the favoured replacement. These fashions in nomenclature reflect the reaction of the producers (and consumers) of PR to their work status, but they ride on top, so to speak, of an underlying consistency. PR is communicative behaviour designed to win advantage for its sender in a pluralistic competition. At its best, it is distinct from information manipulation and propaganda: at its worst it degrades into them (see Chapter 6).

At the level of techniques, PR usually differs from advertising in that PR in the mass media does not announce itself by buying space and filling that space with favourable self-reference. PR seeks favourable references for its subject through the medium of journalism, which often does not give the source of these references or evaluate the material. PR is promiscuous as regards techniques and seeks communicative advantage (ideological privileging, positive media references, good stakeholder opinion, favourable reputation) through any available means.[6] PR in the UK is done by corporate bodies, either private or public, in the following fields: issue advocacy and management, campaigning, community relations, cause-related marketing, corporate advertising, corporate communications, marketing communications, public information, public affairs, corporate affairs, corporate relations, perception management, conference organisation, employee communications, exhibitions, event management, hospitality management, sponsorship, corporate social responsiblity, and contract/consumer publishing. These join older PR areas, such as media relations and lobbying. New ones continue to appear: cyber PR[7] (Holtz 1998) and crisis communications management (Harrison 1999).

Organisations, and to a lesser extent groups, look on PR as a discrete function done by specialist staff: they have a PR person or department. In terms of organisational and group output, PR produces communications, usually in the form of words, sometimes in photographs, visual and sound designs, and sometimes by mixing these forms with locations and selected people into events. It is simply communications which are being produced by PR, nothing else. PR is an organisational sub-set, just as there are others producing goods or services, marketing and sales, transport and distribution services, financial data, legal compliance, advertising, staff training, and health and safety requirements. Because PR deals in communications about all these activities, it can become identified with their functions to the point of being perceived as them, and in this mistaken unity lies a root cause of the low reputation of PR. PR producers can come to believe that their messages equate with what is happening: what they say is what is. The equation may or may not exist. Insofar as it does, PR is accurate communications; insofar as it does not, PR is boasts, exaggerations, errors, self-deception or lies by its producers.[8]

PR has another mode of operation than through specialist staff: the attitude of mind of organisational and group members and of individuals. This led to the contradictory conclusion that PR is a non-specialist, universalist function. J.H. Brebner in 1949 was one of the first UK authors on PR, and he starts his first book with the distinction[9] between public relations directed at 'people in small defined groups' and publicity for mass audiences. Both are work for specialists and both begin '... as an attitude of mind, a way of regarding and approaching other people. Anyone who in his dealings with other people takes pains to listen well, understand well, and explain well, is putting himself into this attitude ...' (p. 7). Both functions could be done by the same organisation; he appears to have the newly nationalised industries in mind. Public relations involved, for him, scanning the organisation's environment, advising top management on policy and its presentation; publicity was about films, advertising, publications and exhibitions. Brebner's emphasis is on PR as an attitude of sympathetically gaining compliance, to use Cialdini's phrase. This book similarly puts much emphasis on those demanding compliance rather than the compliant:[10] PR is (as usually practised) self-interested, persuasive display-for-notice-and-advantage which should be visible, reasoned and emotionally restrained. It could be argued that it is redundant to make explicit its 'self-interested, persuasive' nature, but this ignores a trend in PR which denies these attributes, and which sees PR as a communicative negotiation between equals or as a form of journalism (see Chapter 4). Rather, PR should always be categorised as persuasive communications.

PR benefits

Before turning to concerns about PR, it is important to state what its low reputation hides: for it has benefits for producers and consumers. As regards markets, PR is the principal flow of information by volume – excepting word-of-mouth – to enhance buyer choice in retail and wholesale markets. The persuasive nature of this information is generated by engaging the acquisitive, competitive, enquiring, fear-avoiding, nurturing, sexual and status instincts of buyers, through the use of presentational techniques such as emphasis, repetition, simplification, selection and testimonial. The linkage of instincts to persuasive techniques makes PR attractive to its producers and to its consumers. It is flexible communications and comes in many forms – from speaking to small groups to mass mediated communications. Indeed, PR is so data-, information- and opinion-enriching for buyers that, if it was stopped, advertising and word-of-mouth would be reduced to much thinner communications flows on which to base consumer decisions. A government commissioned report (1994)[11] found that 'PR is gaining ground in relation to other components in the marketing mix'.

As regards electoral politics, PR is a popularising activity to draw attention to policies and to rising politicians among citizens in a way which gives substance to important, positive features of liberal, democratic society, such as voter understanding and involvement, issue and policy awareness for the public, and personal profile building for politicians. Political PR keeps the political class and the electorate in contact with each other and is often linked to focus groups for feedback. Politics is done through policies and through personalities, and it is appropriate in a representative democracy that the political class has to compete through persuasion for voters' support.

As regards cause, interest and pressure group politics, PR in its lobbying form is the communicative modality for linking these elements of civic society with each other, and with the public policy–decision-making process. In the group competition for advantage which is a distinguishing feature of societies like the UK, the quantum of information available to make efficient decisions about public policies would be less without lobbying by all affected interests. Moreover, PR presents this information in a simplified form to a society teetering on the edge of communications overload.[12] Lobbying PR and representative politics are so allied that they are for all practical purposes inseparable. Furthermore, PR has inclusive-making tendencies for public policy formation by offering to outsider groups a low-cost resource for access to public debate and politicians. It is the means by which many groups – both inside and outside the Establishment – realise their opportunity to be heard in public policy-making.[13]

As regards individuals who seek to be celebrities, PR is the route to this status. A category of PR agency exists to create them, often in liaison with the media. Such confections add to the entertainment role of the media and in many ways, some unintended, add to the gaiety of the nation. On balance, celebrity PR is harmless – in small doses. PR is also an opportunity to be heard for aggrieved individuals who seek to overturn official acts against them. Victims of miscarriages of justice, hostage support groups, and employees mistreated by their organisations are among the most frequent resorters to PR.[14]

As regards the media, PR is a major supplier to the media of public interest stories involving outsider groups (e.g. radical road protester groups) and aggrieved individuals, of balancing information and comments so that reports can carry the views of multiple parties, of public information campaigns on, say, health and safety issues, of government thinking on public policy, and of lighthearted news and gossip for entertainment columns and shows. PR adds validity to the claims of the UK media that it reports much of what happens in the UK: PR brings news, opinions, events and people to the newsroom and studio at little cost to the media; it subsidises page and programme production and is indirectly a price reduction pressure for readers and audiences. It is an information subsidy to the media.[15]

The benefits of PR for its producers and its consumers are multiple and significant: otherwise it would not be funded or its outputs sought after. These benefits can be brought together under the heading of free expression in a liberal, democratic, market-orientated, capitalist society. People as individuals and as groups have the right to express their interests persuasively within the law as they judge right for them. None should be prevented from this expression and PR is a legal, popular, accessible and inexpensive form of public communication. In particular, business has benefited from the use of PR as an agent for the reproduction of its ideological beliefs and values throughout the UK political economy. Since the 1960s, other interests, many of them radical, have increased their use of PR, and where these groups have achieved their goals, PR has been *the* communicative resource contributing to those successes.

Other benefits can be identified when PR is looked upon as job creator, as service provider to business and non-business sectors of the economy, and as a purchaser of capital and consumable goods. PR in the UK is an industry of £2.3 billion turnover and employs more than 25,000 people – perhaps up to 50,000 (see Chapter 2).

This statement of benefits is a summary, because their presentation at length would be a repetition of the contents of most UK books about PR, which are positive beyond the effusive to the evangelical. There is therefore a deficit of critique about PR which needs to be reduced: the aim is not to bury PR but to introduce more balance into judgements about it. PR is not an aberration from some other, unstated proper way of communicating in the political economy and civil society of contemporary UK society. It is not going to disappear. It is a communicative consequence of basic material and ideological structures of that society (its market capitalism, interventionist government, group and value pluralism, adversarial mode of public expression). PR is likely to become more pervasive as those structures evolve and intensify. It is their expressive consequence in the form of communications. It is culturally adapted and technically developed. To say that UK society will be better without PR is an idealism: PR exists because of UK society. It is a communicative consequence of the strengths and weaknesses of that society. What it is called is a matter of changing fashion. There is no stasis for PR: it will change (regress or reform from the viewpoints of its producers and consumers) as the balance of material and ideological interests in the UK plays out.

With this statement of benefits in place, the case for arguing its disbenefits at the societal level are explored in the rest of this Chapter and the next, and are examined at the institutional level in Chapters 7, 8 and 9.

The American experience

On balance, the evidence from the academic literature is that the principal[16] use of PR in liberal, market-orientated democracies in the twentieth century has been by big business, in defence of their economic and political interests, and by governments, to maintain power or to promote a social engineering agenda.[17] The major conclusion is that PR has manipulated public opinion in favour of ideas, values and policies which economic and political elites have favoured. The manipulation is a consequence of the type of PR employed: its hidden sourcing, concealed intent, low reason/high emotional content, and elitist, one-way communication flow. There has been little scholarly rebuttal of that conclusion. It is endorsed by the public's low estimate of PR, which it senses to be a device for gaining people's compliance in a way that is less than honest and trustworthy (see Chapter 2). PR has been an effective, one-way communications resource on behalf of the 'big battalions' in US and UK societies.

This conclusion of PR as manipulation and propaganda can be aligned with the neo-pluralist perspective of authors such as Dahl, Lindblom, Useem and Vogel who argue that business in Western democracies is the single most powerful interest facing government, even though businesses are divided on specific issues (Lindblom), and are stronger or weaker over time (Vogel). The business interest in market-orientated, capitalist economies is dominant, in the sense of having more power than any other interest, but that dominance is fractured and is under challenge. To maintain its dominance, business uses PR at two levels: via the mass media to maintain support or induce acquiesence for its ideas and values from the general public, and via the private lobbying of government for favourable public policy (Moloney 1996).

It is not, however, the business or government commission of PR which is the matter of most concern, though it does raise important questions about the balance of interests in a democratic society. Rather, most concern is reserved for the manner of its usage: the manipulative (see Chapter 6). It has been used to build and set societal agendas by economic and political elites in Western society in a top-down, guided and managed version of democracy. Where this management of opinion was later endorsed by elections, the manipulation has the thinnest of defences; where the elites did not seek or want acceptance by voting, there is no defence against the charge of PR as manipulation against democracy.

The manipulative use of PR has been most identified in the USA, where such usage took hold from the birth of modern PR in the last quarter of the nineteenth century. Indeed, PR came into existence to defend American business interests. McElreath (1997, p. 8) records that 'The modern roots of public relations were established in an anti-big-business environment brought on ... by the "public be damned" attitude of powerful capitalists'. Tedlow (1979) tracks the pioneering use of PR by American business and its peak organisation, the National Association of Manufacturers, for 50 years until 1950. It was used as propaganda to ward off trade unions, government regulation and to increase sales. Ewen (1996) has written a history of American PR as defensive activity by business and conservative interests to control mass public opinion.[18] He notes that before World War I the major emphasis by public communicators – the political progressives, the muck rakers, the growing number of PR people – was on facts and reason as the dominant influence on public opinion; after the War, it was on emotion. He stresses (pp. 131–45) the influence of war for this switch of emphasis and how, by 1920, observers had identified the success of the Committee on Public Information (the Creel Committee) in increasing public support for the war. Indeed Goldman, for whom PR was 'the most common form of opinion engineering' (1948, Foreword), judged that its PR campaign 'dwarfed anything that American businessmen had ever imagined in its magnitude and its results' (p. 12). Public communicators believed by then that emotion played a more persuasive role in message reception than reason. Ewen quotes Roger Babson, an influential business analyst, as saying in 1921: 'The war taught us the power of propaganda ... Now when we have anything to sell to the American people we know how to sell it.'[19]

Many authors (Ewen, Goldman, Herman and Chomsky, Sproule, Tedlow) have noted the success of the American government, via the Creel committee, in promoting involvement in World War I through the use of PR and propaganda. American government was later to make PR integral to the dissemination of its policies and to become a major producer. Mattelart and Mattelart (1998, p. 27) note the use of PR people (information officers, photographers, films) by the Roosevelt administrations in the 1930s: 'The Roosevelt administration aimed to mobilise public opinion in favour of the welfare state in order to bring the country out of the Depression. Opinion polls were created as tools for day-to-day management of public affairs.' Pratkanis and Aronson (1992, p. 225) note that in 1936 the Roosevelt administration employed 146 full-time and 124 part-time publicity agents who issued seven million copies of 48,000 press releases. Pimlott (1951) remarks on the Federal Government's use of PR in the New Deal, calling it (p. 95) 'official publicity or more bluntly, governmental propaganda' and judging (p. 100) the mass media as willing partners with official information services. This government/PR connection confirms Habermas, noting of the negative effects on the public sphere of the involvement of the interventionist state. He argues that the social welfare state and business together diminished the public sphere: now it has been 're-feudalised': these elites present determined opinion to the public when once it was the public who formed it. The interventionist state continues in the USA, encouraging a PR response. Dartnell (1996, p. 291) estimates that US business is regulated by 116 government agencies and programmes, and that it is represented by 500 PR firms and 3,000 trade associations in Washington, D.C. One of these firms, Hill and Knowlton, were shown to be involved in false stories about Iraqi troops removing 312 babies from incubators in Kuwait in October 1990, just before American involvement in the Gulf War. McNair (1995, p. 185) calls this 'public relations of the type frequently used in wartime – what is sometimes referred to as ' "black propaganda" '.

From the perspective of a history of ideas, American PR grew up into its modern shape, fearing a breakdown of social order brought about by the strengthening of democracy. Central to this was a conservative concern that the masses were 'getting into the saddle' and the bourgeois elites were losing control. Bernays was aware of this mood and shared it (Tye 1998, pp. 91–111). Gustave Le Bon (1896 *The Crowd: A Study of the Popular Mind*) thought that the human unconscious was a significant motivator of action and that the unconscious was converted into a civilising process in the hands of elites, but that mass democracies threatened this civilising power of the superior few. The masses were the 'crowd'; Sighele (1898 *Psychology of Sects*) wrote of its suggestibility, and of less psychological self-control of people in collective movements. Wallas (1908 *Human Nature in Politics*) wrote to challenge what he called the intellectualist fallacy which asserted that reason played a major role in politics. He argued that politics consisted largely of the creation of opinion by the deliberate exploitation of subconscious, non-rational inference. Wilfred Trotter (1916 *The Instincts of the Herd in Peace and War*) put emphasis on instinct as a human motivator. Walter Lippmann (1922 *Public Opinion*) doubted the involvement by a mass democracy in the rational debate needed to form policy and direct a government; instead the governing elite should use symbolic systems such as film to persuade.

Carey (1995, pp. 80–4) includes Lasswell in this conservative pessimism. In the 1933 *Encyclopedia of the Social Sciences*, Laswell wrote that propaganda is 'the one means of mass mobilisation which is cheaper than violence, bribery or other possible control techniques'. Propaganda was essential in a democracy because 'men are often poor judges of their own interest'.[20] Mattelart and Mattelart also note (1998, pp. 26–7) that Lasswell regarded propaganda as necessary for 'governmental management of opinion'. 'For Lasswell, propaganda was henceforth synonymous with democracy, since it was the only way to generate the support of the masses. Moreover, it was more economical than violence, corruption or other comparable techniques for government. Since it was a mere instrument, it was neither more or less moral than "the crank of a water pump". It could be used for good or ill.' The media was useful for 'circulating effective symbols' to a passive audience.

Bernays, Lee and Grunig

Edward Bernays (1892–1995) and Ivy Lee (1877–1934) are widely regarded as the two founders of modern public relations – but both are embarrassing nominations for modern PR people. Bernays was influenced by his uncle Sigmund Freud, by the new emphasis on mass psychology as a social control technique and by his work for the Creel Committee. Sproule (1997, p. 18) says that he associated PR with propaganda after the end of World War I. Bernays' second book was *Propaganda* (1928). Today the readers of such a title would expect a critique: in Bernays they find praise.[21] The first chapter is entitled 'Organising Chaos' and opens with the following two sentences: 'The conscious and intelligent manipulation of the organised habits and opinions of the masses is an important element in democratic society. Those who manipulate this unseen mechanism of society constitute an invisible government which is the ruling power of our country.' He has a caution about the misuses of this manipulation, but it is subordinated to its contribution to 'orderly life' (p. 12) and he ends positively: 'Propaganda will never die out. Intelligent men must realise that propaganda is the modern instrument by which they can fight for productive ends to bring order out of chaos.' Bernays maintained these views until at least the 1980s.[22]

Emphasis on the reduction of social 'chaos' was the theme of his first book, *Crystallising Public Opinion* (1923). Bernays refers to Lippmann's influential *Public Opinion* (1922) and notes (p. 38) that 'the significant revolution of our modern times is not industrial or economic or political but the revolution which is taking place in the art of creating consent among the governed'. He takes from Lippmann at least two foundational ideas for his PR philosophy. The first is Lippmann's new concept of stereotype as the basis for influencing public opinion; the second is how Lippmann's 'pseudo environment' (human nature plus social conditions) and 'pseudo facts' concepts (pp. 15–29) can be actively used to influence people.

By managing stereotypes through news creation, the public relations counsellor 'is the pleader to the public of a point of view' (p. 57). The counsellor must represent the public to his client and vice versa, must understand how public opinion is formed and maintained (p. 76), and must understand social psychology and, in particular, stereotypes (p. 99), which are the mental phenomena used by people in the formation of public opinion, because the counsellor works through them (p. 162). The PR counsellor creates news (p. 171) to strengthen, weaken or amend stereotypes. They include categories of people (capitalist, boy scout, chorus girl, woman lawyer, politician, detective, financier (p. 98)), slogans (President Theodore Roosevelt's 'square deal' (p. 163)), and visuals (the American flag).

Bernays was comfortable with these social psychological processes: he was practised in recognising and harnessing them and his pioneering talent was to relate them into a body of PR knowledge. He moulded them into 'an art applied to a science' and used them for clients in commerce and in politics, these two fields combining, as when he lobbied Washington in 1951 on behalf of the United Fruit Company against a Guatemalan president with land reform policies.[23] The processes were subsumed into the larger one of propaganda which is 'a purposeful, directed effort to overcome censorship – the censorship of the group mind and the herd reaction' (p. 122). In this way, he appears to make PR a sub-set of propaganda which was a larger and positive societal process of manipulation; propaganda makes for order through the promotion of 'good' ideas, values, events, people. The 'good' is not defined but the implication is that that which serves order in society is 'good'. The role of the PR person described by Bernays is reminiscent of the Gramsci's organic intellectual whose task was to actively gain consent on behalf of the interests they spoke for.[24] Tye (1998, pp. 264–5), Bernays's latest biographer, concludes that he refined PR to make it become more effective in creating consent, sometimes for benign purposes, but that he remains 'a role model for propagandists'.

At the same time (after World War I), the psychologistic basis of PR was also being emphasised by Ivy Lee, often named as the other founder of modern PR. Ewen (1996) reports Lee saying in 1921 that 'publicity is essentially a matter of mass psychology. We must remember that people are guided more by sentiment than by mind' (p. 132). Later that year in a lecture on PR at Columbia University's School of Journalism, he invited his audience (p. 132) to 'come down and let us show you our library, see the extraordinary collection of books on psychology, all the elements that go into the making of crowd psychology, mass psychology'. He added: 'You must study human emotions and all the factors that move people, that persuade men in any line of human activity. Psychology, mob psyschology, is one of the important factors that underlay this whole business' (p. 132).

Lee's contribution to PR development was earlier than Bernays but is not so much referred to as Bernays' who wrote fifteen books.[25] Lee is credited with urging leading American capitalists, known as 'robber barons' in the last quarter of the nineteenth century, to be more communicative about their businesses. He was successful in this to the level of more open PR, but there is doubt about his influence in opening up core business functions such as production planning and pricing to any public scrutiny. More of a legacy was his usage of press releases and conferences, providing more rather than less information, and listening to press and public opinion rather than dismissing it. His *Declaration of Principles* put it as 'All our work is done in the open' (Hiebert 1966, p. 48). Before Lee, it was 'the public be damned'; afterwards, it was 'the public be informed'. Hiebert in his sympathethic biography of Lee details this technical contribution, but regrets the company Lee had to keep. He writes (p. 316): that 'less ethical contemporaries used his techniques to create an image as a façade to cover the truth' and editorialises that 'much that parades under the title of public relations today is nineteenth century press agentry in bankers' clothing', and 'as a result Ivy Lee and his present day counterparts while serving a useful function in society still suffer from a widely held and deep-seated suspicion of being fixers, propagandists and ghost thinkers' (p. 317).

What can be said now of Lee and Bernays is what is said about contemporary, conscientious PR people. Both served their principals well, were sought out but claimed more than they could deliver. Their contribution to relations between the public and business was at the technical level of more efficient PR. Tedlow (1979, p. 201) in his survey of 50 years of American business PR up to 1950 concludes that 'This pattern of essentially peripheral influence of PR can be traced down to the Watergate scandal' and that PR people 'who have self-consciously set about to reform their employers as the first order of business ... most likely met with failure more other than success'.

Today few PR people or writers would enthuse about the closeness of the propaganda/PR relationship and there is an unspoken but palpable feeling that Bernays, particularly because of his literary legacy, is an embarrassment. The rejection of the link with propaganda is found in the European and American experience of the rise of Fascist dictatorships in the 1920s and 1930s, and of the Cold War from the late 1940s. These experiences stripped away any positive connotation from the idea and practices of propaganda (and by implication, of any communicative manipulation). Propaganda came to be perceived as the practice of Nazis and Communists, anti-democrats, oppressors, and murderers.

In the light of this historical experience, PR had no future as a popular concept or practice in liberal, democratic societies if it was defined as linked to propaganda and manipulation.[26] That Western governments practised propaganda, at least against their external enemies, is not recalled frequently but would be another reason for disassociation.

Whether the connections between PR and propaganda are organic or not, what is clear is how time gives its own gloss to ideas about PR. Shortly after Hitler came to power in 1933, Lee worked for the the German Dye Trust to improve American–German relations. He met senior Nazis including Hitler (Hiebert 1966, p. 288), which led to the charge that he was a Nazi sympathiser. At the same time, Bernays was told over dinner by a journalist witness that his book *Crystallizing Public Opinion* was in the library of Goebbels, the propaganda chief of Nazi Germany.[27]

The successor to Lee and Bernays as the most influential thinker of their generations about PR is the American academic James Grunig[28] (see Chapters 4, 6, and 10). As their heir, he inherited, by way of public perception and conceptual construct, the close association of propaganda and PR. His and Hunt's (1984) four-part typology was a historically sensitive and conceptually nimble rejection of that link, and it is the basis of the contemporary academic and operational paradigm about PR. It does, however, involve the admission that much PR is manipulative and propagandistic. Their model equates PR with these qualities in its press agentry, public information campaigns and two asymmetrical forms, forms which they call asymmetrical PR. Grunig later acknowledged that 'such a mindset defines public relations as the use of communication to manipulate publics for the benefit of organisation. "Persuade" is a softer word often substituted for "manipulate" but changing the word does not change the mindset' (1989, p. 18).[29] He and White further acknowledge (1992, pp. 38–42) that this asymmetrical PR 'steers' towards 'unethical, socially irresponsible and ineffective actions' and that it 'has dominated' the practice of PR. Elsewhere Grunig (1992c)[30] equates press agentry with propaganda. Grunig and Hunt, however, break the link with propaganda by going on to posit a symmetrical PR which is two-way, balanced, dialogic communication which is tolerant and respectful of the public. 'We estimate that about 15% of all organisations today use the two-way symmetric model', and they are mostly big businesses regulated by government (Grunig and Hunt 1984, p. 26).

Further critiques

This is no such fracture of the PR/propaganda link for Habermas. He (1962, pp. 193–6), in his historical analysis of the development of liberal public opinion and of the public sphere concept (a rational, disinterested public opinion, accessible to all citizens), argues that PR was publicity to advance the political interests of business as advertising was publicity to advance its market interests. He notes the contribution of Bernays and equates PR with opinion management done through stressing public interests and de-emphasising, if not hiding, private business ones. He thought pro-business PR was American in origin and came to Europe after 1945, dominating the public sphere.[31] PR managers insert specially

designed material into the mass media and create events to gain its attention. It is a form of social engineering done with communications to gain
the consent of public opinion for capitalist interests. If historically and
conceptually, the public sphere was a notional space where there was universal access to rational, disinterested debate about matters important to
liberal societies, PR was one development to politicise that space in favour
of business interests. Holub (1991, p. 6) also lists the mass media and
party politics, as well as PR, as negative factors in the late twentieth
century which put the disinterested exchange of ideas under threat.
Webster (1995, p. 101) argues that PR is degrading the public sphere
because it disguises its sources and is not disinterested.

Herman and Chomsky (1988) posit a 'propaganda model' to describe
the behaviour of the US mass media which serves the interests of social
and political elites by the 'manufacture of consent'. They note the influence of Lippmann's view that propaganda is 'a regular organ of popular
government'. They use case studies to show that various filters (including
PR material supplied by business and government, and PR people as
'flaks' disciplining journalists) leave only 'the cleansed residue fit to print'
(p. 2) in the media. Gandy (1982) developed the supply of PR material by
'the modern public relations firm' (p. 64) on behalf of 'those with economic power' to the media into the concept of 'information subsidy'. The
media accept the material because it reduces their publishing and broadcasting costs. PR 'plays the central role in the design and implementation
of information subsidy efforts by major policy actors' and about this
subsidy, he says that '... the source and source's self-interest is skilfully
hidden' (p. 64).

The most robust restatement of the 'manufacturing consent' thesis is
by Stauber and Rampton (1995, pp. 205–6) who note that 'PR campaigns
do not invite individuals to become actors on their own behalf but treat
them as a targeted, passive audience' and that positive uses of PR 'do not
in any way mitigate the undemocractic power of the multi-billion dollar
PR industry to manipulate and propagandise on behalf of wealthy special
interests, dominating debate, discussion and decision-making'.

Herman and Chomsky, and Gandy are identified with American left
and progressive scholarship. From the right and conservative tradition,
there is the argument of Olasky (1987) who declares that he writes from a
pro-business stance for 'political conservatives and libertarians' (Preface)
inter alia to warn that corporate PR is 'designed to minimise competition
through creation of a government–business partnership supposedly in the
public interest'. He calls this corporate collaborationism.

Carey (1995) associates PR with what he calls 'corporate propaganda':
it is about 'taking the risk out of democracy' – the risk to big business.
'Commercial advertising and public relations are the forms of propaganda
common to a democracy' (p. 14). Corporate propaganda has two
objectives: to identify free enterprise with 'every cherished value', and to

identify interventionist government and strong trade unions 'with tyranny, oppression and even subversion' (p. 18). He identifies what he called grass-roots and treetop propaganda – the latter aimed at other leaders of society (p. 88). Carey argues that after 1900, when the reputation of American business was low, public relations was used by business more; he notes the careers of Lee and Bernays. The same happened in the 1930s' Depression when business used both violence against workers and 'a protective screen of public relations activities' in their industrial relations. After World War II, there was also a shift to more PR (pp. 26–7). Carey goes on to quote Brady (1943, pp. 288–9) that 'broadly speaking the power of public relations ... decreases as one moves away from countries with long and deep-seated liberal, democratic and parliamentary institutions'.

Brady based his study of the USA, the UK, France, Germany, Italy and Japan and their business PR in the 59 years up to 1940. Carey's references are mostly to American and Australian PR and in the introduction Lohrey, his editor, writes: 'As an Australian politician for almost fourteen years I have had direct experience of the methods by which government reactively and continually place business interests before public interests.' He introduces the negative concept of 'democratic propaganda'. Earlier, Pimlott (1951) had picked up on the connection between business and PR, describing the PR person as 'plutogogue' (p. 206), used by business to counter attacks on capitalism (p. 207). He thinks that PR was generally unpopular in post-1945 America: PR people were identified with 'unworthy causes', they were thought to use dishonest methods, and their claims were 'eyewash' (p. 205). He quotes Barnard, a senior businessman turned author, writing in 1938 that 'the inculcation of motives' of people in organisations is done with propaganda (p. 152).

Tedlow (1979) concludes that PR is corporate propaganda after his review of its use by American business. 'Scholars from various disciplines have discerned a movement away from physical force to persuasion as the chief method of social control in twentieth-century America. Public relations can be seen as part of this movement' (p. 202). Marchand (1998) is explicit. He tracks the use of PR by American business between 1900 and 1950 to legitimise itself in the face of the various charges of monopoly, size, remoteness, profiteering and social irresponsibility. He quotes a PR man at AT&T, one of the first businesses to be PR active, in the early 1920s as saying that he aspired 'to make the people understand and love the company. Not merely be consciously dependent on it – not merely regard it as a necessity – not merely to take it for granted – but to love it – to hold real affection for it.' Packard (1957) notes that PR people were 'mind moulding' (2nd edn. 1981, pp. 177–8) on behalf of business alongside the 'Hidden Persuaders' of the advertising industry. Sproule (1997) classifies PR as propaganda in his review of the latter's relationship with American democracy. He uses the phrases 'mind managers', 'engineered persuasion' and 'opinion engineering' without quotation marks when he writes of propaganda. Korten (1995) notes the close connections between business, PR and a 'corporate-dominated' media, while Nelson (1992) chronicles the use of PR firms by global businesses to protect their markets and open new ones. Mallinson (1996, p. 10) notes the rise of modern PR in the USA, evolving from a press agent function 'with an element of propaganda' to a form of mass marketing. To some PR people, however, corporate propaganda is an obligation. Robert Dilenschneider (1999) writes in a newsletter for business communicators: that 'it is incumbent on business to sell aggressively the benefits of capitalism – to workers, at least – because the system is sure to be attacked'.[32]

Summary

The pervasiveness of contemporary PR, both as an industry and an attitude, prompts the view that a more critical, balanced view of it is needed than is on offer. This need is not diminished by the difficulty of defining PR. Indeed, the search for a tight functional definition is misleading about a phenomenon which is flexible in form, which is both highly structured into an industry and expressed as personal, promotional behaviour, which colonises other forms of communications, and which is a communicative expression of liberal, democratic, market-orientated, capitalist societies such as the UK.

Looked at in this inclusive way, it is not surprising that PR has many benefits. They fall into three categories. The first are the functional ones which flow from the operation of PR in relation to three important public institutions: markets which claim to be free, politics which describes itself as democratic and representative, and mass media which describes themselves as independent. The second category comprises the wealth creation benefits brought about by an industry with a £2 billion plus turnover and a 50,000 strong workforce. The third type of benefits flow from the promotion of values and ideas in favour of business, an important role in a society which has become increasingly market-orientated and capitalistic since the late 1970s, and also in favour of active governments seeking electoral approval and implementation of social welfare.

There are, however, two contrasting and balancing sets of concerns about PR. First, there has been its use, at a societal level, as manipulative communications to promote business in many Western societies, principally the USA and the UK, and to promote governments (these are societal functional concerns). PR and propaganda have been seen as largely synonymous. Most analysis of this linkage has been done about the USA. American PR grew up in an intellectual climate pessimistic about a mass democracy's influence on public affairs. Its first use was to defend 'robber baron' American capitalism. It was then deployed effectively by the Federal government in support of World War I and of the New Deal. It became associated with 'corporate propaganda' and mass psychology as social control. Its American pioneers (Bernays and Lee) were supportive of these uses and saw PR's linkage with propaganda positively. However, after the American experience of the fascist regimes of Mussolini and Hilter in the inter-war years and of the Cold War with Communism after 1945, PR had no future as a legitimate, sustainable social function in a liberal democracy unless the link with propaganda was fractured. That fracture was achieved conceptually by Grunig and Hunt in 1984.

The next chapter looks at the UK experience and expands the analysis of relationships between PR, manipulation and propaganda. The second set of concerns about PR are more institutionally located. Chapters 7, 8 and 9 explore the impact of PR on markets, politics and media.

6 PR as manipulation and propaganda

The UK PR industry, being established some 80 years, is younger than the American. Nonetheless, early influential PR people[1] in the UK, all of whom were associated with either business, government or official bodies, viewed their work in a similar light to their US colleagues. They saw PR as a method of social control. They wanted to manage social and commercial developments at home.

These senior British PR people in the 1920s and 1930s sought control through communicating reassurance about the stability and continuity of a traditional UK when the country was facing radical social changes. These included an adult population with a nearly universal franchise, organised working-class interests, a growing welfare state, and a popular press and radio with national audiences. Like their American counterparts, they were aware of the very active use of propaganda by the totalitarian regimes of Mussolini, Hilter and Stalin; unlike them, they were concerned about their country's declining power in the world. They wanted to manage internally a public opinion, which was no longer made up of just the respectable, middle classes and the aspiring working class, but of the great mass of working people as well. It was the unknown and perhaps uncontrollable power of a new, empowered mass public opinion which worried them.

They believed stability and continuity at home as well as overseas would come through education provided by propaganda (a term which had mostly positive connotations until after 1918), which subsumed public relations.[2] They sought to project a confident and prosperous UK through the Empire Marketing Board and the British Council. PR for them was mass communication of official messages via newspapers, the BBC, advertisements and posters, lecture tours, exhibitions and conferences, and other events involving direct contact with the public. They were more likely to call their work 'publicity', 'propaganda' or 'public education' than 'public relations', a term which was largely unknown in the 1920s.[3] As time passed and the term 'propaganda' took on totalitarian connotations through its association with fascists and communists, 'public relations' was used more.

These early UK PR people would have welcomed what Deacon and Golding (1994) later called 'the public relations state', government as active persuader of its citizens.[4] The idea of the modern state and mass persuasion are intertwined. Many PR people helped to build that state as they built up PR. Harrison notes (1995, p. 20) that 'the history of public relations in Britain, largely based on work done to explain government policies or promote government-backed bodies and services, reflects the public information, propaganda and persuasion phases' of PR development. This was PR as social engineering by means of manipulative communications. L'Etang (1998) shows that the Institute of Public Administration, founded in 1922, saw PR as a means of communicating to the public growing state provision of social welfare, and as a means of feedback about public opinion. The National Association of Local Government Officers shared similar views about the link between PR, service provision, public opinion. They also saw that it was a means of enhancing their own work status. Black (1989, p. 200) believes that 'the first stirrings of organised public relations were probably the efforts made by the Insurance Commission in 1912' to explain the new concept of national insurance. It involved presenters going around the country telling employees and employers what national insurance was (Gillman 1978). There was a housing information office in the health ministry in 1922 (ibid.) and by 1939 'virtually every department in Whitehall has accepted publicity and/or public relations as a legitimate part of its functions' (Grant 1994, p. 248). Harrison (1996, p. 20) reports that after World War II, many former government information officers started up in PR and advertising.

Grant also notes (p. 252) that the minority Labour government of 1929–31 'were willing to use publicity' in the form of public information campaigns by pamphlets, lectures and meetings to further policy. Pimlott (1951) notes that the 1945–51 Labour government used PR to promote its social and economic reforms. The phrase 'PR state' – the publicity seeking state – succinctly catches the readiness of modern UK governments to use mass persuasion for policy implementation.[5] There is circumstantial evidence of this in the corrrespondence between the period of most public utility privatisations from 1987/8 to 1992/3 and declining government advertising expenditure from £90.5 million to £47 million in the same period, as the number of sell-offs declined. Similarly, expenditure rose under the impact of New Labour welfare policies from £69.4 million in 1996/7 to £105 million in 1998/9.[6]

Public information campaigns by government, however, raise concerns for democracy. The campaigns range from the uncontroversial (e.g. adult literacy, drink-driving campaigns) to topics still in political contention (e.g. pro-privatisation, pro-poll tax and pro-Euro campaigns). They may be considered universally beneficial – as in drink-driving – or highly controversial – as in joining the Euro; in both cases, it is their one-sided presentation, their national dimension and the difficulty of mounting any large-scale counter to them which are causes of concern.[7] The means of their delivery is also an issue. Government advice on reading skills for illiterate adults has been inserted into the scripts of popular soap operas such as *Eastenders* and *Brookside*. Such insertion is frequent.[8] Reading advice is benign but the principle of inserting official messages into entertainment in an unsourced way raises questions about how audiences are viewed and whether they are treated with the respect due in a democracy.

Early PR in the UK

After World War I, the UK was a less violent, more class-stratified, deferential, centralised, poorer country than the USA, but it was exhausted after four years of machine-age war, unsure of its world role. The UK political economy was enfeebled: that of the USA emboldened. The context of PR was different, even if the response of senior PR people was similar. In overseas politics, the UK's relative power was declining and two policy initiatives were framed to achieve their goals through PR. The first was the Empire Marketing Board (EMB) set up to promote trade with the colonies and the Commonwealth after the UK had failed to introduce preferential tariffs and to make UK citizens more 'Empire Aware'. It was headed by Sir Stephen Tallents, a major figure in the development of PR in the UK. He believed in promoting British interests through effective, modern communications. He saw film documentaries as such, and encouraged John Grierson and the nascent film documentary movement at the EMB and later at the General Post Office (GPO). The EMB staged exhibitions as part of a marketing strategy to increase consumer awareness, and it was among the first to use the technique of indirect promotion for a product, i.e. it promoted pineapples by displaying tropical landscape, not the fruit.[9] The second policy initiative was the British Council, set up in 1934 after the failure of the EMB, with a wider 'soft' diplomacy remit. It started work when the European dictators Mussolini, Hilter and Stalin were building totalitarian states. The Council was a sympathetic base from which to operate conventional PR techniques such news management, corporate identity creation, arts promotion, and event management.

Inside the UK, PR was taken up by many leading commercial bodies, both private and state. Editorial Services was the first PR agency in the UK in 1924 and by 1933 had handled 400 accounts, including home ownership for the Halifax Building Society. The Gas, Light and Coke company, later the North Thames Gas Board, developed the 'Mr Therm' marketing campaign in the 1930s. London Transport was active in the creation of its corporate identity through the famous underground map, posters, station design and carriage furniture. Southern Railways had a PR director in 1925 and promoted its electrification programme through active media campaigns. The BBC had a controller of public relations in the inter-war years, while ICI and British Overseas Airways Corporation and the Port of

London Authority had similar posts. The GPO, which had a public information campaign in 1854 (Gillman),[10] made many films, including the famous *Nightmail.* Shell Mex was also active in films and in branded visual design for its publications encouraging car-based tourism. L'Etang (1999, p. 15) shows for how long documentary film was seen as an effective PR technique. She quotes from one edition of the trade magazine *Public Relations* as an indication of the industry's attitude in the 1950s and 1960s towards film: '[t]he documentary uses its money to do a job of public relations and instruction'.[11]

The propaganda work done in World War II gave a strong impetus to the growth of PR in the UK. L'Etang (1998, p. 433) records how in 1945 there 'was no dismantling of the Ministry of Information but a transformation to the Central Office of Information'. Writing at the time Williams[12] (1946, p. 130) argues:

> An intelligent democracy must be prepared to make the fullest use of every available method of informing its citizens of what is essentially their business. Information is a weapon of democracy. But to refuse to use it is to turn one's back on one of the ways in which the enormously complicated business of modern government can be made comprehensible to the ordinary person. There cannot be public control without public understanding.

These comments are perhaps understandable from a journalist turned propagandist for the Ministry of Information during World War II, but it is nonetheless the language of social engineering, manipulative communications and guided democracy: the mind sets of war were being transferred to civilian government. Earlier, Williams writes (pp. 77–84) about 'the Growth of "Public Relations" ' from the 1930s to post-1945 and in that description he makes no distinction between propaganda and PR. Franklin (1998), in his analysis of news management by the New Labour government, notes a centralised information policy controlled by Downing Street and changes to personnel, who were 'expected to be more energetic in pushing the government agenda' with the result that 'the fourth estate risks being overrun by a "fifth estate" of public relations and press officers' (p. 4). Modern government PR people have testimonials to their influence from unexpected sources. The revolutionary Irish leader de Valera is quoted as saying: 'Any government that desires to hold power in Ireland should put publicity before all' (Coogan, 1993, p. 362). He went on to found his own newspaper group.[13]

By the 1950s, relatively obscure firms used PR actively. Steelmakers Samuel Fox used film, as did Dexion in the form of employee communications to reassure workers about moving to factories in the new, unknown 'garden suburb' town of Hemel Hempstead. More prominent firms had long been PR productive since before 1939: Anglo-Iranian Oil (predecessor to BP); Imperial Airways (forerunner of British Airways); ICI; Rootes cars and the corner-house restaurants of J. Lyons. By the 1960s Shell had 200 people in its PR department. Outside of commerce, PR was well established in local government through the efforts of the officers' trade union and through encouragement from the learned body in the field. The London County Council and its successor the Greater London Council were noticeably active in PR. As local government delivered many planning, hygiene, leisure and regulatory services to the UK population, PR allowed message delivery and feedback from the public.

What marked out this early stage of UK PR (up to the 1960s) was how it responded to particularly British needs – in the first place, support overseas to strengthen the weakening UK and Empire international trade position, and to bolster British influence via cultural activities when fascist and communist ideologies were growing. Second, it was a communicative response to the expanding provision of social services. Third, it was associated with cultural productions which are still appreciated today. It encouraged a new art form, the film documentary, for its own motivational and educational purposes, and it promoted good visual and graphic designs, in what are now considered to be classics. What it shared with American usage was patronage by business and government interests who thought of propaganda as socially purposive and legitimate and who saw PR as inextricably linked to it.

PR and manipulation

The theme of manipulation is witnessed in contemporary PR by Michie (1998). He is a PR man and, therefore, his book *Invisible Persuaders* is important in the UK literature: he admits that PR does social harm. This is an admission which is rare, if not unique for few, if any, PR people take a balanced view of costs and benefits.[14] He asks (p. 69): 'But what happens when [PR's] vigilance to protect [companies] against disaster and [PR's] positive policy steering turn into a campaign to distort the truth? What about companies which, in the face of environmental and political sensitivities, use PR for altogether more evasive purposes? It is in this quagmire that PR becomes an instrument of perversity and deception.'

He turns to this question after making the case for socially beneficial PR: that PR puts information into the public domain and is a precondition for informed choice in a democracy (p. 57). He is critical (pp. 57–8) when 'a company really does only *act* according to the public interest, giving the appearance of heeding concerns and expectations rather than genuinely doing so'. He adds: 'In such circumstances, PR becomes the means by which the wool is pulled over the public's eyes, the propaganda by which a company's profits and power are protected.' He believes this propagandist PR is more likely to happen in 'broader corporate PR' outside of take-over battles for companies and outside of PR about financial matters. Another author, Alistair McAlpine, a businessman, goes beyond reporting (1997) about manipulation. He urges it on the 'image twitchers' (his soubriquet for PR people): 'By using half-truths and convenient words, the image twitcher's job is to make certain that the world knows that the employer is well armed' (p. 154). The political journalist Nicholas Jones (1999, p. 11) writes about the miners' strike in 1984–5 as 'textbook example of media manipulation'.

Both in the USA and the UK, the historic, principal use of PR has been the manipulation of information in the interests of PR producers to alter thinking and behaviour in their interests. Robins *et al.* (1987, p. 16) nominate PR as one of the 'active persuasion industries', along with advertising, in nation states of late capitalism where information management is 'inherently totalitarian'. PR is an active persuasion industry, but the bleak view that it contributes to an inevitable, propagandistic information culture in the UK is rejected. The publicly adversarial nature of accelerated pluralism and a reformed PR (see Chapter 11) will avoid any such condition. A beneficial PR which is a form of reasoned persuasion, which encourages symmetrical communications, and is respectful of its audiences is possible. But first, its antithesis, manipulative PR and its pure expression propaganda, needs to be examined.

Modern PR lends itself to manipulative communications because it shows characteristics associated with the type and because it often operates in societal circumstances which encourage manipulation. Its sources are frequently undeclared, thus making its messages appear to be free-floating from any originating interest. They are often couched as being in the general interest, e.g. 'Sunday trading is good', 'flexible labour markets are necessary'. If the message originator is unknown, it is likely to follow that the purpose of the communications is not known or is suspectible of several interpretations, a condition which often suits a manipulative communicator. Second, the data in PR messages is often asserted rather than referenced or argued. Third, PR communications are often grounded in negative emotions to achieve their persuasive effect, and they downplay reason. They can appeal to powerful, intolerant, solipsistic motivators, such as greed, envy, social superiority and lust. The removal of these manipulative flaws in the internal construction of PR communications constitutes the case for reform through education and regulation.

PR is a flexible mode of communications. It is visible in the form of public PR: corporate identity campaigns, sponsorships, news stunts. It is invisible in the form of discreet lobbying which levers private interest into public policy, as well as in news management. Modern lobbyists, often for hire, are political fixers, usually for business (Smith and Young 1996) and they thrive among the intermediate institutions between the state and people. PR is flexible in regard to message content (a sentence or an event), adaptable as to channel of message delivery (press release or lobbyist) and often concealed as to originating source (mediated through journalists, politicians and funded, front groups). In these ways, PR has played a part – alongside economic dependency – in the acceptance, voluntary or otherwise, of business interests, especially of big business and its related class interests in finance capitalism,[15] in UK society. Similarly, PR has played a part in transmitting, through public information campaigns and through relationships with journalists on unattributable, lobby terms, policies for which governments have had little or no mandate. Examples are steel nationalisation in the 1940s, civil nuclear policy in the 1950s,[16] trade union reform in the 1960s, currency decimalisation in the 1970s, privatisation in the 1980s, and the poll tax in the 1990s. From the 1920s until 1960s, business, government and official bodies had been near-monopoly users of PR.

Michie argues (1998, pp. 81–92) that this pattern of manipulative PR continues in a form called 'greenwashing', which he describes as '... the process whereby a company, rather than earning a good reputation, buys one. It can involve anything from simple window-dressing to undertaking a much more fundamental shift in opinions towards issues and industries.' It is 'one of the most pernicious uses of public relations'. His description is a wide one, covering changes in both marketing tactics and corporate strategy, altering just the packaging and moving towards sustainable production. The examples Michie gives are critical of chemical, oil and tobacco companies, car makers and nuclear energy producers. His examples (both named and anonymous) are of misleading advertising about human health dangers, exaggerated claims about environmentally safe production, 'environmentally friendly' petrol containing the carcinogen benzene, and lobbying against catalytic converters and airbags in vehicles. Other examples are a campaign to change public attitudes against environmental groups, setting up apparently independent advisory boards and networks such as the Business Council for Sustainable Development, but formed by the American PR agency Burson Marsteller, commissioning research from sympathetic scientists and academics, funding an anti-green writer, inviting known public figures onto industry lobbying bodies such as the pro-smoking group Forest, and voluntary codes of conduct to head off mandatory regulation. Michie argues that these activities, often carried out through increased PR budgets and hired PR agencies, amount to a corporate 'green backlash' against the environment movement. Gabriel and Lang (1995, p. 136) make a similar point about corporate behaviour towards consumers when in the early 1990s recession, 'neither the employees' jobs nor the overall product quality matters as much as the maintenance of an effective image and an intensified public relations exercise to keep the confidence of shareholders and fund managers'.

But this corporate communications manipulation is under challenge as the resort to PR techniques and attitudes by non-dominant groups grows in the accelerating pluralism which characterises contemporary UK society. Since the 1960s, social movements, the pressure and cause groups

to which they give rise and business-challenging organisations such as consumerists, environmentalists and trade unionists have used PR (see
Chapter 3).[17] They challenge business PR with their own PR and often
start heuristic rounds of public statement and counter-statement which
enrich the public domain with information to the benefit of consumers
and policy-makers.

This challenge is essential where the liberal, pluralistic, inclusive and
empowering aspects of UK society are favoured at least as much as the
economic efficiency and market ones. Where business and government
resort to persuasive communications, the tendencies are for one way flows
of information and opinion, and the decline of adversarial debate. This
unbalances the egalitarian and libertarian aspects of UK society, weakening civil society and suppressing value and group pluralism. In the past,
PR has further privileged the already privileged in UK society. This argument, however, does not lead to the same conclusions when PR is used by
small- and medium-sized businesses (SMEs). For them, PR is a marketing
aid and is consistent with market competition if the appropriate conditions apply. Their lobbying is done via their trade representative bodies.
Given the market position of SMEs, PR does not have the monopoly-
inducing tendencies it has with oligopolistic businesses (see Chapter 7).
They have, nonetheless, benefited from the traditional use of PR by big
business to manipulate public opinion in the interests of business as a
sector.

PR is a set of communicative attitudes and methods and cannot be
'blamed' for the power of business or government in a market-orientated
political economy. PR is not inherently pro- or anti-business or government, but the historical record shows how PR has been an instrument for
maintaining, if not increasing, those powers. This neutral, instrumental
view of PR needs to be consciously asserted after reading the content of
PR trade journals, so dominated are they by business news and values
(Chapter 11). As an agency service to businesses in particular, PR people
have been content to charge what their clients will bear; as employees,
their skills as professional persuaders have been enthusiastically offered
and well rewarded.[18] PR has been expensive or, rather, has made itself
expensive in the service of business, but it does not have to be. Second, PR
people as a group have accepted uncritically or welcomed positively business values. It could be said that they have believed in those values or that
they have succumbed to compliance. PR by and for business is not a cause
of the power of business: its extensive use by business over decades is an
expression of the power of its paymaster. The sources of business power
lie elsewhere, in the slowly changing human, material and value structures
of UK society. PR does not create these sources of power for business or
any other interest. Rather it is used by those – groups, organisations, individuals – who have the resources or the personal skills to promote their
ideas and values via an array of public, private, flexible, low- and high-cost

techniques. PR is an agenda builder through its multiple displays-for-attention-and-advantage, but it has built mostly in a manipulative way.

PR and propaganda

Most academic authors, including the most influential modern PR academics, and some writers about PR (Bernays, Carey, Herman and Chomsky, Ewen, Gandy, Goldman, Grunig, Habermas, Hawthorn, Hiebert, Korten, Marchand, McApline, McNair,[19] Michie, Moore, Nelson, Olasky, Robins *et al.*, Pimlott, Stauber and Rampton, Tedlow,[20] Tye) conclude that PR has been manipulative communication, or they have conflated it with propaganda. A senior British PR man notes the elision: 'For what is perceived as propaganda by some is labelled public relations by others. Some commentators see no distinctions between the two as to purpose or practice.'[21] Indeed, Moore (1996, pp. 79–97) argues that 'public relations is fouled up with propaganda: it ranges over the ground between compulsion and free persuasion'. It becomes propaganda, he believes, when it is imperative in tone, offers no alternative facts or views and is formulaic. Only Grunig has offered a developmental model for transformation towards a better PR.

There has been little literature refuting this conclusion, which is embarrassing to most PR people, little broached when they talk of their work, and avoided by the great majority of PR writers.[22] The Americans Kruckeberg and Starck (1988) note that the historiography of PR in the USA is underdeveloped: in the UK it has only just started. Mostly, they argue, the development of PR is treated as the Whigs treated history: a progressive evolution to better times. They cite the views of the respected PR authors Aronoff and Baskin (1983), that PR evolves through three stages: manipulation, information, and mutual influence and understanding. 'Significantly, they note that while the stages generally have been sequential all three have coexisted from the beginning' (p. 8). They conclude that 'it would be grosssly unfair to paint a picture of public relations today as consisting of hucksterism and propaganda as it was often practiced in the past. Yet, to many people, the distinction would be blurred' (p. 7).

The critical writers generally develop their conclusion of manipulation or propaganda without precise definitions of these phenomena, relying instead on their structural analysis of unequal power in the political economy and on their experience of PR. The alternative methodological approach is via definitions. Jowett and O'Donnell (1992, p. 4) take it and define propaganda[23] as 'the deliberate and systematic attempt to shape perceptions, manipulate cognitions and direct behaviour to achieve a response that furthers the desired intent of the propagandist'. On that definition, much of PR, past and present, has been and is propaganda. The definition includes manipulation, and posits propaganda as an extreme form of one-way communications imposing attitudinal, cognitive and behavioural outcomes on people. Grant (1994, p. 11) notes the phrase 'tampering with the human will'.

Propaganda is 'the magic bullet' version of persuasive communications while manipulative PR is weak propaganda. Jowett and O'Donnell (p. 8) make a typology of propaganda which allows this shading. Propaganda is 'white' where its source is known and the information is accurate: the examples given are the Voice of America radio network and the BBC overseas. It is 'black' where it is credited to a false source, is misinformation, passes on lies and deceptions and is based on emotion alone. Cold War propaganda would be an example. In between, there is 'grey' propaganda. On this shading, much PR is 'white' or weak propaganda. O'Shaughnessy (1996) lists characteristics of propaganda as bias,[24] intent to influence, high-pressure advocacy, simplification and exaggeration, ideological purpose, avoidance of argumentative exchange, and reluctance to give and take views.

Another problematic with propaganda concerns the intentions of its producers. Grant (1994) notes (p. 18) how Grierson saw propaganda in a positive way as an empowering, educative agent which increases citizens' knowledge and decision-making capacity in a democracy. The other view[25] in the UK after World War I reflects the conservative, American intellectual climate of the same time. Propaganda was a negative phenomenon because it works through the susceptibility of the common people to the 'herd instinct', and in the wrong hands leads to loss of control by elites. Both views were understandable in the 1920s and 1930s when the meaning of the term was in transition; both permitted their proponents to use propaganda: one to further a progressive ideology; the other to sustain a conservative one. The word still carried favourable connotations but ones which were first undermined by the success, ironically, of UK and American official propaganda campaigns at home and abroad in favour of war. If governments could propagandise successfully in wartime, they and other interests could do the same in peacetime. It was, however, the experience of totalitarian propaganda by fascists and communists throughout those years which relieved the word of positive meanings.

Positive attitudes to propaganda, like Grierson's, informed – and still informs – many public information campaigns. It is hard to mount a sustained critique of the 'Drink More Milk' campaigns of the 1920s and 1930s as a threat to liberty (pp. 194–224). The motivation behind such campaigns was an amalgam of many influences, including Whitehall departmental self-interest and dairy trade politics, but it did include a health education concern about low nutritional levels among the population. The campaigns have to be seen in terms of the political and social discourses of their times when official pronouncements were authoritarian in tone, and education and literacy levels were lower than today. One-way communications with the public were the norm. People were not expected to speak back. The 1960s saw the end of such silence and deference by the public; since then, while the urge to propagandise remains strong in elites and in government, the effectiveness of propaganda is more in doubt.

In these ways, the term 'public relations' replaced 'propaganda' as the popular descriptor for persuasive mass communications, excluding advertising. What has dogged PR ever since is whether the semantic change also reflects a change of meaning and practice. This change, however, sits inside a much larger and more important conclusion. What has become clearer since the inter-war years is that mass involvement in politics is not ruinous for a thriving political economy, but that manipulative and propagandistic mass communications is.

Response to the propaganda charge

No type of manipulation or propaganda is acceptable in the internal communicative behaviour of a democracy and where PR is either of those, it is in need of reform. Optimists about democracy will note the argument of Abercrombie *et al.* (1980) that less powerful groups in society can resist the ideas and values of dominant forces (often conveyed by propaganda) by developing a popular culture and their own organisations. Propaganda undermines citizenship because it is posited on giving to an elite control over the many. In particular, propaganda is disrespectful of reasoned, public argument, a methodology which must be the basis of the public life of a democracy. In the overseas affairs of a democracy, there are some exceptions in the case of war when the manipulation/propaganda is aimed at the enemy, but it becomes unacceptable when it is directed at home journalists.[26] Reform of this debased PR can be classified into two categories: structural, via the encouragement of an adversarial climate of public opinion derived from strong pluralism in a liberal society; and institutional, as in relation to markets, politics and the media and its own internal organisation.

Favourable literature (by academics and authors who have worked in PR) adopts various approaches to the propaganda link: ignore it and/or define PR in a way which dissolves or reduces the linkage. Most UK textbook writers (Black, Jefkins, Hart, Heywood, Kitchen,[27] Smythe *et al.*, White, White and Mazur) give PR a clean bill of health. The discussions, references and examples are invariably to businesses, usually big, and how PR markets goods and services, and lobbies public policy decision-makers. The link with business is stated unproblematically: 'It has to contribute directly to business success.'[28] The link is taken as self-evidently beneficial at the level of values and influence on the political economy: any critique offered is technical in an instrumentally rational way and there is not much of that. The government's use of PR is similarly treated in an unproblematic way.

The American textbooks widely used in the UK are very favourable and more comprehensive in their coverage of PR for public and voluntary sectors organisations than UK ones. Again, the approach is the instrumental rational. For example, Cutlip, Center and Broom in their eighth edition (2000) do not list 'persuasion' or 'propaganda' in the index, but nevertheless note on p. 3 that 'the one-way concept of public relations relies almost entirely on propaganda and persuasive communications'. A few UK writers have written of PR in its non-business uses (e.g. Keen and Greenall, McIntosh and McIntosh, Silver, Ward,[29] West). Second, some authors manage to write without mentioning the term, especially in the public and voluntary sectors. An example is Ewles and Simnett (1985) who have pages on press releases, campaigning, mini-case studies of health issue lobbying and 'looking good and sounding good on television and radio' (p. 177) without mention of PR. Third, another version is name 'rebadging' as when Dolphin (1999) in his textbook on corporate communications (p. 4) moves his subject further away from PR with the comment that the latter 'has metamorphosed into a wider business and organisational discipline'.

The current paradigm for conceptualising PR in the UK does not ignore the propaganda link and offers a typology of PR which both includes and excludes manipulation and propaganda (see Chapters 5, in relation to persuasion, and 9, in relation to the UK teaching of PR). It presents PR as moving from a practice of disrepute (the output of press agents) to the practice of virtue (two-way communications between negotiating equals). In PR historiography, taken as a whole, the paradigm has rescued the idea of PR from its propagandist connotations. It presents the subject as a continuum from 'bad' to 'good'. The first category in the continuum is false information delivered to a passive and ignorant audience in the interests of the PR producer; the second is accurate information presented in a one-sided way to the same audience; and the third is two-way communications researched and amended to strengthen the PR producer's interest without regard to the audiences'. The fourth category is seen as the conceptualisation of optimum communications in a pluralist, liberal and democratic society – two-way communications between negotiating equals and described as 'excellent'.

The paradigm founders, Grunig and Hunt (1984), speculate that the great majority of PR (85%) is in the first three categories. These categories are described as manipulative or propagandistic according to the degree of message accuracy and symmetry in their communications. Only symmetrical or balanced PR is free of manipulation or propaganda. In offering an evaluative scale, the paradigm has allowed judgement about the practice of PR. The scale is essentially about amounts of manipulation and propaganda. In this way, the paradigm puts one type of PR apart from propaganda.[30] It has made PR respectable. It has made it teachable at public expense.

Summary

This chapter continues to look at the use of PR by business and government, this time in the UK. Modern PR has been established in Britain some 80 years and its early, influential founders shared the same fear of social change as their more established American colleagues, and the same resort to manipulative and propagandistic PR as social control. Such forms were widely accepted, for propaganda in the 1920s and early 1930s still carried positive connotations, at least when practised on domestic populations. PR is shaped by the political economy in which it is found and early UK PR was influenced by specifically British circumstances. It was a public communications system able to tell the population about new national state services; it often took the form of filmic, visual and graphic work which is still appreciated today; it was market support for large, prestigious businesses, state commercial bodies and Empire countries. It was used to promote trade and diplomatic policies overseas. It was very much official and establishment communications.

Most UK PR has been, and still is, principally manipulative communications, merging into weak propaganda at its most manipulative – more 'ordering' and 'telling' than 'listening' and 'talking'. Three sources of evidence confirm this conclusion: the academic literature looked at in this and the previous chapter; the current PR paradigm which classifies much PR as propaganda; its low reputation in public opinion (Chapter 2). Modern PR lends itself to debased forms because its sources are often undeclared, making it difficult to establish the motives and intent which produce it. The data in its messages is asserted rather than argued; reasoned persuasion is downplayed and emotional appeal is strong. Its sources are often hidden and it is misleadingly presented to audiences as journalism. These flaws in the internal construction of PR make a case for reform through education and regulation. Furthermore, the accelerated pluralism of the UK since the 1960s challenges one-sided communications in a more adversarial, democratic culture (Chapter 11).

PR as a concept had to be rehabilitated when propaganda became associated with totalitarian state communications. The current paradigm for conceptualising PR allows a graded differentiation between propaganda and 'excellent' PR. Its four-part typology is based on degrees of symmetrical, dialogic communications between PR producer and consumer.

The first set of concerns about PR in liberal, democratic, market-orientated societies, set out in this and the previous chapter, flows from its use by their most powerful single interest, business, and by their governments. The second set of concerns is with the negative effects of PR on markets, politics and mass media (the institutional concerns). The next three chapters (7, 8 and 9) look in detail at PR's involvement in those institutions.

7 Communicative equality and markets

The second set of concerns about PR revolves around the effects of its operation on three important public institutions: markets, politics and the media.

Chapter 2 presents PR as representing a paradox: so popular, yet so disparaged. That disparagement expresses itself in the low reputation of PR as evidenced in derogatory references by politicians and journalists, a negative, popular linguistic usage by the public, and some poll data.[1] The low reputation is a consequence of specific concerns about its operation. Chapters 5 and 6 look at a systemic concern: that PR has principally served – and still is serving – business and governmental interests and often degrades into communicative manipulation and propaganda. Another set of concerns is more specific to individuals. Those concerns reside among the general public in their roles as citizens and consumers, and in their roles as members of organisations and groups. Individuals can be seen as either PR consumers (receiving PR messages) or PR producers (sending them), and many people have both roles. For example, individuals read about food and wine *and* are active in Friends of the Earth campaigning against genetically modified plants. Concerns about PR in relation to markets and marketing are discussed in this chapter and in relation to politics and the media in Chapters 8 and 9.

Among the UK general public, PR is often perceived as having negative effects on important aspects of their public lives. PR causes concern by offending against a traditional, popular and conventional view of the British about themselves. It offends a cherished ideal of equality, the British common sense of fair play. To write of fair play is to put the case colloquially: more formally, it can be expressed as equal and proportionate access to markets and to political decision-making via mass-mediated sources of information. The concerns about PR come alive when it reduces, or is perceived to reduce, through manipulative communications popular access to three institutions which are near-universally viewed as important public goods. Those three institutions are free markets which claim to give choice and value, a political system which claims to be democratic and representative, and a media which calls itself independent.

PR puts itself in the dock before public opinion when it is seen favouring powerful, sectional causes and vested interests at the expense of broader public ones: when it deforms itself into manipulation or propaganda (see Chapters 5 and 6). The three institutions of the market economy, the representative political system and the mass media are among the principal social mechanisms through which the welfare of UK citizens is enriched or impoverished. The market and the political system together can be seen as forming, at a distance from the individual consumer and citizen, the basic societal platform on which material and ideological resources are collectively shared out to classes and groups, and so later made more or less accessible to individuals inside classes and groups. The mass media is important to this collective and, ultimately, individual distribution of resources because they are the 'binoculars' through which UK consumers and citizens can observe, evaluate, approve of or disapprove of that share out. UK consumers and citizens are wary of communicative manipulation by PR, the media and lobbying which interferes in that distribution against their interests, and are watchful for an equitable share out of material and ideological resources. Their interests are served by communicative equality, flows of factually accurate, reasoned persuasion equally available to all.

This conceptualisation can be characterised as the 'auction house' model of PR, in which citizens and consumers need accurate information and substantial confidence in communications before they commit themselves to buying in markets, to assessing the honesty of the public policy decision-making process, or to believing what the media say. This characterisation can be developed further. The auction catalogue (the mass media) should be comprehensive, up-to-date and accurate. The objects on offer (public policy-making, market goods and services) should be open to inspection and should correspond to their descriptions. There should be confidence that there are no price-fixers (hidden political decision-makers and market monopolists) in the audience. The auction officials (politicians and businesses) should be honest and contactable (accountable). This auction house model is cast from the viewpoint of PR 'consumers': the people who are the receiving end of PR, the citizens and retail consumers of the UK. It is not a model from the viewpoint of PR 'producers' and 'players'. Its focus is on the effects of PR on people as citizens and consumers. The PR literature in the UK lacks this perspective to a great extent, being technical in tone and focused on organisational needs. The critical literature from media and cultural studies only touches on PR effects in a fragmentary or illustrative way. Indeed, it is a surprise how little attention PR as a distinct mode of media production receives in mainstream academic work. There is room for a PR effects literature alongside the media effects one. It would fill a gap in understanding: how do individuals, organisations and groups react to PR produced for them? An example would be how PR influences consumers as conceptualised in the nine roles Gabriel and Lang (1995) have set for them (see Chapter 11).[2]

Free markets and PR

PR as a form of marketing communications can cause concern among the general public. That concern arises when people – in their role as consumers instead of citizens – conclude that an economy, which claims to provide value for money through a wide choice of safe goods and services priced in free markets, is exploiting them through flows of inaccurate, misleading or unsourced information. There are several aspects to that concern. The first is the tension between legitimate marketplace values sought by PR, such as high profile and good reputation and, on the other hand, the use of PR as 'education' and/or 'objective' information. It is good marketing for Walt Disney to use PR to promote its cartoon characters, but is it an intrusive private interest debasing the public interest when they are used to teach French schoolchildren about the Euro currency?[3]

The second area for questions centres on information flows into markets: whether the PR is manipulative or beneficial, whether all suppliers use PR equally in markets, whether all consumers are affected equally, and whether its sources are known to consumers. In so far as the answer is no, PR in markets puts some consumers at a disadvantage vis-à-vis other consumers. The third area lies in the sheer volume of persuasive communications in our society today: the continuous pumping at citizens and consumers of promotional material: adverts, mail shots, telephone selling, logos, brands, sponsorships, press releases, competitions, exhibitions, special events and T shirts with corporate messages. Even plastic bags have messages. The internet is sprouting adverts. Is this volume overwhelming non-marketing sources of market information? All communications are persuasive, but not all should be from markets.

The starting point for an analysis of PR's effects on markets is to establish what PR people do for the marketing of goods and services. The large-scale involvement of PR with marketing is a relatively new practice (Kitchen and Papasolomou (1997) and Harris (1991)).[4] The evidence suggests that this involvement is substantial for PR people as a work group: 55% of respondents in a 1998 industry survey[5] said that their budget is derived from marketing resources. The same survey showed that a quarter of PR in-house departments report to the marketing director and 9% to the marketing manager. One rule of thumb has it that 70% of PR jobs are marketing public relations.

These jobs are often gathered up inside the generic title of marketing communications which, besides PR, includes advertising, direct marketing, and relationship marketing, because all are ways of sending persuasive messages about goods and services to consumers. The PR role inside this title is now called marketing PR (MPR). This PR work is sometimes, in marketing jargon, said to be 'below the line' work as opposed to 'above the line' activity, such as advertising and personal selling.[6] This 'above' and 'below' distinction, however, becomes less important as marketing propositions become more complex. The reason is that the PR and marketing disciplines are together better able to handle multifaceted propositions. The rise of 'lifestyle' is an example. Fashion marketeers have 150 years' experience of persuading people to buy a suit with an advert alone; it is a complexity beyond a single medium's ability to persuade people to buy all the products of apparel, personal accessory, food, drink and domestic surroundings which comprise the 'lifestyle concept'. PR and marketing techniques together offer the marketeer a wide-ranging variety of expressive modes (words and visuals) and multiplicity of message distribution channels (e.g. product photos and competitions) to communicate the complexity persuasively.[7]

Writing is a major element of marketing PR (MPR) and is probably the core activity, but what else is included is hard to predict in any particular PR operation. Moreover, inclusion is subject to change over time. In the 1970s when sponsorship was a relatively new and underdeveloped promotional activity, it was relegated to PR by the more powerful marketing departments; now sponsorship is controlled by marketing departments, or often stands alone. The writing side of marketing PRs is twofold: to write media releases about goods and services for the national, local press and specialist press, and to write promotional copy for brochures, leaflets and exhibition stands. The task is to create promotional statements (newsworthy enough to win space in the media or informative in a persuasive way for brochures, direct mail and in-store display) which support the good or service being sold. There is also the related work of developing ideas with journalists and visual designers for take-up in feature articles, programmes, brochures, exhibitions and visuals, and the organising ability to integrate these activities into campaigns.

MPR and 'soft' selling

In the contemporary UK marketplace, MPR is a prominent component of marketing communications. Goods and services producers since the 1960s have been inclined to favour it more vis-à-vis advertising[8] and MPR has developed or been associated with new techniques (e.g. corporate hospitality, cause-related marketing, celebrity endorsement, conferences, exhibitions, product placement, sponsorship, special events and roadshows) in ways which have expanded its skill base beyond writing. New cars, for example, have traditionally been advertised, but that persuasive act is today only the most visible item in a set of marketing communications. Now, they are 'launched' at exhibitions. Journalists are flown overseas to test drive them. The new models are 'placed' for audiences to see in TV programmes and are associated with celebrities. 'Advertorials' about them appear in the local papers based on technical superiority and buyer advantage. Customers are invited to dealer showrooms on Sunday afternoon for wine and an inspection. The cars are on stands at summer shows. They are found in the entrances to supermarkets as competition prizes. Cars, like many retail goods, are given the 'soft' sell treatment. MPR is the contemporary title for the 'soft' sell.

In the language of applied economists and consumer behaviourists, UK retail markets deal not in commodities but brands, which are differentiated from substitute purchases by product features, both physical and perceptual. Brand management requires that these differences are communicated in all markets at all times in order to maximise opportunity-to-see by consumers. MPR is a cluster of techniques inside marketing communications opening up more routes to the marketplace for product and brand differentiation messages. The statements about the value of PR to society made by Graham Lancaster (Chapter 3) are echoes of marketing propositions translated into professional discourse: he talked of PR 'using third-party endorsement and data-driven campaigns to achieve what PR does so much better than advertising – anticipating and then filling the vacuum of consumer uncertainty in purchase'. An example of the power of third-party endorsement is the case of Delia Smith and the aluminium frying-pan, not named but shown by use on her BBC television cookery programme in October 1998.[9] Markets are information distribution systems, as well as product ones, driven by persuasive communications.

Three common MPR techniques for creating newsworthy copy are through surveys which make a point in an 'independent, scientific' way favourable to the product; second through association of 'celebrities' with products; and third, through the creation of 'news events' (e.g. the unveiling of new tailfin designs on airplanes).[10] The following headline in the London *Evening Standard* (8.7.1998, p. 15) is a good example of the PR technique of commissioning and publicising surveys. It reads 'New Woman "changes her man more often than her duvet" '. There are 12 column inches of this story by the paper's shopping correspondent plus an accompanying chart of 'What the Lad-ette likes' and the conclusion that single women in the capital 'change their men four times more often than they buy a new duvet'. The source of the data is a 'new lifestyles survey commissioned by DuPont (UK) Limited, the leading manufacturer of fibre fillings for duvets and pillows'.[11]

MPR can be a creative activity in the way that striking or at least bizarre ideas generate attention in the media.[12] *The Observer* (23.8.98, p. 7) reports that Bournemouth and Brighton are in active competition over attracting visitors and that a poll in southern England has voted Bournemouth 'Britain's sexiest resort'. Bournemouth is repositioning itself as nightclub capital of the south coast with the name 'BoMo', a place full of 'Bo Monians'. To this end, the tourism department of the council paid for advertisements on Brighton buses with the message 'Bournemouth, the resort with MORE style' underneath a photo of the English international footballer Jamie Redknapp who has connections with the town. Brighton replied in *The Observer* with the name 'Yawnmouth' for Bournemouth. One reaction to such coverage is that it is both journalism and PR as froth, and its effects innocuous. Who could object to this harmless fun which fills papers in the silly season and which makes residents in two towns aware of how tourism officials spend their council tax?[13]

Kemp (1988, pp. 127–8) provides another example of imaginative MPR – the Budgerigar Information Council, 'born out of one of the most inspired public relations briefs, or, more precisely, one of the most inspired marketing briefs … It was the Petfoods division of Mars that initiated the Council at a time when the birdseed market had come to an apparent standstill'. The market was saturated and the solution was 'to expand the budgerigar market'. 'There were endless budgerigar clubs and shows, pamphlets, articles, press conferences, books – a real orchestration of activity designed to start a budgerigar craze. It worked.' Harrison (1995, p. 162) gives another example of the imaginative. A PR company devised a campaign for the launch of penny novelty sweets called Fruity Foam which included a children's tasting panel, competitions in comics and a video on how to sell the sweets.[14]

A currently developing form of joint PR and marketing is cause-related marketing where a business, its goods and services are linked to a cause, e.g. the supply of 29,000 computers to UK schools by Tesco, funded via coupons from customer purchases. It is defined by Business in the Community as a 'commercial activity' to 'market an image, product or service for mutual benefit. It is an additional tool for addressing social issues of the day.' It emphasises goals such as 'enchanced reputation', 'awareness, improved loyalty'.[15] Research indicates that 86% of consumers are more likely to buy a product or service associated with a cause given that price and quality are not an issue; also, that the technique 'offers a unique means of emotionally engaging the consumer'.[16] Cause-related marketing lends itself to PR involvement in two ways: its existence can be promoted via editorial and publishing channels with the aim of corporate and/or product differentiation, and its outcomes are those of PR. Business in the Community says that 'there are a variety of different tools that can be used to implement and leverage Cause Related Marketing programmes. These range from advertising, PR, direct mail and sales promotion.'[17] Most of it is controlled by the marketing departments of the sponsoring businesses, but it seeks both the volume goals associated with marketing and perception goals associated with PR.

Relationships with marketing

Five characteristics (domination, subordination, separation, equality and identity) have been attributed to the PR/marketing relationship but the major trend identified in practice and in the literature over the last four decades is integration. This is the fusion of the two forms as equal but different, or as indistinguishable.

The starting point is the work of Black (1962), one of the earliest UK authors to publish on PR, and who had no chapter on marketing nor index reference to it. He did not observe or advocate integration and, even by 1989, his *Introduction To Public Relations* has only a short reference to MPR, mentioning media relations and events such as themed weeks and 'the selection of beauty queens'. Wragg (1987) is one of the few UK texts given over to MPR. He develops (p. 10) the themes of more credibility for products through MPR and its complexity-handling ability, themes taken up later by other writers.

> The value of PR lies in the greater acceptability of a message conveyed by the journalist, who is regarded by the audience as being an impartial commentator. . . . Public relations is more subtle than advertising. It capitalises on certain strengths at certain times: specifically it exploits news or feature value. . . . A detailed message might not be palatable or possible in an advertisement, but a lengthy feature in a quality newspaper or trade and professional journal will often work.

To the PR and journalism critic, this is PR material presented unprofessionally by the media as journalism.

Heywood (1990, pp. 156–7) picks up the integration theme: 'some companies with a strong marketing orientation have put all their public relations muscle behind their brands' and MPR 'can be used to support marketing in many areas'. He goes on to specify 11 such areas, including creating sales leads and motivating the sales force, distributors, wholesalers and retailers. Fill (1999) develops the integration theme. He puts MPR in the 'promotions mix' (pp. 6, 414) alongside advertising, direct-response media, sales promotion and personal selling. This 'mix' is itself part of the standard 'marketing mix' for achieving marketplace goals. He characterises PR as a cost-effective means for delivering messages, with a high degree of credibility. 'However, the amount of control that management is able to bring over the transmission of the public relations message is very low' (p. 395). He notes that MPR should be used alongside corporate public relations (see Michie above), and he quotes an American source that MPR is 'not only concerned with organisational success and failure but also with specific publics: customers, consumers, and clients with whom exchange transactions take place' (p. 401). MPR is media and sports sponsorship, publicity, sales promotion (p. 403), press releases (pp. 405, 419) which produce sales leads. Fill finds it difficult to separate out MPR activity from corporate public relations and overall he judges that the shift in importance of PR 'is a testament to its power and effectiveness' (pp. 393, 401), leading to increasing use (p. 418).

The introduction by Kotler to Harris (1991) is a restatement of the integration argument and goes on to privilege MPR with strong, situational persuasive power: 'To win the consumer's dollar ... companies must first win a share of the consumer's mind and heart. They must know how to build strong consumer awareness and preference.' But in an over-communicated society, consumers develop communication-avoidance routines. Advertising is losing some of its effectiveness and 'message senders are driven to other media. They discover or rediscover the power of news, events, community programs, and other powerful communication modalities.' PR offers these other, newer channels for reaching the consumer. Kotler adds:

> Marketing public relations represents an opportunity for companies to regain a share of voice in a message-satiated society. Marketing public relations not only delivers a strong share of voice to win share of mind and heart: it also delivers a better, more effective voice in many cases. Messages are more effective when they come across as news rather than advertising. Companies capture attention and respect when they sponsor cultural events and contribute money to worthwhile causes.

For the critic, these points raise the PR-as-manipulation argument.

Harris says that PR and marketing combine to create 'integrated marketing communications' (p. 35). MPR creates news, events, community relations and atmospheres and is to be used for product launches, for keeping products prominent in markets throughout their life cycle and for defending products at risk. Media relations, he writes, is 'one of the balanced set of communications tools used by the company to drive target audiences through the purchase path from 1) awareness to 2) interest to 3) desire to 4) action'. He takes the same view as Fill about the marketing/PR relationship: 'that the two functions are rapidly converging concepts and methodologies' (p. 42). He supports the argument that PR creates more credibility for product messages (p. 44). He picks this theme up in his final chapter by noting that the growth of MPR has benefited 'from government restrictions and regulations imposed on advertising of certain products or categories' (p. 288), citing health products. 'As a result, many marketeers have turned to public relations to carry their message to the consumer.'

Fill and Harris touch on a longstanding debate[18] about the relationship between PR and marketing, one which gives rise to professional and academic 'turf wars' (Kitchen and Papasolomou, 1997). To give the debate a shape, they borrow from Kotler and Mindak (1978) the five part typology of the relationship. One part is PR as part of marketing, a view which Bell (1991) takes. His view is interesting because he is a PR man[19] with his own agency and he stresses PR as a business. All PR techniques 'relate back to the "bottom line" (which I use, as a phrase, in its widest as well as financial sense) and are therefore part of the overall marketing process' (p. 27). Overall, the drift of the academic writing and reports from the field are that PR and marketing communications[20] are integrating, as equals or as an identity.

The recent literature and evidence from PR people and practice suggests three views on the historical development of MPR. van Riel (1995, p. 15) argues that until the latter half of the 1960s, marketing communications meant advertising alone and that other techniques were then added. Harris, Fill and Kitchen and Papasolomou date MPR as a development of the 1980s. A third view is that PR in the service of selling to consumers is as old as PR itself, a conclusion corroborated by a look at the cinema in the early twentieth century (Moloney 2000).[21]

It is clear that the inventory of marketing communications methods has grown in range over the last 30 years and that MPR is a significant part of the growth. This developing inventory can be linked to the pro-market ideology and policies of the Thatcher, Major and Blair governments[22] from the end of the 1970s, and it is likely that the list of methods will grow, given the dominance of marketing thinking in today's UK. But from the viewpoint of consumers in retail markets, what is the balance of advantage and disadvantage created by MPR?

PR as marketplace information

Consumers in retail markets (and buyers in business-to-business markets) benefit from this burgeoning growth in marketing communications, and MPR makes a contribution to that general benefit. The UK retail marketplace has structural features beneficial to consumers (product variety, price competition, new products) and communications about these features leads to more consumer choice and satisfaction. For example, the arrival of new products onto the market needs to be announced and MPR is the largest single channel for delivering such messages to consumers.

There are two mediated sources of communications into markets:[23] MPR (as part of marketing communications), and market information from non-producer sources. The producers of goods and services are the source of marketing communications/MPR, for it is in their economic interest to disseminate data and opinion to consumers. Most communications into markets come from them. They are the originators of MPR for, in the language of marketing, MPR leads to more 'informed' consumers. All these marketing communications by the producers of goods and services are persuasive. Economic self-interest ensures this. Kotler in Harris writes about 'winning' the consumers' hearts, minds and money. Bell (1991, p. 24) says 'if you are a PR consultant you're in the persuasion business'. Thorson and Moore (1996, p. 1) write of 'integrated marketing communication' that 'its aim is to optimise the impact of persuasive communication on both consumer and non-consumer'.

The second mediated source is from market observers such as UK government departments, official regulators, consumer groups, market critics and commentators, and business data sources. These observers are either neutral or critical towards the producers of goods and services, but they are active communicators and they use public relations techniques such as press releases, brochures, briefing packs, exhibitions, conferences and lobbying. For example, the UK Treasury 'names and shames' pensions companies for mis-selling and for tardiness on paying compensation, the rail regulator rebukes rail companies for inadequate service, fair trade pressure groups tell supermarket customers about third world labour practices, and business information services sell company news on the internet. Information from them can be called *market communications* which are intended to aid or stop the selling or buying of goods and services, as opposed to *marketing communications* (including MPR) which are designed with one exception to aid selling. (The exception is product withdrawal communications, usually for safety reasons.) Market and marketing communications combine to make up the category *mediated marketplace communications*, the sum of all communications in a market, except word of mouth.

Taken together, marketing/MPR and market communications add to the volume and source pluralism of communications flowing to consumers, and so provide the data and opinion foundation on which to make purchase choices. But identification of these two communications sources (producers and market observers) raises the problem of whether all marketplace communications are persuasive. It is clear that the Dupont survey on duvets mentioned previously is designed to be persuasive. Can the same be said of Nestlé when it takes a newspaper advert to warn against eating Lyons Maid New Cascade Toffee Ice Cream Dessert?[24] Is a press conference by the Consumers' Association putting non-persuasive information into the public domain? When the Treasury lists insurance companies mis-selling pensions, is that intended as a persuasive act? Is a leaflet from the Vegetarian Society persuasive? Are all marketplace communications – both marketing and market – intended to be persuasive by their senders?

The answer here is 'yes', for marketplace communications are part of a larger debate about communications. There is an extensive literature on persuasion in communications and one of its presuppositions is accepted, namely that communications are of their nature persuasive, where persuasion is defined as a communicative process designed to influence others and is a quality embedded in messages for that purpose (Jowett and O'Donnell 1992). Such a presupposition does not deny that communications can have other intents (e.g. giving information) as well as persuasion. It also allows questions about the relationship between persuasion and reason in message construction (a vital relationship for a socially beneficial PR), and it keeps in contention the proposition that reason is persuasion in cognitive rather than affective form. Nor does it rule out the view that persuasion, reason and emotion are inseparable entities when done by humans, and that they are presented in the literature as distinct constructs to satisfy the necessities of exposition.

Debate on these propositions might amend, but would not deny, a general conclusion that communications are persuasive in their intent. Miller (1989, p. 47) puts the point grandly: 'that persuasion as a chief symbolic resource for exercising environmental control remains an indispensable and irrevocable dimension of human existence'. Nor would debate deny the dependent conclusion that the sub-set of communications known as marketplace communications (market and marketing) are persuasive in particular. Markets are one of the great sites in our society for the playing out of persuasion exchanges, where persuasion is offered through communications by goods and services producers and/or by market observers, and where it is accepted or not by consumers. If they apply the *caveat emptor* (let the buyer beware) rule to evaluate communications (a necessary condition), consumers can gain marketplace benefits, e.g. product knowledge and comparison, judgements on source credibility.

Consumer friend or foe?

The argument of consumer benefit, however, is problematic because it rests on four assumptions: first, that marketplace communications achieve their persuasiveness by reasoned persuasion based on accurate data, second, that all marketplace communicators are active and equal in their output, third, that the persuasive quality in their communications acts equally on consumers, and fourth, that the communications source is evident.

First, the presupposition that all marketplace communications, even official ones, are persuasive cannot avoid the question of whether they are beneficial for consumers. It does, however, leap over the sterile assertion that information and persuasion can be separated in marketplace communications. Instead, the fruitful assertion here is that they cannot[25] and with this in place, the central question becomes: 'What sort of persuasion in marketplace communications benefits consumers?' From the consumers' viewpoint, this is persuasion which has appropriate amounts of the following in its make-up: accurate data, reasoned argument, limited and benign emotional appeal, and declared sourcing. If the persuasiveness of marketplace communications has more of those qualities than their opposites, consumers are benefiting. It could not be sustained rationally that persuasion based on no data or false data, irrationality, destructive emotions, and hidden sourcing was beneficial to its recipients. That is manipulation at its extreme, propaganda.

When PR people view MPR from the perspective of consumer benefit, it is apparent that they touch on ethics. For example, if they look at the IPR and PRCA codes of conducts, the code of the American Marketing Association or at frameworks for ethical decision-making,[26] they see statements about moral behaviour for themselves and about how to construct consumer-beneficial MPR. It is another project to discover the proportions of MPR in the UK which fit into the continuum between the beneficial and the manipulative, but it is safe to assume that puffery constitutes a large amount. A generous judgement is that puffery – defined by Chonko (1995, p. 5) as 'sales representations that praise the product or service with subjective opinions, exaggerations, or vague and general statements with no specific facts' – is the last stop before MPR becomes manipulative.

Second, it can be measured empirically whether producers are active in their markets, and marketing theory can help predict timing and quantity. Product life-cycle theory posits that the quantity of communications is high at the beginning of the cycle, and low to non-existent at the end. It is also an aphorism of the marketplace that some products 'sell themselves'. Thus consumers considering buying long-established products in a marketplace may have no communications, including MPR, except for word-of-mouth between consumers. It is also likely that monopoly suppliers to markets are relatively inactive and that suppliers of generic goods as opposed to branded ones will also be passive about communications: for both these groups, there is no advantage to be gained from producing communications.

Conceptually and empirically, it is unlikely that all marketplace communicators are equal in their output. Indeed, PR theory can be developed to offer an explanation for an unbalanced output of marketing communications, one unrelated to product life and linked instead to the size of the producer. Gandy (1982) offered the thesis that corporate public relations done by large businesses to influence government is an information subsidy favouring companies with substantial public relations budgets. This information subsidy concept can be extended to goods and services from big businesses; such goods and services are likely to have more MPR developed for them than are products from smaller businesses with smaller budgets. Thus, large-scale producers are financing an MPR communications subsidy for their products. These MPR subsidies create by their existence a form of communications bias in the marketplace. They fill Lancaster's role for PR 'anticipating and then filling the vacuum of consumer uncertainty in purchase' set out in Chapter 2, but do so in a skewed way. To say this is a reminder that communications (and therefore persuasion) are influences in the marketplace and that the flow of MPR to markets reflects producer concentration in the form of monopoly and oligopoly.

Third, the equal persuasive impact of marketplace communications on actual and potential consumers is measurable, in theory at least, but extremely difficult to imagine being made operationally quantifiable. The task, moreover, faces the conventional difficulty inherent in measuring adverts: do respondents admit the extent of any persuasion done to them? Furthermore, measuring the extent of persuasion on those who 'nearly' bought but just failed to, is methodologically difficult.

The fourth assumption, that the communications source is evident, is the most concerning when it comes to assessing consumer benefit; if this assumption does not hold, MPR is manipulative. Advertising is self-declaring about its originating source: the name of the good or service *and* its producer are carried – almost without exception – in the advertisement itself. Second, consumers are habituated to the highly flagged advertising discourse and read it in the context of paid for, explicit, selling messages. But this self-declaration is not apparent in MPR. In the case of the media, journalists too often appear to be the communications source about the good or service, passing on the opinions and facts in PR messages as if they were their own. Indeed, PR people say that their work gains persuasive power precisely because of that quality of non-declared source: they talk about the value of third-party testimonials by journalists. Non-declaration of source extends to other MPR activity. Goods and services are associated with celebrities in such a way as to appear to be natural endorsements when, in fact, the association is a commercial contract. These forms of source invisibility suit PR producers but not consumers, for the latter are put at a disadvantage by this form of communications deficit. If 'free' markets claim to have many of the characteristics associated with what economists call 'perfect' ones, all players in the marketplace – producers, consumers and observers – should be equally knowledgeable about message sources, contents and delivery. The communications flows should be the same to all market players, otherwise some – other producers and all consumers – are at the relative disadvantage of a communications deficit.

The same point about communications deficit can be made in a judgemental or ethical way. West (1963, p. 118) provides an example. He quotes Martin Mayer, author of *Madison Avenue, USA*:

> Advertising, whatever its faults, is a relatively open business; its messages appear in paid space or bought time; and everybody can recognise it as special pleading. . . . Public relations works behind the scenes; occasionally the hand of the PR man can be seen shifting some bulky fact out of sight, but usually the public relations practitioner stands at the other end of a long rope which winds around several pulleys before it reaches the object of his invisible tugging.

Michie writes that the best PR is never noticed. He quotes one spin doctor (1998, p. 4): 'PR is very much an invisible art and it doesn't serve our purpose to reveal how much we manipulate journalists and the public.'

This is a dramatic and anonymous statement, perhaps said boastfully by a preening professional. But source invisibility is a characteristic of much PR: much MPR (especially product information via the media) does not self-declare and is not easily detectable. Kotler (1997, p. 672) writes that 'some experts say that consumers are five times more likely to be influenced by editorial copy than by advertising'. To the MPR 'producer/player', this invisibility is an operational strength. To the MPR consumer, source invisibility is a communications deficit. Taken together, MPR subsidies by large-scale producers of retail goods and services and the undeclared sourcing of MPR are matters of public concern, for they distort the operation of free markets. The nature of this concern is economic: outside of that, undeclared sourcing raises questions of journalistic conduct and of manipulative intent towards consumers by PR people. These latter two points raise the question of regulating MPR like advertising (see chapter 11).

Overall, MPR (and other marketing communications) and communications from market observers create information flows inside markets. They do so positively because the flows are a mechanism for bringing more information from many sources to consumers: all of it persuasive in design, much of it competitive about products, and some of it cautionary and critical. The overall balance of benefit and harm to consumers from MPR is as follows. Consumers benefit from multiple flows of communications from competing sources because such flows aid informed consumer choices. But this benefit depends on consumers behaving in the sceptical and cautious way required by the *caveat emptor* rule and in particular on four conditions external to them: that MPR is more data-based and reasoned than affective; that all producers selling into a market create equal MPR flows for their goods and services; that MPR impacts equally on consumers; and that the sources of such flows are known to all market players. Where these conditions do not apply, the flow of marketplace communications favours suppliers, and builds up a concentration of advantage in their favour and against that of the consumer. In these circumstances, MPR is manipulative.

MPR as noise

The argument so far about the balance of advantage from MPR has been in terms of markets, principally retail. An aesthetic critique can also be made in that MPR is one prominent item in the array of communications – and therefore amounts of persuasion – aimed at UK citizens in their role as consumers. The overall effect on UK society of this search for new and more marketing communications is more and more 'walls of sound' around consumers. This metaphor is a title in Moore's *An Introduction to Public Relations* (1996) and it captures a sense of people being trapped before a rising quantity of marketplace communications. Even street furniture is part of the 'wall' now, with roundabouts sponsored by Chinese restaurants. Pay for a parking ticket in a public car park and the reverse side is a special offer for a 'McChicken sandwich and fries'. The public service bus is covered with company logos. MPR is making a contribution to an excessive marketisation of public spaces in the UK. Pratkanis and Aronson (1992, p. 11) write about a 'message-dense environment', in which the average American will see or hear more than 7 million advertisements in a lifetime. The process is becoming more targeted and refined, and making a contribution to what Gabriel and Lang (1995, p. 2) have called 'the final stage of commodification, where all relations between people are finally reduced to usage and exploitation'. For example, the advert hoarding has been blocking the off-road view at the roundabout for years; now the smaller sponsorship sign is strategically placed just in the eye-line of the oncoming driver. The result is that the UK citizen/consumer can find fewer and fewer physical or mental spaces where marketing communications are absent. The UK consumer is finding it increasingly difficult to avoid persuasion exchanges.

PR and financial markets

PR is widely used in wholesale financial markets as well as retail ones and is therefore involved in City of London wholesale market operations, venture capital operations, company takeovers and mergers. Whether these operations are controversial or not, PR people are often the holders of price-sensitive information and how that information is sourced, held and released concerns City regulators. The Financial Services Authority (FSA) is the regulator and there is little sign that PR specific regulation is to be introduced. The informed view is that common and statute law plus the general regulatory framework covers these 'financial communications professionals'' and journalists well enough. They are already affected by three Acts of Parliament, the Stock Exchange Yellow Book, the Takeover Code Blue Book and the Stock Exchange's price sensitive guide.[27] The 400 member City and Financial Group of the Institute of Public Relations (IPR) has voted on regulation by the FSA via a code of conduct on 'market abuse', such as the release of price-sensitive information. The vote was evenly split but on a low turnout. Members appear to be more interested in professional continuing education than in regulation as the route to raise standards.

What these events say about the regulation of PR is interesting: first, that PR is a regulated activity in so far as it is an integral part of other market operations which are regulated; second, that there has been censure in the past;[28] third, that for the FSA one regulatory regime covering all cases is preferred; fourth, PR people are divided on the need for outside regulation. They would prefer the issue not to be an active one on their professsional agenda, and will not volunteer to be regulated (see Chapter 11).

Summary

PR has benefits for its producers and its consumers in markets, politics and the media. This chapter has reviewed from the consumer's viewpoint the balance of advantages and disadvantages created by PR in markets. Marketing PR (MPR) takes many forms and they are likely to grow in number and volume because it is a highly adaptable form of persuasive communications. Many have noted that it has higher credibility than advertising, especially when journalists uncritically publish its messages in their work. It is often called the 'soft sell'.

MPR by the producers of goods and services and market PR by government, regulators and pressure groups constitute a flow of marketplace communications which lead to more informed consumer choice. These communications are always persuasive and to take benefit from them, consumers must observe the *caveat emptor* rule (let the buyer beware). Consumer benefit from MPR will be optimised when four assumptions hold: the persuasiveness of the communications comes from data, reasoned statements and appeals to benign emotions; all MPR producers are active and equal in their output; the persuasive quality in MPR acts equally on consumers; the originating source of any MPR is evident. Unless the rule and the assumptions apply, MPR creates communicative deficits and prevents consumers from getting value for money because of distorted flows of communications.

MPR is growing as an element in the total mix of marketing communications and is well adapted to handle complex marketing propositions such as lifestyle. But this growth, and the growth of all sorts of marketing communications, is leading to an aesthetic assault on the public space which is now excessively marketised.

The next chapter looks at PR and politics where there are concerns about equal and proportionate access for citizens to public policy decision-making.

8   PR, electoral politics and lobbying

It is hard to distinguish between PR and forms of modern politics. The roles of spin doctor, lobbyist and politician are merging, making the distinctions of less presentationally conscious times harder to grasp. The contemporary cultural dominance of marketing and PR with the primary emphasis on self-interested display and exchange is the underlying reason for the conflation. There is, however, a paradox in this overemphasis by politics on the presentational. While increased emphasis on PR is a response to the need to maximise electoral support in a mass media-saturated, democratic system, PR as spin doctoring and as lobbying reduces the accountability of elected politicians to electorates. PR in politics tends to take power away from politicians and transfer it to experts. The task of reforming PR in politics is to reverse that transfer.

The presentational urge of display-for-attention-and-advantage is very strong in PR as spin doctoring, and in electoral politics. The urgent search for media coverage is shared. Politics has taken on the PR and marketing tasks of research into what electors want through focus groups, of sensitivity to presentation, of event management, of sponsorship, of creating pseudo-events,[1] and of constructing new corporate identities. There is a conscious, visible transfer of skills from mass markets and business to politics.[2] The general term most frequently used to describe this is political marketing, and its most striking feature is the attempt to know what the mass wants. The search to know mass public opinion and satisfy it is a new political phenomenon, only 140 years old in the UK. Until the 1860s, political persuasion was not a mass process, previously taking the forms of Establishment and professional class networking through personal contact, and of corruption with drink or money of householders who had the vote. In the UK, there never has been a golden age when politics and persuasion went separate ways. The incremental spread of the franchise and the rise of modern political parties from the mid-Victorian period, and the development of mass persuasion techniques at the end of the period, meant that politics and persuasion entered a phase of 'massification'. Modern PR makes the connections manifest (see Franklin 1994, Rees 1992, Scammell 1995), and they are not to all politicians' liking.

There is, however, the irony that politicians are good at PR but could not possibly comment on their proficiency: Harold Wilson, who was twice Prime Minister, is alleged to have said PR was 'degrading'.[3] But there is no escape from PR and the persuasive mode for the modern democractic politician: mass electorates oblige them to be more persuasive than they were in the age of limited democracy. McNair (1996, p. 52) is correct, but perhaps not extragavant enough, when he notes that 'mass democracy is inevitably *populist* democracy in which appearance and image, as well as policy substance, have a role to play'. Democratic politicians have to behave as suitors as well as policy-makers.

The specific contributions of PR as electoral politics and PR as lobbying are profiled in the concentrated circumstances of general elections, the 24-hour influencing of media agendas, the daily persuasion of voters[4] and the constant leverage of private interest into public policy-making. Politics, however, is about ends as well as means: PR is only a means to an end. The forms of presentation of PR and politics are coalescing and persuasion for politics is parasitical about means; but politics, as the non-violent resolution of conflicting interests, is the master activity, using PR tactically. The coalition may be tactical but there is an imperative on politics to use PR. Schlesinger and Tumber (1994) identified the imperative in their study of source-media relations about criminal justice, and it can be extended to all public policy areas: they found evidence 'for the existence of an inescapable promotional dynamic that lies at the heart of contemporary political culture' (p. 271). It is hard to construct an extended role for PR (and marketing) in politics outside of the presentational and its foundations in market research – all done to maximise support (see Wring 1997). That is honourable enough work in a liberal democracy: there is no need for PR or marketing to extend their instrumentalities into policy-making. In markets, marketing activity identifies aggregates of preferences for actual and possible goods and services, and matches them against profitable supply by business. Politics deals principally in a currency of incommeasurable values, goals and behaviours between which equilibrium may or may not be produced. Presentational skills alone will never make for peace and justice in Northern Ireland.

There is, moreover, a case to be made for PR as electoral politics and as lobbying in that they bring benefits to mass democracy. Spin doctoring is the most common form of PR as electoral politics and is political news management between political parties, government and the electorate. PR as lobbying is usually a more private persuasive communications in the competition between interests for a favourable public policy. PR as lobbying comprises one or both of the following: the private activity of negotiating, often face-to-face, with policy-makers, and the public activity of media campaigns to win public support and so put political pressure on policy-makers. The benefits created by PR in politics are those which come from information flowing between parties, government and the public/electorate. PR is a major flow of information between rulers and ruled, and when democracy is seen as an information system about public goods, its contribution is important. McNair (1995, p. 191) elaborates this: PR and other political marketing techniques make politics a more attractive 'mass spectator sport' to an electorate who are adept at winnowing out manipulation and propaganda from useful information and opinion in political communications.

The work of spin doctors is particularly important at elections and most of the literature concentrates on that period with intense operational descriptions. There has been, however, little attempt to generalise the data into a descriptive or predictive statement. Holbrook's (1996) model of campaigns may be an adaptable basis, for he models information/publicity as a campaign effect. He argues that information/publicity in election campaigns influences the gap between a party's or a candidate's actual level of support and their expected one. If the difference between 'actual' and 'expected' can be sustained in this context, the following could be hypothesised: where actual support is lagging behind expected support, the effect of information (e.g. via spin doctors) in campaigns can reduce or extend the gap.

Spin doctors as folk devils

Freidenberg (1997) judges that American political consultants – his 'ballot box warriors' who use cable TV, videocassettes, email, polling and focus groups – are in a field 'which is almost certain to grow' (p. 209), because of, among other reasons, the growth of corporate issue management and new technology such as the internet. He notes the rise of the political consultant as celebrity.[5] This is flattering to UK spin doctors who will find job satisfaction in such attention. The Prime Minister's Press Secretary is better known than most Cabinet Ministers, and has more media references to his work than many of them. Charlie Whelan, the sacked spin doctor to Gordon Brown, Chancellor of the Exchequer, has gained a new career as a football writer because he was a flamboyant spin doctor. Their work is media management at the centre of government, high intensity PR activism for 10 Downing Street. Nicholas Jones's (1999) observation of it, as a journalist working with it and against it, suggests that government is the largest PR producer in the UK. He describes a 24-hours proactive management of news which builds a news agenda and tries to avoid reacting to one, which is pushed at the media through twice daily briefings and selected ministers for interview, which is ready to rebut stories it does not like and is quick to scold offending journalists, and which is crude and hectoring in tone. There are two opposing views of political communications: debate among voters and politicians, versus presentations by politicians to voters. In the marketing culture of contemporary Britain, the latter view is prevalent. Spin doctors are master presenters.

Freidenberg's category of political consultant is, however, a less populated one in the UK, with fewer specialist species in it,[6] but his observation on celebrity has picked up on a trend concerning government news management. In the 1950s and 1960s, the civil servants and party officials doing this work were called 'press officers', 'information officers' and 'press secretaries', titles too prosaic for contemporary self-presentation. Spin doctors have always been with us: they have laboured under other job titles. Rosenbaum (1997) dates the appearance of the modern political campaigning to between the mid-1950s and mid-1960s. From that period, press officers started their evolution into spinners: they adopted a more active, challenging, less respectful attitude towards the media, suggesting a new balance of influence between politicians and the media.

Their role and the associated one of political consultant continue to expand. Just before the summer 1999 ministerial re-shuffle, one minister's promotion prospects were reported to be diminished because his team of press officers was not as good as others. An Irish MEP seeking re-election hired a PR firm on a temporary basis for the campaign,[7] a move with great implications for the ability of parties to control their electioneering. This expansion, however, of the political adviser role should not hide the extensive and continuous political PR coming from politicians themselves. Political consultants and spin doctors are not operating among a nervous collection of innocents: they are invited in by PR's sophisticates. Indeed, one survey is reported to have found that MPs regarded a television interview as 'worth more to them' than a speech in Parliament.[8] Parliamentary proceedings can be seen as pseudo-events designed to optimise persuasive, if not partisan, information flows to the media. House procedure is manipulated in content and time by party business managers and whips. By crafting their words for the TV cameras and press gallery above them, MPs act as their own PR agents. Parliamentary politics is a showcase for PR techniques (see Tutt, 1999).

Political press officers – or spin doctors – have attracted much attention since the early to mid-1990s and the word 'to spin' has entered the language for glossing over matters so as to put them in the best light.[9] Two reasons can be identified for this prominence. The first is cultural and is a development in the contemporary fascination with celebrity status for individuals, and corporate personality and identity for organisations and groups. This attraction to presentation (of others and self) has spilt over into interest about how it is done, an interest observed by Boorstin 30 years ago about the public wanting to see the 'wires and pulleys' behind news management. Spin doctors are part of the backstage of politics made visible.[10]

Another cultural aspect to the attention given to spin is related to the pervasiveness of the PR mentality in the contemporary UK and its inclusion in popular culure (see Chapter 2). The word 'spin' has entered the general language as popular slang. People may or may not know what political spin doctors do but they have recognised intuitively an attitude and behaviour which is integral to modern living. These easy, frequent references to spin suggest that spin doctors are a new variant of folk devil; 'wicked' creatures in the vernacular sense of the word; persons to be half-admired, half-feared, but wholly needed. These joshing references by journalists, competitive politicians and the public have a political importance in themselves: public ridicule is a form of control in mass liberal democracies (Moloney 2000). We know what they are doing and it is coded into satire. McNair puts it formally (1996, p. 53): 'Our best defence against such efforts [manufacturing consent] is, as it has always been, to gain knowledge and understanding of the process (including, crucially those aspects of it which politicians would rather keep secret).' This is the *caveat emptor* rule applied to politics. The references also signify another social phenomenon. Linguistic appropriation of spinning into the demotic suggests a knowing tolerance of politicians and their ways, because spinning ways are the publics'/voters' ways too. To be aware of spinning in politicians is one step from being aware of it in oneself. Is not spinning well known in daily lives? It goes, however, by another name: it is 'getting your own way', 'pulling one off', 'sliding one past them', 'playing both ends against the middle', 'sneaking it through the back door', 'it's all in the small print' at work and in dealings with the powerful and the official. The declension out of the political into the personal is a natural one.

The second reason for the prominence of spin doctors lies in the particular configuration of UK politics in the early to mid-1990s. This was a time when public opinion was ebbing away strongly from the Conservative Government and the Labour Opposition was exploiting a mood of 'it's time for a change' through news management. Labour's political press officers – most noticeably, Peter Mandelson – were the semi-visible political operatives exploiting the mood through favourable media coverage, a process analysed by Franklin (1997), Jones (1995 and 1997) and McSmith (1997). The management was successful because it was congruent with the national mood, and this observation was widely shared by the media: Labour spin doctors were working with majority public opinion and the media wanted, for editorial and commercial reasons, to reflect the balance of national opinion. This concurrence of Labour news management and majority public opinion accounts for the weak resistance by political journalists to Labour spin doctors. In this way the influence of spin doctors is dependent on the degree of favour their party has with majority public opinion. The 1997 general election continues this dependency: the high standing of the Labour Government up to 1999 is matched by its continuing emphasis on news management. Labour doubled the number of special advisers employed by the Conservatives,[11] bringing the new total to over 70. Most advisers seem to be involved with PR. Franklin (1998) has described this as a policy of centralised control over all government public relations, directed from Downing Street and operated to narrow the distinction between informing about policy and promoting it.[12] 'Stay on message' summarises the policy.

The power of spin doctors over journalists is a restraint on the 'freedom' which the UK media claim is their professional goal, and ought to be reduced. Their power is a function of a government's or political party's standing with the electorate in the competition for votes. It is thus only weakly subject to institutional control, but it can be moderated. Against that macro setting, the working culture and arrangements between political PR and journalism should be arranged so that there is a distinctive balance of advantage in favour of the media. The arrangements can best be conceptualised as an exchange of information to journalists by politicians in return for publicity to politicians by journalists (see Blumler and Gurevitch 1981). The point of public information policy and work practice should be published as the provision of information to the public (and thus journalists) on an open government basis. Securing that declaration in the ways discussed below is the reform task facing political PR, for change will result in greater access for the UK public to political decision-making via a media which claims to be 'free'.

Franklin (1998) argues the case for change. He (p. 20) recommends two reforms of government machinery to maintain the distinction between informing the public about public policy and promoting it. First, that two daily press briefings in Downing Street by the Prime Minister's Press Secretary be televised; second, that special advisors who deal with the media follow the same code of professional conduct as the 1,000 civil servants of the Government Information and Communication Service. The first is welcome, for it would make public the source of quotations and opinions about policy and events which is now half-anonymous and shrouded in the euphemism of 'well informed sources'. This is not the language of accountability. If government declares for an open information policy, these briefings are important information transfer points and they should be open to public inspection. Morever, televising them provides a public record if questions of accuracy come up. Jones (1999, pp. 285–90) makes this point, and notes that a public record favours government as well as journalists and reminds us that parties already acquiesce in the recording of their policy statements, reactions to events and open forum questioning: party news conferences during elections are televised automatically. Televising the briefings recognises the importance of the briefers: the Prime Minister's press secretary has become more influential than some Cabinet members in a 24-hour media system with increasing outlets. The most substantial argument against televising the Downing Street briefings is that journalists are given information ahead of Parliament. This precedence is another sign of the general decline of Parliamentary influence and is difficult to accept. A starting point, perhaps, is the recognition that the media are the principal scrutineers of UK government on a daily basis and that Parliament should concentrate on detailed policy scrutiny over time through strengthening select committees.

Franklin's second point about putting special advisers, who do much public relations work for their ministers, on the same contract as professional civil servants will flounder, for it blurs a significant distinction which a convention of UK government weakly tries to maintain. The distinction between informing and promoting is too fine to maintain in operational public relations work and politicians implicitly acknowledge this by having preferences about who should be their spokespeople.[13] The career history of Charlie Whelan, the former press adviser to Chancellor of the Exchequer Gordon Brown is a case in point. It is untenable to maintain that his spin doctoring made a distinction between informing and promoting. He was a political ally of Brown in opposition and his *alter ego* when talking to the media. Whelan did not inform journalists about policy as opposed to promoting it: he informed only in order to better promote it.[14] It is better to recognise the distinction as a major one which cannot be maintained in one PR person and have two categories of press officer – civil servant and political – presenting policy. Their job titles should be recognisably different, but both should be subject to a code of openness written into their contracts. All political press officers would be temporary. The civil servant press officer would brief on public administration aspects of policy, the political one on party and governmental reasons for policy.

Finally, it is possible that the internet will be a force for reform in that it multiplies the number of primary sources about public matters and government policy. The Lewinsky scandal become public via private websites; the Starr report was first read by public and journalists on the internet.[15] In these ways, spin doctors and conventionally placed journalists in press corps and lobbies would be redundant after their intermediary role is abolished by direct electronic publishing. This would be reform in the shape of extinction.

Lobbying for advantage

In the climate of accelerated pluralism which characterises organisation and group competition in the the UK today, PR as lobbying is a technique with the potential to add strength to weaker, 'outsider'[16] groups seeking policy advantage. It is an accessible set of low-cost techniques, not difficult to acquire. It aids these groups in that it publicises their interest and so socialises the conflict which is to their advantage (Schnattschneider 1975).[17] This is PR as a conduit for bringing in government and public opinion to rebalance the contest between interests of different power and influence. Equally, it can aid stronger, 'insider' groups to maintain public policy in their favour and this has been the principal use of lobbying in the UK.[18] But if accelerated pluralism continues to grow and there is lobbying regulation, this predominance will weaken and PR as lobbying will be a means to more equitable outcomes in the competition of interests.

Lobbying has been a growing industry since the beginning of the 1980s, with estimates of a doubling or trebling in turnover for lobbying businesses who hire themselves out. It is, however, much harder to measure amounts of lobbying done by the employees of organisations such as businesses, for the cost is rarely identified. Identification is even more an obstacle for the amorphous voluntary sector. Whatever the measuring problems, lobbying in the UK will grow because of accelerated pluralism. It will also benefit from a new kind of pluralism – constitutional devolution. Lobbying always follows politics: Westminster-based lobbying firms have opened offices in Edinburgh, Cardiff and Belfast as government has been devolved to these regional centres.[19]

PR as lobbying is a communicative resource in the competitive struggle over public policy; it is seen at work in the genetically modified (GM) food controversy. Early on, the government's stance was set out by the Prime Minister.[20] Surrounding the immediate policy questions, he said, were two 'broader issues': 'we need to be guided by good science, not scaremongering' and 'we should resist the tyranny of pressure groups'. These remarks illustrate the political pressure which can be generated by the PR of groups: for 'scaremongering' read using media relations, organising petitions, designing news events to build public awareness and political pressure; and for 'tyranny' read combining these PR techniques into a sustained campaign which influenced government to modify its policy. PR by voluntary groups can generate great public opinion pressure and therefore political influence when it is done by those immediately affected and not by paid professionals. West (1963, p. 127) makes this point: 'The Jarrow march won more supporters than any handout.' This most successful of early, modern UK pseudo-events raises questions about the artificiality or otherwise of news management.[21]

The case for PR as lobbying being communications for negotiation and compromise between interests has been variously made. L'Etang (1996, pp. 30–1) reviews the mostly American claims to this non-governmental 'diplomatic' status: one claim talks of PR 'as the lubricant which makes the segments of an order work together with the minimum friction and misunderstanding'. Banks (1995, p. 19) favours a definition of PR as altruistic, mediating and translating activity in the communications of a society. He joins Kruckeberg and Starck (1988) in developing a communitarian view of PR, one concerned with its social consequences because it is constitutive of communities of interest. There is a strain in European thinking which also emphasises PR as the communicative aspects of social cohesion.

This European approach is different in focus from the current paradigm in UK and US practice where institutional needs are primary.

Indeed, PR regards lobbying (and community relations) as a specialism, but one perceived in a utilitarian way as enlightened self-interest for the organisation engaging in it. At its least self-interested, this institutionally based model sees lobbying as a two-way symmetrical process where listening, amending, negotiating, compromising are the modes of communications. It is lobbying PR as a practice of virtue in the competitive struggle between interests in society, and not as a practice of supremacy on behalf of the powerful against the less powerful.

The upper class voice

The case against lobbying PR is various. The case against it as negotiation and compromise is that historically it has been a technique mostly available to powerful interests: in Schnattschneider's phrase, pressure groups usually sing in an upper class voice. Lobbying has been a resource shut off from organisationally weaker or unarticulated interests by cost and organisational ability. Moreover, its internal architecture of message construction easily degrades into manipulation and propaganda. This case against accounts for the hostility towards lobbyists and the aversion shown by those who do it themselves towards the term. The American literature is replete with anecdotes of contempt; in the UK, lobbyists in print and public statement will search for any managerialist-sounding euphemism under which to trade.[22]

Another source of this hostility is 'shoot the messenger' behaviour. When we hear lobbying (and, in general, public relations) messages, we are hearing communications designed to further an interest, a group or organisation; if we do not like the interests and its groups, we will not like the messages or the messengers. Lobbyists (public relations people) are often 'shot' because they carry statements which are unpopular with listeners. Other sources of hostility are the use of discrete, if not 'hidden' contact with politicians and senior civil servants; the deployment of free gifts and favours to policy-makers; and the promiscuous nature of the hired lobbyist, serving any cause for money.

The Americans Stauber and Rampton (1995, p. 14) are the severest critics: lobbying entrenches the already powerful by dubious means. They argue that PR-as-lobbying is captured by powerful interests and by government:

> ... ordinary citizens cannot afford the multi-million dollar campaigns that PR firms undertake on behalf of their special interest clients, usally large corporations, business associations and governments. Raw money enables the PR industry to mobilise private detectives, attorneys, broadcast faxes, satellite feeds, sophiscated information systems and other expensive, high-tech resources to out-maneuver, overpower and outlast true citizen reformers.

They are not critical of a beneficial PR, serving non-corporate interests: 'Citizens and individual PR practitioners can use ethical public relations techniques' (pp. 205–6). Beneficial PR is based on social movements, citizen reformers, grassroots groups, often in contest with powerful, vested, public and private interests.

Lobbying is sometimes considered the most influential component in PR. Whether to beneficial effect or otherwise, what do lobbyists do? Their work can be broken down into four components:[23] the supply of information about policy development, the supply of administrative support, the supply of policy advice, and the supply of access to policy-makers. Most of the work is humdrum in that it involves the collection of data, the writing of position papers and the administration of events, where their principals are in contact with politicians and policy-influencing civil servants. On balance, the professional lobbyists tend to be more involved with policy processes than policy contents and goals, since policy-makers prefer to talk to their principals. With volunteer lobbyists working because of commitment, there is a better balance: these lobbyists often experience the consequences of present policy and want to change it. They lobby because they experience policy consequences.

Lobbying is done from three organisational positions: full-time, professional employees inside organisations, professional, hired help from lobbying firms, and volunteers in groups lobbying out of commitment. There are also lone individuals with a sense of grievance who use PR in the 'cottage industry' and 'personal kit' ways described in Chapter 3. Whistleblowers and people claiming wrongful conviction are examples. There are handbooks for voluntary sector PR on how to lobby.[24] All four lobbyist types are found in accelerated pluralism, and while the volunteer and individual categories are difficult to count, the media evidence is that they are present in large numbers. What unifies all types of lobbyists as PR is the display-for-attention-and-advantage behaviour, much of it discretely and directly done to the policy-makers without the mediation of newspapers or broadcasting. It is identifying an organisational or group interest; spotting opportunities and threats to its advancement; building supportive alliances; blocking hostile ones; aligning self-interest with a larger interest; expressing the interest persuasively in the language of the policy-makers; building up pressure on them directly and indirectly. Many professional lobbyists reject their inclusion in PR, joining the flight from it as a work title and preferring euphemisms such as government relations, political communications and public affairs specialists. For these separatists, PR is public campaigning via the media, as opposed to their private and confidential approaches to persuade powerful persons face-to-face. PR loyalists in lobbying are a minority.[25] To the unkind, this networking earns them the soubriquets 'corridor creeps' and 'influence pedlars'.

Evaluating the contribution of lobbying to a policy decision is difficult, if not impossible. A decision is the subject of an array of variables: a short list starts with stated government and party policy; disagreements amongst policy-makers and their changing, factional influence; media and public opinion; the balance of all lobbying efforts on policy-makers; the secrecy of policy-making; government willingness to be representative. There is no literature on a proven methodology for successful lobbying outcomes, but there is a considerable one on how to conduct a lobby. Working lobbyists themselves are cautious about claiming success for their efforts. They write about influencing policy, not about changing it. They can associate themselves with favourable outcomes; they cannot demonstrate that they caused them. Lobbyists may boast of knowing senior politicians and civil servants but the compliment is not returned; a phrase most unlikely to pass the policy-maker's lips is 'All that lobbying changed my mind'. The government's proposal to exclude policy advice, the economy and relations between devolved assemblies and parliament from freedom of information legislation will not increase public knowledge about the influence of the lobbying. Lips are not being opened.

Spin doctoring and lobbying are two prominent, contemporary manifestations of modern PR. Both can be construed to yield benefits and costs. If the 'new variant folk devils' perception of spin doctors needs examination, so does the 'naughty and nice' image of those dubbed the most influential part of the profession of the decade, lobbyists.

Reforming lobbying

The case for lobbying is made in constitutional terms as the right to petition and to seek redress of grievances, and in political economy terms as the expression of the competitive struggle between interests vis-à-vis public policy. Viewed as a liberal, constitutional right, the case for lobbying is strong; as an influence in the actual, existing UK's political economy, however, it can be objected to on the grounds that it entrenches the power of the already powerful and makes policy-making less transparent and accountable. Observation of the influence of lobbying on UK policy-making from 1985 to 1998 reinforces the conclusion of inadequate transparency: this was the period when 'sleaze' entered the political vocabulary; when 'cash' could get questions asked and meetings held with the powerful. Politicians and lobbyists were mired in allegations of trading their privileges for rewards.

Unless this corruption was reversed, UK politics was heading for a crisis of confidence with the public. The trend was at least staunched by the appointment of the Nolan committee on standards in public life. Its ten members were alarmed about the low public reputation of politicians. In their first report (1995, p. 15) they wrote: 'There is no precedent in this century for so many allegations of wrongdoing, on so many different subjects, in so short a period of time.' Its findings amount to the first, significant reform of lobbying in the UK, the significance lying not in the technical changes to MPs' behaviour but in the evidence given to the committee of public anger and contempt for their behaviour. Their findings and their adoption by the House can be summarised as permitting MPs to offer paid advice to outside interests, but not to do paid advocacy for them. These reforms adopted in 1995 showed up the previous pusillanimity of the House of Commons on matters of its members' self-interest (see Jordan 1998). They were a reminder that meaningful change for more open and accountable government was unlikely to be put through by Ministers or MPs without public pressure. Greenwood and Thomas (1998) note that regulation is 'openly inspired by issues of declining public confidence in public life', and that public disclosure is the agent of effective change. It is a high irony that it was an act of lobbying – with public evidence taking – by the Nolan Committeee that led to lobbying reform.

Lobbying regulation is increasing over time in the UK: the question is whether it is effective. MPs now have to give the House of Commons Register of Members' Interests more explicit information (contract details and remuneration levels) about contracts with outside interests: those organisations and groups outside Parliament which they advise on policy development and Commons procedure. Remuneration has to be declared in bands of £5,000. MPs can accept monies for advice but may not receive payment for performance of Parliamentary duties. The ineffective Members' Interests Committee has been replaced by the Standards and Privileges one, and there is a Parliamentary Commissioner for Standards who maintains the Members' Register and who can investigate breaches.

By May 1999, all three trade bodies representing lobbyists – the APPC, PRCA and IPR – were in favour of statutory regulation. The IPR were the last to declare with an accreditation scheme for 'IPR Registered Lobbyists'. It was part of their evidence to the Neill Committee (successor to Nolan) investigating whether there should be statutory regulation. The PRCA and APPC, with an eye to business competitors, also called for lobbyists from law firms, charities and pressure groups to be regulated. The same process of an extending net of regulation is evident in other parts of the EU.[26] A useful addition to any code of conduct would be an undertaking by lobbyists to publish retrospectively a diary of meetings they arrange with decision-makers (ministers and senior civil servants). If they counter with the claim that this would infringe their clients' confidentiality, the Neill committee should recommend that ministers and senior civil servants publish retrospectively every week on the internet their schedule of meetings with outside interests.[27] The committee also heard that the example of the Scottish Parliament should be followed: MPs who do not declare interests are liable to face criminal charges, and that lobbyists who seek to be Ministers' special advisers should have a two-year cooling-off period before joining government.[28]

There is one area of lobbying activity which has escaped specific reform, that which is known as 'intrastate lobbying' where public bodies hire lobbyists to find out about government policy. It is reported that there are over 60 such uses of tax payers' money to discover what other parts of the public sector are doing.[29] That such public expenditure is allowed is a sign of the cultural acceptance by the political class that paid lobbying is a normal technique for managing affairs. The question as to why the senior management of these public bodies does not lobby in person on their own behalf should be asked by public auditors.

Overall, the reform agenda has touched lobbying more than any other PR specialism. It is apparent that reform is drifting towards statutory and self-regulation of lobbyists. This is welcome but it is the least effective of two approaches. The other is to ban all payments of any sort to MPs for representation of interests in Parliament. This representation is now lobbying via advice instead of advocacy, but the objective of influencing policy is the same. To do their representative work, elected politicians do not need to be paid by outside interests: they are paid salaries out of public funds to do it. Representation is the task of MPs. They should represent any interest they like. Why, however, should they accept payment from those whose affairs interest them? Politicians who accept money from interests are effectively asking to be paid twice. That this double-payment happens and that reformers have to argue against it is an example of the marketisation of politics. This is a complex phenomenon and expressive of the marketing paradigm as the leading cultural form of contemporary UK. It has three expressions, however, relevant to politics and PR. First, it regards politics as another forum where services are exchanged only or principally for money. Politics viewed as the exchange of benefits is a sympathetic environment for the growth of lobbying PR. Second, marketisation transforms politics, in Franklin's phrase, from a market-driving activity into a market-driven one, in which policy is principally determined by what attracts more votes. It points up PR's role as the attracting wand. Third, PR in politics amends further any extant versions of liberal, democratic theory that politics is pure, rational deliberation. The presence of PR as persuasive communications makes clear the role of self-interest in politics and prompts the question of how it is rationally integrated with other interests.

The spread of marketisation and PR has nearly driven out of the political vocabulary the idea of 'public spiritedness'. If Parliament banned all payments to MPs other than their public salary, it would be in part a reassertion of the idea of politics as service. The ban would be both a material and symbolic act simplifying the reform task. First, it would focus the responsibility of maintaining high standards in public life where it should be fixed: on those who have asked for public support in elections. They are 650 identifiable individuals with security of tenure for five years who volunteered for membership of, formally, the most important instituition in the country. Let them set the benchmarks for high standards.

Second, the whole private and public apparatus of public registers for lobbyists could be dropped. These documents imply that the constitutional right to petition and to seek redress is being tiered into varying categories of access to politicians. At some stage, the words 'you are not registered: you cannot put your case to an MP' will be uttered. It will be costly and litigious to maintain any public register and it will confer commercial advantages on lobbyists for hire who are in the last resort business people.

Summary

The kinship between PR and modern politics is made plain in the rise of the political spin doctor, a job which demonstrates the marketisation of politics and therefore the importance attached to policy presentation in media-saturated democracies. The post is the skills transfer into politics of the corporate PR spokesperson managing relationships with the media. When politics is presentation rather than policy formation, such imports are very hard to resist. Spin doctors, moreover, represent a rebalancing of government information policy towards the manipulative and propagandistic. The machinery of government should recognise this new tilt, title them clearly in this role and hive them off from the civil servant information officer who describes policy rather than promotes it. The promotional role of spin doctors is intuitively understood by the public/electorate, who have knowingly taken the word 'spin' into daily language as 'putting the best verbal gloss on people and events'. In so doing, they catch the spin doctors at work, make them figures of ridicule and do service for more open government. This is the *caveat emptor* rule reworked into politics as satire.

S.E. Finer famously ended *Anonymous Empire* (1958) with a call for more light to shine on lobbying. It was some 40 years before the Nolan committee came along to put its finger on the switch. The House of Commons consistently failed to provide the light of effective self-regulation when it was most needed: from the 1980s onwards when a growing number of lobbyists sought the favour of MPs and ministers in an ideological climate which encouraged the view of politics as a market exchange of self-interests.

Political PR is a major, expanding form of PR in the context of the accelerated pluralism which characterises contemporary UK politics. There is increased competition among a growing number of businesses, organisations and voluntary groups for advantage vis-à-vis public policy, and PR is the communicative aspect of that competition. The struggle over genetically modified food is an example of PR in the service of players manoeuvring for a policy advantage. Accelerated pluralism should see weaker 'outsider' organisations and groups gain more influence in policy formation because their increasing numbers represent more challenge to stronger, 'insider' groups. PR is the technique through which weaker groups mobilise public opinion and so reduce the advantage of stronger groups seeking private, favoured contact with policy-makers.

Apart from these structural changes following through from more pluralism, the internal architecture of lobbying is being reformed by self-regulation codes put upon itself by the lobbying industry. But these are weak, second order reforms; more important are the post-Nolan changes to MPs' freedom to profit from outside interests, i.e. organisations and groups on whose behalf they can lobby. More changes are needed, the most effective – a complete ban on earnings by MPs from outside interests – being the most difficult for the metropolitan political class to accept. When MPs accept payment from outside interests, they are being paid twice – from public and private purses.

After more than 40 years, Finer's light is only shining weakly on lobbying. But even this thin illumination will always find some form of PR in its path, for politics and PR as lobbying are also cousins. The commonality, as with spinning, is self-presentation-for-attention-and-advantage and not in policy-making, where there is no role for PR. The next chapter turns to the effects of PR on the media and journalism.

9 PR, journalism and the media

The expansion of the mass media is before our eyes, ears and fingers every day. Since the 1980s, the UK public has had more information, entertainment and opinion sources to choose from than any other generation. The established media has grown exponentially: witness the multiplication of radio and TV channels tenfold by digital technology, more pagination in newspapers, and more magazines. A new computer-mediated media has appeared; increasingly the internet is filled by media services with access to both mass markets and to specialist e-communities. There is 'crossover' between old and new media.[1]

This expansion has been, is and will be a major opportunity for placing PR ideas and material in the media. Today PR is the biggest river contributing to what has been called the Niagara of supply bearing down on a media waiting to be filled up.[2] Baistow (1985) notes how in the past PR benefited from developments in British print journalism: its penchant for 'action' and 'human interest stories', rather than what he calls 'significant information' and its need for 'ready-made early copy' to suit pagination determined by advertising. He writes (p. 68) that 'all are grist to [the] busy and profitable mill of what one might call the Fifth Estate, the creators of copy that is in effect subsidised, usually with a commercial profit in view, and, at its most sophisticated level, the practitioners of news management'. Holtz (1998) judges that business PR will communicate via the internet both with its traditional audiences and a relatively new one made more powerful by cyberspace – activist groups.

The arrival of 'e-comms.' is a reminder, however, to distinguish between technology and promotional techniques. To read the 1906 account by the 'muckraking' journalist Ray Stannard Baker about the PR campaign by American railway companies to stop Congress passing price-capping legislation is to note that the latter are static. The contemporary investigative journalist would see that the companies used the word 'campaign'; that their first target to influence was the media; that they hired a 'publicity bureau' with 'high class clients, notably Harvard University'; that the agency took on extra staff and opened up five new offices; that the largest branch in Chicago had 43 staff; that they did daily press clippings;

that they visited editors and kept their profiles updated in a central file; that they changed their copy to interest local papers; that they evaluated the clippings, e.g. Nebraska was turned around in eleven weeks from 212 unfavourable references and two favourable to 202 favourable and four unfavourable; that they stirred up opinion formers against unfriendly editors; that the agency did not want publicity about its role; that they gave away tickets as 'freebies'; that they sent out media releases of favourable Congressional speeches; and that the railways' in-house PR departments were working in parallel with them, sending out briefings and copy, as well as an offer of paying for any extra printing costs. Change the date and today's investigative journalist would hardly know the difference. Indeed, from early twentieth-century America comes the most succinct argument for PR vis-à-vis the media and Baker's 1906 account provides an empirical basis for what Lippmann wrote 16 years later (1922, p. 344). The latter argues that 'the enormous discretion as to what facts and what impressions shall be reported is steadily convincing every organised group of people that whether it wishes to secure publicity or avoid it, the exercise of discretion cannot be left to the reporter'. The modern question is about how little discretion the contemporary reporter has got.

The same contemporary journalist, if in the UK today, would, however, welcome some changes in PR practice. The first is the historical decline from the eighteenth century until the mid-Victorian age of government using working journalists as covert or open propaganda agents, usually paid. Grant (1994, pp. 10–54) traces the decline of this working journalist-as-government-publicist role, its temporary resurgence around World War I and then its decline in the inter-war years. Journalists also lost out to advertising people and to civil servants as advisers to government on publicity. They were replaced by people such as Frank Pick and Stephen Tallents[3] who showed public relations talent, a talent in Grant's phrase (p. 249) for the 'sale of ideas'. This reliance on professional persuaders, rather than journalists, for propaganda or public relations advice to the state continues with the contemporary pre-eminence of the Saatchi brothers, Tim Bell, Sir Bernard Ingham, Peter Mandelson, Philip Gould and many of the 72 special advisers to the Labour government. Their rise in influence and the relative decline of journalists' – the partial exception is Alistair Campbell for he has become a PR man – is welcome, for the liberal, democratic state needs the scrutiny role of journalists more than it needs their advice on publicity. Journalists should not be partisan persuaders for government.

If journalists have escaped a historical propaganda or PR role for government, they are ironically in greater danger from contemporary, pervasive PR. They are being colonised by it. There is a PR-isation of the media happening in the UK. This is a growing identity in the attitudes, behaviours and personnel of journalism and PR.[4] It implies a growing dependency of journalists on PR, leading to the disablement of their critical faculties. A similar process has been described about the American media by freelance journalists Blyskal and Blyskal (1985) who identify the 'great bulk of stories that are the product of assembly-line factory journalism' (p. 35). It is the PR industry in the USA and UK which is supplying the prefabricated pieces. These relationships of journalistic dependency need to be reversed into independence. The more distance between journalists and PR people, the better for an open, liberal democracy.

A love-hate relationship

Baistow's comments are typical of some journalists' attitudes to PR: hostile (see Chapter 2). Tedlow (1979, pp. 176–82) tracks the hostility of American journalists back to the end of the nineteenth century: its two sources were diverting advertising revenue from papers and confusion over what was news. Hostility by some UK journalists is not new: some twenty years before Baistow, West wrote *Fifth Estate*, which is an early version of Michie's 1998 book – critical but sympathetic to PR. The title is a powerful, compressed description of the status of PR today, more accurate than in 1963. More journalists need to be more wary of it.

West records both the attacks on and defences of PR (pp. 90–107) and they illustrate both the cultural mood of the period and some perennial themes. He notes the public debate between journalists Macolm Muggeridge, Michael Frayn and Cyril Ray (who founded The Society of the Discouragement of Public Relations) and Alan Eden-Green, of Wedgewood Pottery and President of the IPR. West says (p. 127) that 'if a case is good, its supporters can state it themselves', a reply to the argument that PR is needed to make a case. In PR's defence, he notes that politicians and journalists also claim to be persuasive, that journalists do not reveal their sources or the entertainment they accept, and that all are entitled to promote what they believe in.

When journalists attack PR, it is often the sound of pots name-calling kettles. West quotes a right-of-centre journalist Godfrey Hodgson of the *Observer* saying journalists have a mixed attitude towards PRs and that part of their dislike is 'snobbish'. He notes that journalists enjoy PR lunches and that there should be more PRs. Anti-PR critique came from 'quality' papers, while less exalted journalists said they were in the 'same racket' as PR people and that if you have a family to keep, you welcome the 50% more paid by PR. He notes that Frayn had written advertising copy for *The Guardian*.

West also describes Frayn's invention of Rollo Swavely, 'the well known public relations consultant' and observes that Frayn has hit at 'the worst vice of the PRO: his belief in telling the public what he thinks the public will want to hear'. He says, however, of PR critics: 'PR arouses the Puritan in them. It is a smooth, deceiving, soft-talking, politiking Romish thing to be answered by clear and honest English. Above all PR is bought with gold, can corrupt other weak ones with gold, if the Valiant-for-Truth of journalism do not lay bare its wickedness. This puritanism can easily turn to priggishness.'

Valiant-for-Truth can also repeat a long-standing attack on the hidden sources of much PR. West quotes (p. 97) from a letter of Muggeridge to *The Times* (27.6.61):

> Persuasion is obviously a legitimate and necessary social activity. Clergymen try to persuade us to behave like Christians, politicians to vote for them, prostitutes to desire them, salesmen to buy their wares, and so on. In this sense, public relations men are only engaged in doing, on behalf of their employers, what lawyers do for their clients, leader-writers for their editors and strip-teasers for their managements.
>
> Where, however, PR persuasion differs from these other forms is in being, more often than not, hidden behind a camouflage of objectivity and hospitality. It is, as it were, wrapped in slices of smoked salmon, aromatic with cigar smoke and delivered, not as a sample, but a gift package.

West notes a political dimension to attacks on PR: 'It is argued, too, that since public relations is merely another form of salesmanship, any attack on it and on advertising should logically be extended to an attack on capitalism' (p. 107).

Much of the above is satire and as such a reminder that in having to deal with journalists, PR people have got themselves critics who are skilled trumpeters. In a liberal democracy, the critique is to be encouraged, so that there is no complicity between media systems to the disadvantage of the public. Indeed, these exhanges underline the persuasive role of journalists and point up that they can manipulate by having hidden sources. This is an important point for building a reform agenda for PR and for pointing the trumpet back at journalists.

PR-isation of the media

Too many journalists are passively – or actively – accepting colonisation by PR. They are content to accept 'newszak', news designed for a market and delivered in small bits for easy consumption, from their PR suppliers.[5] For journalism as public gossip and as entertainment, this colonisation is entrenched. It is often active collaboration in the cases of celebrity news, entertainment columns, lifestyle and consumer sections, and may not be immediately damaging. PR colonisation, however, is immediately destructive of journalism as scrutiny, as the review of spin doctors in politics in the previous chapter shows. For all journalists, scepticism up to polite hostility is the proper response of a media which calls itself 'free' and 'independent' of PR. Such a media should not be beholden to the suppliers of news, real or pseudo. There should be an apparent, critical distance between a wary media and a supplicant PR industry. Reliance on PR creates a dependency culture in journalists, taking out their critical edge of independent view, substituting meretriciously the views of another for their own and leading to the editorial deception of readers and audiences.

This distance is shrinking over time. What is unsaid by media commentators is that journalists are complicit in the in-take of PR material. They seek the material, use it to fill expanding editorial space and benefit from any audience or reader increases. But how does that complicity come about in the face of journalistic hostility? Is dislike not enough to keep the two groups apart and stop any PR-isation? There are two related explanations which explain this contradictory mixture of hostility and complicity. The first is that journalists are too weak as a professional group to halt PR-isation. They are caught in markets in several ways. There is a structural process of marketisation happening to their institutions which is sucking in PR material to fill space. Moreover, the labour market position of journalists is weak. There is too much supply for too few jobs, undermining – through easy replacement – any principled stance against the process. In this marketised environment, some journalists are hostile to PR, but they are too few. Their opposition, moreover, is undermined by the concept of 'the total newsroom', where the distinction between journalism and marketing is weakened by the co-ordination of the editorial, advertising, promotion and circulation aspects of a media outlet.[6] The position of regional and local journalists appears the weakest, leading to this irony: Harrison (1998, pp. 167–8) argues that 'the professional local authority PRO, often a fully trained and experienced former reporter, is a more reliable source of news for the local authority than many local reporters acting on their own', and 'that the town hall is becoming the last bastion of good municipal journalism'.

Second, journalists' attitudes are suggestive of something else which is unsaid: the most powerful news managers are working journalists. They select events and people, and shape words and visual images into a 'product' they call news which is 'manufactured' (e.g. Glasgow University Media Group 1982; Cohen and Young 1973) by their professional routines and values; they present this process as an objective one to their mass audiences. This 'manufacture' sometimes itself becomes a news event, as when the *Sun* airbrushed a woman in a wheelchair out of a picture of the English cricket team celebrating victory against the South Africans at Headingley.[7] Moreover, it is not that there is too much news for too little space: there is too much space for too little news (Curran and Seaton 1997, p. 278). In this ways, journalists have become embroiled with PR because of changing work organisation and professional behaviour.

Journalists are also complicit with PR in more internalised ways. Traditionally, most of them omitted PR material, challenged it or found alternatives. Now they are more likely to accept it. Journalists have increased their reliance on secondary sources (including PR), especially when these sources produce copy in a pre-prepared, journalistic form. Journalists thus rely more on official and company spokespeople as primary definers of events. This reliance gives the sources the ability to co-operate or obstruct depending on the favourability of journalists' copy. It is also a rejection of the most effective journalistic methodology – personal investigation. Furthermore, reliance means that journalists are accepting the work subsidy which PR represents in the form of information subsidy (Gandy) and are ceding some control over the news agenda, an advantage much sought by PR people.

Reliance has wider consequences beyond the individual journalist: a spiral of work consequences has set in which reinforces the PR-isation process and makes journalism as scrutiny more difficult to do. News room budgets and numbers are cut as journalists move towards more passive re-working of PR material. More young, inexperienced and low-cost staff are taken on. Fewer tips needing follow-up are phoned in to news desks, who do not want the delay associated with investigation and who insist on new copy for morning/lunch/evening/night editions. Reliance on secondary sources means journalists reduce face-to-face contact – which is when they transform scrutiny into journalism through observation, investigation, questioning, admission and indiscretion. Withdrawal into the news room means journalism becomes invention. Open letters to the Prime Minister or to the Governor of the Bank of England appear, for example, on the front page of regional evening pages. Once, and this is appropriate if the Prime Minister visits or if a factory closes. Twice, and it is a refuge from investigation.[8]

At the level of ideology, the dominance of the marketing culture aids the PR-isation process. The culture of self-interested exchange, outside markets as well as in them, is an operating environment to which PR has easily been adapted. Historically, it has been used mostly in favour of private interests, societal passivity, submission to elites, and to consumption and acquiesence *over* public interests, societal criticism, popular creativity, abstention and conflict. This balance may not be harmful to journalism as public gossip or as entertainment, but it is maladaptive for journalism as scrutiny. Markets encourage endorsement and repetition and tend towards the conservative. Journalism as scrutiny promotes critical engagement and tends to rupture with the status quo.

Journalists should have more regard for their own working practices and ethics when they criticise PR people.[9] In Boorstin's account of the rise of the pseudo-event, which he entitled 'From News Gathering to News Making', it is clear that journalists, politicians and PR people worked together. If pseudo-events are those created to be reported, they need journalists to see the light of day. The conventional relationship between the two groups usually devolves to love-hate, but sometimes it degrades to love-love (see Chapter 2). An example of the latter is the 'freebie' culture, where consumer and lifestyle goods are loaned to journalists; other free-bies are free travel and free holidays. New cars are used in this way. The loans are sometimes declared by 'thoughtful' journalists who see that acceptance of them disadvantages readers if not declared: 'The less thoughtful ones worry that they are not working in enough plugs to keep the PR people happy.' 'Honest' can be substituted for 'thoughtful', for freebies are a black market of hidden favours traded at the expense of media audiences. Another freebie area is personal finance journalism, where the connection between editorial endorsement and sales of a product is a tempting line to shorten by favours.[10] Even PR people are sometimes shocked at its extent.

These relationships are detrimental for journalists. More journalists should be more cautious, prudent and distant in their relationships with PR people than they are. PR-isation of the media has set in too far and journalists are too complicit with it. It is journalists who have travelled more to PR than *vice versa*. Indeed the Fourth Estate has watched on pas-sively as a Fifth Estate has settled on its boundaries, if not inside them. It is not a phenomenon which is new, for Tye (1998, pp. 169–71) describes over-close relations between Bernays and American reporters who were covering the political difficulties the United Fruit Company (Bernay's client) was facing in the early 1950s from a reforming Guatemalan govern-ment.

Expansion into journalism

If journalists want help from PR people, there are many they can call on. Franklin (1997, p. 10) estimated that there were nearly as many PR people (25,000) as journalists who were members of the NUJ (26,800). Pilling (1998, pp. 193–4) notes that 'on most local papers fewer journalists are working harder and being far more selective in their coverage of local affairs than they were a generation ago', and that 'the "sweatshop journal-ists" are aided in their need to fill space by the press releases of resource-rich organisations'. This understaffing weakens the ability of local and regional journalists to resist PR-isation. Harrison (1998, p. 167) writes that 'their journalists, in many cases hard-pressed, de-unionised, demoralised and poorly-paid, are increasingly reliant on press releases and promo-tional material provided for them by vested interests'.

Dowie in the introduction to Stauber and Rampton (1995) writes that there are 150,000 PR people in the USA as against 130,000 journalists and the gap is widening. Some of the 'best' journalism schools send more than half their graduates into PR – 'an almost traitorous career choice to tradi-tionalists like myself who instruct students how to handle PR executives and circumvent the barriers they erect between the truth and the story they want told about their clients' (p. 3). Messages in PR are integrated with messages in advertising, increasing their reach. Dowie concludes

(p. 4) that 'we' [journalists] have given an 'awesome power to an industry that gravitates to wealth, offers surplus power and influence to those who need it least, and operates largely beyond public view'.

Journalists also collude with PR by training them. A flyer for two conferences organised by Meet The Press 'Britain's biggest PR training company' for February and June 1999 urge PR people to 'Meet Britain's top editors and journalists – Find out from them how to get maximum *positive* editorial coverage'. These sessions were addressed by journalists from *Financial Times, The Sunday Times, The Evening Standard, Independent Radio News, The Sunday Telegraph, BBC TV News* and *The Daily Telegraph*. Many journalists are also involved in media interview training for senior business people, in being the compère and interviewer for corporate videos, and in chairing business conferences.

Spinning is not confined to politics. Anthony Hilton, City editor of *The Evening Standard*, London, writes[11] about a 'constant barrage' of PR and that newspapers 'seem to be losing their independence of judgement'. The structural cause in the case of financial journalism is the evolution of the City of London away from long-term relationships in finance capital towards making deals. In operational terms, this change creates more PR opportunities. There are public announcements to make about a deal which is the optimum solution for any given set of circumstances, a deal that is better than the alternatives, and a briefing that, on- or off-the record, competitive deals are inferior. Deals are also easy to personalise when business people are involved: they are a competition amongst opposing teams struggling with market forces, an easy representation for PRs and journalists to portray. Hilton concludes that 'the press has moved away from being an observer of the business scene to a participant in it', and 'media manipulation has become a legitimate way for increasing shareholder value'. He notes that the media 'have been relatively starved of resources', that talented journalists go on to be PRs, that 'more and more copy appears in newspapers as the PR people want it', that finance houses are as much 'on message' as ministers, that the media lacks investigative journalists, and that critical journalism will be met with non-co-operation by news sources.

This analysis by a working journalist is reflected by Franklin who adds other factors to account for the weakening of journalism vis-à-vis PR. He notes (1997) that journalists are now dealing with collaborators and competitors who have communications skills similar to their own. Terms and conditions of service and pay have fallen for journalists; the National Union of Journalists has been weakened by the introduction of personal contracts. Vocational education has also played a part in the weakening. It has educated and trained large numbers of graduates in journalism and PR on courses where many skills, such as news sense, copy writing, electronic layout, internet publishing and presentation are interchangeable. It has not emphasised the professional differences of attitude and motive between the two fields and often uses the same lecturers on both sets of courses. These graduates leave to find researching, writing, editing and electronic publishing skills in both news rooms and PR offices, and they think that the work is the same. Journalism graduates know that jobs are fewer than PR ones. New journalists are entering a labour market where there is over-supply, at least at the level of a liveable wage. A move into PR using transferable skills is tempting. There is already noticeable job traffic between PR and journalism: gossip, for example, about the freelance journalist who also does PR work for the local MP and runs a PR business as well; trade news about the former journalist who is now a PR manager.[12] The opposite flow of PR people into journalism is much smaller but is detectable. It will grow with the media's increasing use of pre-prepared soft news – especially in business, lifestyle, fashion sections of the press, in magazines and in contract publishing – which originates from PR people. This material was significant in the 1970s[13] and threatens journalists' professionalism: it is hard to identify what value they add to it. In this and other ways, the boundaries between PR and journalism are becoming less dintinct.

Tabloids and PR

The tabloidisation of the media is another example of the skills merger between journalism and PR. It is a merger which favours the media acquiring the features of markets. Peter Golding has characterised this in four dimensions:[14] more soft news; shorter stories and more pictures; change in mode of address – readers and writers are of the same status, a move away from the didactic to the diadic; market structure in which media are businesses, with the broadsheets trying to increase market share. His research shows that in the periods 1952 to 1992, word counts in *Times* stories have decreased but *Mirror* counts have increased; in the same period, entertainment stories (animals and celebrities) have increased in the tabloids from 6% to 17%. The tabloid coverage of politics has increased from 3% to 6% of content, and 10% of broadsheets are entertainment. This 3% to 6% doubling suggests that one positive outcome of tabloidisation is that it makes politics more reader-friendly and that more coverage is encouraged. A more negative outcome is that when the media see audiences as consumers, all topics, even politics, are treated in a personality-based, gossipy, unchallenging way in order to increase circulation.

These developments are broadly sympathetic to the genre colonisation of journalism by PR. They contribute to what Langer (1998) has named 'the lament', a sense that the journalism necessary for citizens to contribute effectively to a liberal democracy is threatened by the expansion of soft news, human interest stories, tabloid TV, 'insignificant' and 'other' news. This expansion is aided by media managers seeing journalism as a commodity creation activity for the building of audiences more numerous than those attending to the competition. The insertion of PR attitudes and material into creating this 'other' news is the colonisation of journalism by PR. Soft news and PR are synonymous (but not exclusively so, for political PR deals with news concerning liberal democracy). Soft news is highly promotional about itself and often announces its arrival by a showy vanguard of presentational effects which strain for audience attention (see Humphrys 1999). It is the news category into which most PR material falls, for 'soft' is conventionally taken to mean that which is positive and pleasing about personalities, policies, events and organisations. Indeed, PR published in the media from a traceable source has that 'soft' quality in journalistic form, for PR cannot publicly criticise its own source and is loathe to attack others for fear of retaliation. (Invisibly sourced PR has different qualities.) Further, the supply of soft news eases the process of marketisation of the media by turning editorial attitudes away from costly investigative, independently minded journalism which has to be created from small, uncertain beginnings.

For media market-makers, whether managers or journalists, the point of a readership or audience is to make it grow. This is done through soothing, entertaining editorial, constantly adjusted to attract the largest number of paying individuals in that market segment. Marketeers call it choice. This is not the voice of a thunderer, of an independent thinker, of a principled dissenter, of a critic. Marketeers call that negative thinking. This is not persuasion on behalf of an opinion which may cost the persuador a loss of self-interest: this is persuasion on behalf of an opinion constructed to increase self-interest. Markets have a dynamic of increased production, and media market-makers show that propensity in more pages and more air time. The soft news generated by PR is a cost-effective filler of space. It transfers the costs of its own production from the media market-maker to the PR source. It does not have to be sought out: it is offered freely – in superabundance, in binfuls. As consumer markets provide most PR and as the marginal media space is mostly devoted to consumer goods, services, entertainment, fashion and lifestyle, both the demand and supply from media market-makers and PR providers tends to rise. Journalists as market growers will assume that their reader-, listener-, viewer-consumers want more and that they should create more journalism in reply. Journalists as social observers will know that they have to wait upon events.

There is an allied process of celebrity manufacture going on. Celebrity news is news about people and is therefore another strand in PR-isation. It is not new, for it was noticeable at the time of the rise of the film industry at the turn of the twentieth century, and there have always been press agents at work to fill the showbusiness columns of the tabloid press. Celebrity manufacture, however, has increased and spread since the mid-1980s and Michie (1998, pp. 149–215) has described it from the PR perspective. It has been resurrected in its contemporary form largely through the efforts of Max Clifford.[15] It is a staple component of tabloid, middle market and broadsheet newspapers in the UK, their use of it distinguished only by amounts of column inches and bared flesh. Broadcasting has its 'nice' presenters and news readers.

Celebrities could not exist without PR production and media demand. A person who is known for well-knownness has to knowingly get known. This takes a careful self-presentation, a schedule of outings, entrées and partners to audiences. This is personality construction work, nice for those who can get it. It is a double market with supply and demand for what is produced and for the mechanics of production, for front-of-house perfection and backstage *faux pas*. It is a double market for readers wanting to know how it operates, and for PRs and journalists wanting to boast about how it is done. The personality construction work has been described by Ekow Eshun:[16]

> There is, among, the public today a greater awareness of the process of manufacture involved in creating a star. We know that they are not simply born. Instead … they must seize their moment and spin it and spin it until the result is newspaper headlines, TV appearances and lucrative product endorsements. Thanks to the media's own obsession with spin, we are all less naïve about the collusion between event organisers, agents, paparazzi and stars that helps create a tabloid sensation.

Reform of relations

Journalism and PR should separate themselves as two distinct communications practices. A starting point for this separation is the reconceptualisation of PR as a media system in its own right, alongside print media, radio, TV and advertising. Such a perspective befits the current status of PR as a widespread, noticeable and pervasive activity. Historically, it has developed principally as a service to journalism, often staffed by former journalists, offering pre-prepared copy to fill space. To a lesser extent and differently in terms of an organisational home, PR has roots in the advertising industry, which offers another form of commercial communication. (See Tedlow, 1979 for these historical relationships in the USA.) PR grew by the side, so to speak, of these more established activities: now it stands alone, linked but separate. The literary flourish caught in 'Fifth Estate' reflects this new status.

Like journalism and advertising, PR produces messages comprising data, opinions and values in forms which have grown distinct from them (e.g. media releases, news videos, lobbyist briefings). It distributes this indigenous production directly through its own distribution systems (sponsorship, contract publishing, conferences, exhibitions, direct mail) or indirectly and parasitically via other media systems (newspapers, broadcasts, internet) to predefined groups of people, its 'publics'. With these characteristics of distinct message forms, own and shared distribution media, and aggregations of people which it seeks to persuade, it can be viewed as a media system in its own right. Moreover, PR is done by people, on both a paid and voluntary basis, who share identifiable skills and attitudes and who can be found in specific geographic locations and/or in posts with titles traditionally associated with PR. Many of these skills are shared with journalists (writing and presentation) but the professional attitudes motivating them (advocacy as opposed to scrutiny) are distinct. These PR attitudes are not effective in the news room and only partially in the ad agency.

PR is colonising print and broadcast media, it is argued, in the PR-isation process and this is a compromise of its separateness. This genre colonisation, however, does not deny separateness, for colonisation can be identified precisely because there is a previous presence – the colonising agent, PR – which is different from the object to be colonised, journalism. PR thus has both an independent zone of message construction and distribution, and a zone of distribution which it shares with at least one other media system (journalism), sharing in a way which vitiates the character of the latter. A reform of PR can be based on the conceptualisation of PR as a separate media system.

All media systems (Schlesinger and Tumber 1994, p. 4) impart a particular characteristic to the communications they transmit and the particular characteristic associated with PR is an intense persuasiveness in advocating an interest. PR is partisan, persuasive communications. This partisan characteristic marks off it from uncolonised journalism which transforms PR material by its scrutiny. Such journalism is persuasive in assessment of the validity of interests by its scrutiny and is not *a priori* committed to an interest. Where journalism is partisan to a media owner or a political owner, it diminishes itself. The intensely persuasive quality of PR is hidden when the PR media system works vicariously through journalistic forms without the latter declaring or amending that quality . This hidden sourcing and the related information subsidies to journalism cause public concern because they present a false identity: a form of journalism but a substance of PR. This falsity amounts to a limitation put on equal and proportionate access of UK citizens to a media which calls itself free (see Chapter 4), and indirectly to a political system which claims to be democratic and representative.

This separateness/colonisation perspective allows the development of the reform agenda of PR in its relations with journalism. These two work tasks should be treated as separate media and this distinctness demonstrated. When PR communications come into contact with journalism, the former should be transformed by journalist work practices. If PR is mixed with journalism, the PR element should be identifed. This visible sourcing of material is an important reform task but is not new. It was a minority and temporary practice in US journalism at the end of the nineteenth century (Stauber and Rampton 1995), and was the practice in the UK *Financial Times* whereby technical press releases were grouped together on one page. Journalists should ask who is benefiting professionally and in status when they train PR people.

The PR media system is developing through internet use, in that it distributes persuasive messages direct to its publics, intentionally cutting out media transformation of the material. One 1989 survey[17] shows that 44 political parties in the UK had websites and that they were principally used as electronic brochures, although left-wing parties attempted two-way communications with e-mailers. But the evidence so far is that the internet is more effective for marketing public relations than for political ones: face-to-face relationships are integral to deliberative democracy. The internet, however, does provide an apparently new and growing site for competition between business and critical pressure groups. These web pages are monitored by firms who have developed PR tactics for response (Holtz 1998, pp. 176–98). It is not clear, however, whether this electronic contest is much monitored by the critical media: it may be that journalists perceive it as a field upon which they have little or no mediating role.

A hindrance to reform in journalism/PR relations is the traditional regard in which the former has been held, as witnessed by descriptors such as 'fourth estate' and 'free press'. It is an uncomfortable fracture of this tradition to see journalists as passive, uncritical processors of PR material. It may be that PR-isation is too strong a process to resist and that some more journalism should attempt to re-establish itself on a non-market basis. Fallows (1996) argues for a 'public' or 'civic' journalism which is community-based in order to be 'journalism in the public spirit'. Electronic publishing on the internet is a testing ground for this paradigm, one which evokes the work of the seventeenth-, eighteenth- and early nineteenth-century politically radical printers and pamphleteers. In today's unreformed circumstances, however, this public service journalism is weak. Too many journalists deny that PR-isation is happening; all PR people proclaim that it is a positive development. This is true for PR in the particular circumstances of a specific campaign but it is a dubious, summary judgement if PR-isation reduces the media to a passive publisher of its material. PR people want their material in the UK media because the latter has had – and is in danger of losing – a reputation for independence of view which conferred credibility on what it published. Publication was a favourable testimonial. PR-isation destroys that and eventually dilutes the self-interest of PR producers.

Summary

Media outlets are multiplying at a time when journalism is declining vis-à-vis PR. The decline has several aspects. The labour market position of journalists has weakened since the 1980s, especially in the regional and local media, and fewer of them are doing more work in more insecure news rooms. The marketisation of the media also weakens journalists in that listeners, readers and viewers are seen by media managers as consumers to be satisfied and increased, rather than audiences to be informed and challenged. Celebrity news is the major filler for the growing spaces in an expanding media, much of it operating 24 hours a day. These conditions together smooth the passage of PR material unhindered into publication and broadcast. The PR industry has become the most important supplier to a media which calls itself 'free' and 'independent'. It amounts to a PR-isation of the media which weakens all forms of journalism, but especially journalism as scrutiny of public affairs. The weakness comes from the reduction of independence of view: there is less journalistic scrutiny. Yet journalists have been complicit in this process: they publish what they get with no or little amendment or delaration of its source; there is a flourishing 'freebie' culture, encouraging a black market of favours. Moreover, many journalists are trainers of the next generation of PR people. These behaviours are too relaxed for journalists to persist with if they want to restore their position vis-à-vis PR people: they should treat PR with scepticism, bordering on hostility. In the long term, the withdrawal of the PR colonists favours their self interest directly by increasing media credibility and indirectly by strengthening adversarial democracy. The next chapter looks inside the burgeoning PR world.

10 Inside PR

It may be some consolation to PR people today, when the reputation of their work comes up in conversation, to remember that lawyers were unpopular in the 1640s and still are today. They will reflect that such unpopularity has not held back the growth, the status or the salaries of lawyers. Indeed, a private disregard for outside opinion and a determined focus on the task in professional hand is intuitively a sound survival strategy for any work group. Thus, many PR people react to the reputation matter with the slight irritation of 'not that again; stop navel gazing; let's get on with the job'. These colleagues can further reflect that politicians, journalists[1] and estate agents also have poor reputations but still they prosper.

However, for PR people at the top of the industry, such reflection is too passive a reaction: they deny any suggestion of their being held in low reputation. City PR people, the heads of London PR agencies and of large businesses PR departments take this view.[2] They often make the comparison between themselves and barristers, one of the highest status occupational groups: that PR people are corporate advocates. Indeed, it is to be expected from those who strive for a good reputation for others that they should see themselves in the same light.[3] This is the halo effect of the bright corporate reputation spreading brightly over all those who make it shine. These conviction PR people are not faced down by low reputation; they reject the stereotypes of film and fiction which has PR as 'a somewhat mysterious occupation populated by unscrupulous practitioners with superiority complexes whose main goals appear to be getting their clients mentioned in the news media, duping their clients, and gaining power' (Miller 1999, p. 27).[4] However, for PR technicians – the majority of PR people – reaction to low reputation is usually shrugged off in the same way that the bricklayer tells the architect about the critic: 'over to you, boss'.

One way of accounting for the poor reputation of PR is to see it as a burden brought upon the industry by itself. That charges of low reputation are made against PR is an irony of Titanic size for an activity which seeks to produce that social outcome for its principals.[5] The irritation today of some PR people with the charge is, in part, built on the knowledge that it is a long standing one and that their industry has flourished since it was first made. Pimlott in the 1940s and West in 1960 noted that PR was struggling with its low standing. The combined careers of the American PR men Ivy Lee and Edward Bernays and the PR academic James Grunig from 1890 to the death of Bernays in 1995, aged over 103, can be characterised as century-long attempts to release PR from association with propaganda, give it a coherent intellectual basis acceptable in a liberal democracy and to raise its status. In this way, the irony becomes richer; the low reputation of the activity devoted to producing high reputation has not impeded its growth: at the operational level, PR's low reputation does not matter much.

Sought outcomes

The impatience of the busy PR person about reputation has sources other than the irrelevance one, for PR seeks other outcomes for its principals and these are not stated so publicly. They can, however, be detected through an inspection of the elusive phenomenon of reputation. Is it distinct from the terms 'image', 'status' and 'worth'? A reputation is held by others[6] and are these holders all significant? How is reputation measured and how does it relate to other phenomena which may be competitive with it, such as success and survival? Is the dissemination of low reputation about PR people done by their natural critics – journalists? Is the reputation of PR confused with the reputation of the organisations, causes and persons it serves? Are the messengers demeaned on account of those who sent them?

Reputation is defined as a quantum with a positive and negative dimension: the amounts of social prestige or social disdain attached to an organisation or cause or person in the perception of others. The assumption is that more social prestige is better for the object of perception, as is less social disdain. However, it is not clear that the assumption holds in all circumstances, and it is this variability which causes problems for PR – problems brought upon itself because of its devotion to better reputation as a master outcome.

Organisations, causes and persons may have to – may choose to – behave in ways which achieve other goals at the price of loss in reputation. In politics, this could be said to be normal behaviour. Indeed, it is a definition of government. In the marketplace, there are similar conflicts between goals for businesses. The reputational goal is more paramount than in politics because buying decisions are influenced by confidence levels of buyers, which in turn depend on the reputation of the good to be bought and of its supplier. The confidence/reputation nexus is probably more important in commerce than in politics, where fear and ideology are powerful motivators which can override confidence. Even so, suppliers of goods and services do trade off their reputations against other goals.[7] For example, Southwest Trains lowered its reputation with users in 1998 when it cancelled services because of the cost reduction policy of sacking drivers. Generally, organisations, groups and persons pursue goals which produce behaviours which have positive and negative effects on reputation. Consciously or otherwise, there is a trade-off among competing goals and there is no imperative for the reputational goal to be always protected.

Looked at from this analysis, PR people are naïve or disingenuous to make reputation their single, desired outcome for their employers and clients. In so doing, they are loading the gun and pointing it at their own professional feet. They did this in 1993 when they added a second definition of PR based on reputation (see Chapter 2). Modern PR speaks in mantra tones about 'reputation, reputation, reputation', and makes itself the guardian of this important, social asset. This places PR people at odds with non-reputational goals of the organisation and puts at risk their public and private internal role of promoting or defending its reputation. This goal competition is prioritised in the boardroom or in the dominant coalition, and PR should associate itself with the master goal of survival of the organisations, groups, causes and persons it serves. Non-reputational goals such as risk ones (growth, diversification, merger, short-termism and share price) may take precedence over reputation. There is also the self-interest of any PR firms working for the organisation: their advice may be coloured by their need to be retained and so they may follow whatever goals are favoured by the internal dominant coalition.

Finally, it is important to discount any claims of functional imperialism made or implied by PR. So far, the assumption has been that it is PR people through their communications who are the producers of reputation. That focus flows from the latter's declared intention to help produce for their employers or clients 'effective communication', 'mutual understanding' or 'goodwill' which will result in better reputation. It could be argued, however, that accountants, engineers, marketeers and reception staff engender those qualities as much as PR people, and that PR is a state of mind to achieve those ends via other functions as well as a distinct, staff function itself. This leads to the startling proposition that all organisational members or cause supporters are in PR. This leads to another irony: that the organisation, group or cause has a high reputation, but its PR people a low one.

The expansion of jobs

Whether at the top, middle or bottom of the industry, PR people have another reason for denial or indifference about their standing: PR will continue to expand. Stories and references about PR abound in the contemporary media and are complimentary in special circumstances;[8] its jargon is part of demotic language; in the PR industry there is a sense of optimism and little awareness that other professional groups could do the same work.[9] There are various reasons for this expansion. It is most likely that the larger category of mass persuasive communications, of which PR is a sub-set, will continue to expand. Such communications are a century-old phenomenon and a consequence of mass production and mass consumption. They will continue in the current, later capitalist, liberal democratic period, facilitated by powerful multi-media systems. Reich (1991, p. 177) in his review of work organisation in a global market lists PR people among the third and most advantageously placed group, symbolic analysts.[10] A culture of accelerated pluralism, both civic and commercial, with more businesses, organisations and groups wanting their advantage and with more opportunities to communicate will be a nurturing societal environment in which to lobby. Moreover, the media and politicians are not likely to turn away from their own use of PR techniques: they gain too much. Three examples of the role PR plays now in accelerated pluralism indicate future trends.

The first shows how PR as an industry helps business respond to new pressures. *PR Week* (4.8.98, pp. 10–11) reports that 'social reporting' by big business is a growth area for the industry (although neo-liberals (Halfon, 1998) would argue that it should not be). This is described as partly a response to consumer concerns on issues such as child labour and sweatshop labour, and partly a response to other stakeholders, such as pressure groups. It has the internal benefit of making management look at the social consequences of their actions and defend, reform or hide them. PR people, with others, will write these reports and then alone disseminate them. The second example is PR as a 'cottage industry'. In early January 1999, the UK media reported the arrest in the Yemen of five British citizens. In response, their families and their lawyers organised coaches from Birmingham for a demonstration outside the Yemeni embassy in London where they handed in a letter of protest, followed by a lobby of their MPs at Westminster. This was widely reported.[11] The third example is from animal welfare, where culling as method of controlling badger populations is strongly contested. The spokesperson for the National Federation of Badger Groups said of culling: 'This would be a public relations disaster.'[12]

PR and journalism are becoming interdependent as they increasingly publish similar material, and as the costs to the media of using it are so low. PR subsidises the media: the media accepts the subsidy and so passes back to the PR industry more job creation, to the detriment of journalists' jobs (see Chapter 9). Furthermore, most PR today, in volume of material produced and in people employed, is for marketing[13] and, given the centrality of markets and of the marketing mentality in the public and private sectors, these trends are likely to continue. PR is well suited to developing the more complex, lifestyle messages associated with contemporary consumer markets (Chapter 7).

If PR is colonising journalism and marketing, it is expanding into other work and becoming part of them. Two examples are found in PR as policing. A documented example is a Strathclyde police PR campaign warning of extra surveillance to combat car theft directly leading to crime reduction.[14] Senior detectives and their PR people in Cambridgeshire devised the strategy to get the runaway Bramleys to return home with their foster daughters; it included calling the Bramleys by their first names and putting up young, junior police officers for media interviews.[15]

Will the low status of the industry put talented people off taking up a job in the industry? This is unknowable but what can be stated is that PR, even with the drag anchor of low status, attracts many more applicants than places. Large London PR agencies measure applicants in their hundreds, university applications are broadly ten to one for each place, communications jobs are highly popular with new graduates, and *PR Week* is full of young faces. Despite all, the public relations of public relations is very successful when it comes to recruitment for itself. This success is striking when it is realised that the industry is in the service sector and subject to fluctuating levels of job security; many 12-hour days, and middling salaries of £40,000 on average in firms and £31,000 in house.[16] So why do people want to enter the industry? Few entrants talk of a vocation: many perceive it as a people-centred, 'sexy and fun', tolerable way to earn a living.

PR as work

To be in PR – for a job, for personal advancement or for commitment to a cause – is to be a wooer, a suitor, a persuader, always displaying-for-notice-and-advantage: usually on behalf of the other (the employer, the client), sometimes for oneself. The work generates great energy, great commitment, sometimes great creativity and is often driven by desire for public acclaim. It is mostly work of mediation, satisfying self through the satisfaction of others. It is important for its sustainability that the PR person's self-presentation is always subordinate, for an invarible role requirement is to stay in the background, be the adviser, the agent for the principal. The PR person self-presents to journalists, usually as an unnamed public source, and to civil servants and special advisers but rarely, if ever, to ministers. If the play of events requires the PR person to be a public spokesperson, such a role is exceptional, low-key and preferably anonymous.

The opposite role of being the story rather than the messenger is a precarious one, putting at risk the principal's interest[17] and is not sustainable. This puts the PR person in what Ericson *et al.* (1989, pp. 8–12) have called the front region of an organisation where its affairs are done publicly, as opposed to the back region where privacy and confidentiality rule; a very small minority of PR people actively seek the front, without wanting to be the story. Moloney (1996, p. 90) has made a similar back/front distinction in the case of lobbyists between those with a backgrounder and fore-grounder style of work. The role of PR persuasion involves dealing with rejection, for not all causes or briefs are to be accepted. But this rejection – frequent – does not appear to damage psychologically PR people, who treat it internally as rejection of the other – the employer or client being served. This is the same quality of rejection as that of the salesperson and lawyer, and the psychological technique of displacement comes into play – 'I win some and they lose some'.

So far the argument is that PR work is low-key, background presentation-of-self for the other. But presentation-of-self is also for self when the PR person is representing themselves, either in terms of redress of a personal grievance, advancement to celebrity status, or promotion of a belief or cause personally believed in. Hesitation at the front–back boundary does not apply in these cases for the other is removed from the professional psychological contract.[18] With this high profile, personalised presentation, more energy, commitment and creativity can be put into the PR task, but when the brief is rejected or the campaign fails, the disappointment is also personal.

As well as rejection, PR people often have to deal with the charge of lying, usually to the media.[19] Most PR people do not lie either because of their innate honesty or because they choose to tell a little rather than tell a falsehood. They are also often protected from the temptation to lie because they are not fully informed about a sensitive situation by their principals. However, such partial briefings open up the possibility of PR people being manipulated by their principals and so unwittingly describing false situations through ignorance. Some PR people do lie (Harrison (1996), Ericson *et al.* 1989, pp. 232–3, and anecdotal reports from students on placement), but they run the risk of eventually being found out and ignored by journalists. It is protective self-awareness in PR to know that personal credibility is an important asset. Another important asset is 'knowing how to deal with people'. This is regarded by nearly all PR people as a skill[20] and is often given as the reason for the large number of women in PR. This is not a flattering attribution; it may be unconsciously sexist since the phrase is the fuzzy, ambiguous code for knowing how to defer to, persuade and/or manipulate principals, journalists, politicians, public officials and competitive colleagues.

The majority of PR people in the UK will be women before long – if they are not already. They have been in the USA since 1985 (Grunig 1995, p. 153). The 1998 IPR membership survey estimated females at 48% with a trend line of 21%, 40% and 44% in the 1987, 1991 and 1994 surveys. In the same year, another survey of the top 150 PR firms showed that women outnumbered men in all work categories except directors/partners.[21] Most students doing PR degrees are female. Respondents to a survey of six cohorts of PR graduates were 73% female (Moloney and Noble 1999). The impression left after looking through *PR Week* is of at least as many female faces as male. There is some American literature which argues that women are discriminated against in PR (Creeden 1991).

When PR people talk about the gender balance (very infrequently), two points often come up. The first is that in the past, many women started as PR secretaries and progressed to PR managers because there was no barrier of formal entry qualifications, and in this way the industry was not discriminatory. The second is that women are 'good at communicating', and is a more polite version of the 'good at dealing with people' attribution. It is rarely clear what good communications means in this context. The connotation is often a baffled male chauvinist one of being under threat for no very well understood reasons. This connotation moves towards the explicit when a sexist line of insult is 'jokingly' made, usually by journalists: PR is for 'girlies' with 'a penchant for organising fabulous parties' in the AbFab tradition.[22] Such joshing is not helped by a near monopoly of male PRs making 'serious' comments in the media.

However, the feminisation of the PR workforce does raise substantial issues: that of pay levels and related questions of job status. Creeden (1991, pp. 67–84) starts her review of the place of American PR women with industry concerns 'about the potential for a decline in status and salaries in public relations due to the increasing number of women entering the practice'. Transplanted to the UK, concern about declining status seems obsolete. As a new variable in the industry's mix of productive factors, it is arguable that more women in PR are as likely to reverse the decline as continue it – a decline started under a majority male workforce. Concern about lower salaries for PR women may be justified. Nationally, the average earnings of all women are 80% of men's, and it may be that PR women's are in line with that discrimination.

If they are being discriminated against, it is not a major debate inside the industry. The great majority of PR people, however experienced they are, are not self-reflective about their workplace or their roles as persuadors or manipulators. Their most common self-analysis is cast in the language of one of the great mantra themes of the late twentieth century – mutual understanding between people through better communication. Such discourse offers the comfort of being quasi-humanitarian aid workers without the risks, and L'Etang (1999) has shown that it is part of the traditional discourse PR has had about itself, even before the foundation of the IPR in 1948. It may be one source for putting job satisfaction at the top of a list of reasons for being in PR. Moloney and Noble (1999) surveyed six cohorts of PR graduates: 76% of respondents gave satisfaction as their most important reason, with money and status at fourth and fifth.

PR as higher education

Many questions are raised about why and how PR arrived (along with retailing, tourism, hospitality, advertising and marketing) on the curricula of universities, principally the new ones. The most common one is hostile: 'how can you study for three years what only takes three weeks to pick up?' The darkest version of this is: 'Have academic PR teachers made a simple thing complicated in the interests of their own professional status?' The standard reply (sometimes more a stuttering defence when the PR teacher's self-image favours the 'don') is that the degree is applied business, communication and political studies, topped off with PR specific skills such as persuasive message construction, copy writing, media relations, small group presentation, document design, event management and campaigning. There are other replies to questions about PR on campus: that the new universities as part of their widening access role should vocationally educate young people, with no family tradition of graduation, for rising industries; that the many young women wanting to do PR work should be given the opportunity of degree level work; and perhaps most importantly, that higher education (HE) in itself is valuable because of the skills of critical evaluation it fosters.

PR represents for university planners access to plentiful student numbers, with about ten applicants for each place. PR graduates go to employment where over half the postholders hold a first degree or higher, where the most common first degree is Arts at 27%, and where 4% have PR degrees.[23] The planners also noted that PR industry bodies were keen for the subject's arrival on campus because it implied more professional status. These bodies in turn ask about what is taught and this brings up the balance of the curriculum. Where does it rest: is the vocational or the academic emphasised? For example, this reduces for the student and teacher to either: 'how to get PR material into the media' or 'why do PR people and journalists want or not want material in the media?' Most of the 16 institutions teaching PR or largely PR degrees tend towards the vocational. PR is also taught as a component of many MBAs and business studies first degrees, but it is difficult to know on how many campuses this is happening. Some old universities are putting PR on the curriculum under titles such as political communications. It is for these reasons that the full extent of PR teaching on UK campuses is difficult to estimate, a task made more difficult if it is accepted that there is a 'flight' from using the words 'public relations'[24] (Moloney, 1997).

Institutions fine-tune their curricula over time, in response to examiners' reports, student opinion, PR practice and professional self critique,[25] but overall the pedagogical tone is that of most vocational courses: instrumental rationality, in which teaching and learning are aimed at doing the subject more efficiently and effectively, rather than probing its interconnectedness with the political economy, ethics and asking normative questions. Given that it is in the former polytechnics where most of the teaching takes place, this bent has been understandable and just about acceptable when it is realised that PR has been on campus for only ten years.

However, a decade of higher education teaching and the size and pervasiveness of the industry combine to make it opportune to re-appraise the place of PR as a university subject. So far it has been under-studied from the perspective of its political economy and in its ethical dimension in the new universities. In the old universities, it is treated critically by media and cultural studies departments, but invariably only as an example or illustration of larger social phenomena and themes. The courses on offer are therefore more teaching and learning *to do* PR rather than teaching and learning *about* PR. They also teach it as a practice of virtue, an assessment which does not sit easily with that of the public (Moloney 1997, p. 1). It is also arguable that PR has been under-studied in the UK, given that it is now a media system in its own right and given the PR-isation of the media (Chapter 9). The study of the effects of PR could be a fruitful growth point for extending the cultural studies agenda.[26]

For vocational teachers, taking a critical stance towards their subject raises questions which, rightly, are uncomfortable. Do the work values and skills taught produce more social harm than good and is there unethical practice? It cannot be right to foster such consequences in society via helping 18–year-olds to get jobs. A critical stance can conclude that the subject produces more social disbenefits than benefits and/or has ethical shortcomings. If this conclusion is accepted, teachers face the urgent task of reassessing their relationship with the subject. Reassessment takes many forms. The easiest is the passive one of accepting the critique and continuing to teach vocationally without amendment. This is professionally and personally unsatisfactory, unworthy of a university teacher. The hardest re-assessment is to conclude that PR brings more costs than benefits: if this is the personal conclusion, the teacher should stop teaching the subject vocationally. Other choices are to continue teaching vocationally as before, but to tell students that there is a critique to answer; or to continue teaching but to amend the vocational content in the light of the critique.

Hopefully, PR teachers in higher education opt for the latter two options. However, the choices are difficult psychologically for those who came to teaching after working in PR: generally, the vocational teacher is loathe to criticise their functional area, for it is impossible to teach well a subject that the teacher does not sympathise with. One solution is to separate out bodily the roles into two: the vocational teacher and the academic critic/researcher. However, this is probably too expensive for most campuses. The other is for teachers to confront these conflicts, and resolve them academically and professionally. Sproule (1997), writing about American propaganda which for him includes PR, offers inspiration towards a role of social critic for teachers: 'Society's muckrakers [progressive critics] never will permit citizens to forget that the communications media play a role in furthering competition among self-serving institutions and that a steady diet of top-down communication can starve participatory democracy' (p. 269).

It is to be hoped that the 50 university and college PR teachers who teach at the relevant sixteen institutions will be more critical to their subject now that it begins its second decade on campus. PR as a university subject is not yet at ease with itself. The next curriculum re-balancing will be towards the critical, and it will find its point of ease just short of where critique kills desire to teach the subject vocationally. A sign of that re-balancing would be, for example, texts for its consumers on how to identify harmful and beneficial PR in markets, politics and the media. The Americans Pratkanis and Aronson (1992) have done such work about propaganda.[27] Finally, there is another reason for a re-balancing: the curriculum is overdependent on the thinking of James Grunig, an American at the University of Maryland, who with Hunt, developed the current paradigm for conceptualising PR in 1984 (see Chapters 4 and 5).

Their bad-to-good typology can be read as a Whig version of PR history, with bad practice associated with nineteenth-century American business and with early Hollywood, and with good practice more akin to two-way symmetrical communications said to be practised now. Their work can also be read as a virtuous path for the PR person to follow in professional development: avoiding PR as propaganda and doing PR as negotiation by communications in a process based on understanding, not on persuasion, and in a process akin to open, liberal politics with all players on equal terms. The latter reading of Grunig and Hunt (1984) and Grunig (1992a, pp. 1–28) has allowed PR teachers to present PR as a practice of virtue, since – consciously or unconsciously – their fourth category has become established in HE teaching as the definition of what PR is rather than what the authors wished it to be, an ideal type.

Overall, the UK PR academy has taken to these two authors with relish, too much so to allow critical distance for amendment. Some lecturers associate the typology with particular forms of PR: press agentry and two-way asymmetrical with marketing public relations; public information and two-way symmetrical types with corporate PR. For none of this are Grunig and Hunt to be praised or blamed, for when the subject reached UK campuses there was no other paradigm on offer. They filled the conceptual void and gave pedagogic comfort to many: and for this their views have become distorted. The first decade for PR on campus can be characterised as the behaviour of a discipline finding its feet, marked by over-reliance on one conceptual approach. The second decade will hopefully be marked with more intellectual variety and more evaluation: marked as much with teaching about PR as teaching PR.

A review of the UK history of PR shows that there is an alternative paradigm and that it has been argued in the past. L'Etang (1998) has shown that in the 1920s and 1930s the journal *Public Administration* understood PR in a literal sense as relations between civil servants and the public. Seventeen articles were published on propaganda and publicity and 23 on general relations with the public. Herbert Finer opined that the extension of state activity led to inevitable and desirable contact between civil servants and citizens. J.H. Brebner, who wrote the first UK book on PR in 1949, also carried that civic-centred sense of PR serving better citizenship. But today that voice is not heard.

Quest for professional status

The Institute of Public Relations (IPR) had 5,650 members of all categories in 1997 compared with 2,908 at the end of 1989 when there were 45% working in business, 37% in agencies and the balance in government and the voluntary sector.[28] This significant jump in members was probably more influenced by exam-based and length-of-service-based membership criteria introduced in that period than by industry growth, for IPR numbers are low in relation to the 20–25,000 industry workforce estimates and they have been so since at least the 1960s.

Whatever the PR industry thinks about its status, it can be asserted with certainty that very few observers would ascribe to it the professional status given to doctors, barristers and, perhaps, to solicitors and architects. The great weight of the literature on work status (see, for example, Haralambos 1985) associates factors such as monopoly control of entrants, specialised knowledge, enforced codes of ethics, commitment to a public good and high earnings with full professional status. Salary levels are a starting point for noticing the distance between PR work and established professions: PR salaries are low compared to doctors and barristers. Training courses with titles such as 'Public Relations for Absolute Beginners', a two-day course 'packed full of invaluable hints, tips and guidelines that will show you how to get the best from your PR effort' is another indicator of the distance PR has to go (Flyer for three conferences, London, by Meet The Press). Inside PR, there are two approaches taken to the professional status debate: that the industry can develop the behavioural characteristics of an established profession, and that the industry cannot achieve this and should concentrate on efficiency and effectiveness levels which will attract the title professional as in 'professional plumber'.[29]

The industry's trade bodies have policies which can be described as increasing professionalisation, but whether there is collective agreement on what form that will take is not clear. The first is to increase education and training, and to this end the IPR has a set of recognition criteria. It is around these criteria that contests will take place about who controls the curricula of publicly funded courses – the universities or the professional bodies. The second policy is an attempt to have the industry speak with a single voice, and there is talk now and then of the IPR and PRCA merging. A complicating factor in the search for unity, however, is that there are other groups representing specific work sectors of PR, and in some cases they distance themselves for the two lead PR bodies, e.g. the Association of Professional Political Consultants, the International Public

Relations Association, the International Association of Business Communicators. Third, there are intermittent efforts to seek charter status for the PR industry, a status awarded to the Institute of Marketing and one admired by the more status-conscious professionals.

The search for traditional professional status is significant for what it says about sectors of the industry. Industry anecdote suggests that it is not a widespread concern around the country: rather it is the preoccupation of older and retired PR people, very often metropolitan, who have seen much of lawyers and bankers at times of corporate take-overs. What is a concern among more PR people is doing work better, setting measurable goals and evaluating results. This is the professionalism of good practice, seeking more secure ground for confident statements to principals (and self) about inputs and outcomes. For the many overworked, job-insecure, ambitious and talented people in PR, this second professionalism is much more meaningful, and it is noticeable that evaluation is much discussed and methodologies for it published. The search for good practice is arguably the demand behind the many PR training courses on offer: they are not so much about continuing education but about a secure foundational education in the first instance.

PR and ethics

Discussion about definitions of professionalism touches on the connection between ethics (rules for moral behaviour) and PR because ethical concerns are a feature of professionalism. This connection is more actively on PR teachers' minds and maybe on professionals' than it has been before. This is because ethics has gone up the general business agenda in the UK since the corporate and political sleaze cases of the mid-1980s onwards. The role of lobbying in many of these cases was a PR specific concern. Most PR people do not talk of ethics when doing their work: they talk of successful outcomes, keeping principals contented, and more profit or salary. This may or may not be exceptional behaviour for UK business people; and it may or may not be consistent with ethical rules. One reason for its silence is the absence of any enforceable code of ethics put on PR people. The weaknesses of the PR industry bodies – i.e. their inability to control entry, their low membership, the lack of sanctions over members – are major causes for this absence and of these, inability to control entry is the most debilitating. It is impossible to have common standards of behaviour when anyone can publicly call themselves 'public relations consultant'. Harrison (1994) noted that although the IPR revised its code of conduct in 1991, enforcement has been difficult for it has the weakest form of regulation – a self-imposed code which is perceived as ineffectual. It is hard to remember any breach of ethics cases being reported in the UK. The same weak regulatory regime applies in the USA. Wright (1993) reports that although 150 complaints were made under the code of the

Public Relations Society of America, only ten members have been reprimanded.

In a liberal, democratic market-orientated economy, ethics is an important aspect of communications and PR people do not pay enough attention to it. If they are to take ethics seriously, it follows that there will be more regulation of their work. That regulation has three sources – the individual PR person, the industry, and government.

There are six aspects to note about higher ethical and regulatory levels in UK PR. The first is that regulation of an activity which is industrially and professionally organised in markets is at bottom a matter of morality, expressed ethically in the form of rules. Ethics is an intervention into the political economy by a set of values from another aspect of human activity – that of moral behaviour based on a respectful humanism. It is a judgement that the activity left to the exigencies of the political economy sometimes produces behaviours which affront moral sensibilities. In a state incorporating both democracy and markets, citizens and consumers should enjoy communicative equality. The second is to admit that PR is always a persuasive activity, and that it easily and frequently descends into manipulation and propaganda. It is, to use Jensen's title, one-sided, hemispheric communication. Manipulative communications, where sources and purposes are not revealed, and where the appeal to emotion is high (see Chapters 5 and 6) are always morally unacceptable in a democracy.[30]

Both these aspects have to confront the argument, made by Barney and Black (1994) about PR in the USA, that it is done in an adversarial society where individuals and interests have the right to select for themselves the information which makes their case and the right to present it persuasively. It is a right in a liberal democratic society for the self to select the content and style of a self-presentation: it is right for the other to make the countervailing case with the same two freedoms. This argument is a reflection of J.S. Mill's view that truth is what is left after the clash of opinion in debate. The regulation of PR does not destroy the right to selectively and persuasively present information: it seeks, instead, to limit it in the interest of a public debate which has the characteristics of being a declared, openly sourced process of reasoned persuasion, in circumstances which others can enter into on terms of debating equality. PR regulation would allow the countervailing principle of thesis calling forth counter-thesis to be more operative. Citizens and consumers in a liberal democracy with free markets expect to encounter persuasion. They need to be protected from manipulation and propaganda which are forms of social exchange associated with elitist states and rigged markets.[31] This argument is not a new one, for the words 'protected from manipulation and propaganda' evoke the thought of protection from 'invisible persuaders' – the title of Vance Packard's book in 1957 about how modern American advertising developed techniques to harness psychological drives to sell more consumer goods.

The third aspect to note about regulating PR is that reform initiatives need to come from inside and outside the industry. People do not impose upon their working practices more regulation than the amount which is unavoidable from law, custom and culture, a point demonstrated by Harrison's review. The major stimulus, therefore, will have to be from outside; left to itself the industry has historically produced only an appearance of regulation. The reform of PR may be a by-product of the general political drives which have led to the establishment of regulatory regimes for the privatised utilities and for financial services since the early 1980s. A few industry voices have drawn attention to these drives, the most notable that of Simon Lewis, the monarchy's PR man (see Chapter 3). He called for the industry to prepare, in the form of an anticipatory debate, for such an outside initiative.

The fourth aspect is that regulation is being reversed into PR, so to speak, by the regulation of public officials and politicians involved in lobbying. This has happened in Parliament with a register of MPs' interests where the acceptance of free services such as hotels and flights has to be declared, and where monies from commercial lobbyists are barred. This regulation of politicians is the agency for regulating PR people working with them. The same is happening with the Financial Services Authority and its general regulation about market-sensitive information. Another example is the European Union where a code of conduct for Commission officials in regard to lobbying by interests groups is being drawn up.

The fifth aspect is that regulation will take many forms. These will include more effective self-regulation via codes for individuals and firms in their contracts, and the presence on the industry's field of play of an official body as the enforcer of last resort. That official body could be an enlarged Advertising Standards Authority (see Chapter 11). Another form will be increased self-awareness by future PR people of their own behaviour. PR education may play some part in this, but a more potent force for change will be the heightened awareness of the need for more open and accountable behaviour towards the consumers of PR. Reflection on events outside of PR will start up this awareness. The costs imposed on the pensions industry by the mis-selling of the later 1980s and 1990s is estimated at £2 billion. There is some evidence that consumers are becoming more aware of the moral dimension to market operations, witness the number of fair trading, environmental and consumerist groups. A thoughtful service industry will note that through its agent/principal relationships to its employers and clients and through these to markets, it is not immune to the larger political and societal pressures for more regulation and auditing.

The final aspect is that the UK industry says that it does regulate itself currently. There is, however, little evidence that it is effective regulation. This situation is pious and self-serving: either regulation of PR behaviour is important enough to be done properly, or it is unimportant enough to be ignored. It is the worst sort of public relations to have rhetoric without performance. That is the very source of the low reputation in which PR is held.

Summary

The contemporary UK PR industry prospers, has more job applicants than vacancies and will expand as a persuasive mass communications sector well suited to multi-media technologies. It also prospers with the growth of lobbying by businesses and pressure groups in the public, adversarial climate encouraged by accelerated pluralism. It is well adapted to promoting complex 'lifestyle' marketing and to continuing its subsidy of pre-packaged 'soft' news to the media. It is largely indifferent to its low reputation, noting how lawyers and politicians have also prospered for much longer. Besides, many PR people know that organisations and groups pay more lip service to having a good reputation than to achieving it, and that it is traded off against other goals such as survival and growth. The industry is entering another growth stage with a search for more professionalisation, but how that goal will lead to more reliable techniques and more predictable outcomes is not clear. It is the latter two occurrences which most PR people want, much more than they wish for regulation of their conduct. But more regulation and ethical awareness are needed if PR is to reduce its manipulative and propagandistic outputs, and if it is to play its part in substituting for these outputs the better PR of reasoned persuasion. If PR reform promotes better PR, it is strengthening the communicative equality appropriate for a liberal, democratic, market-based society. The next chapter looks at an alternative, reformed PR.

11 A beneficial PR

PR is not going to disappear from UK public life. As done by organisations, groups and individuals, it is an expression of structural features in our society. It is a comunicative consequence of liberal, democratic, market-orientated, capitalist societies. It cannot be un-invented. It can, however, be better understood for the benefits and costs it brings to citizens and consumers, to the powerful and to the powerless. That understanding leads to the case for reform because PR too easily slides in intent and consequence towards manipulation and propaganda, what Boorstin has called 'appealing falsehood'.[1] At its worst, PR is in an abusive relationship with the public. Instead, PR should play a part in emancipation rather than manipulation. It needs reform because much of today's public debate goes through it. A beneficial PR will improve the context and the content of that public debate. It will be used by less powerful interests in UK society in order to bring a better balance with the most powerful.[2] It will benefit citizens and consumers by employing more reasoned persuasion. It will be societally beneficial.

But who cares about the reform of PR? Today few inside PR, few outside, and fewer in the past.[3] The reformers mostly concentrate on where PR intersects with government (lobbying and government PR), and here there is a discernible agenda growing. There is no move for reform of PR activity mediated through journalists – the largest area of PR work and the one which coalesces with concerns about journalism. The current balance of power among interested groups may prevent any significant change for some time, even against a widespread public acceptance of regulated public and private services. PR is as it is today because most of its producers and principals benefit. The initial leverage for change will not come from them, though it will eventually bring a better reputation for them. Instead, the leverage will be generated, in piecemeal fashion, by PR's part in scandals involving lobbying, corporate mismanagement or media standards. Public opinion will want reform in the public interest.

There will be no PR reform until outside constituencies become publicly clamorous and they put the issue on government's agenda, as happened in the 1960s when the Advertising Standards Authority was created in response to widespread concern about abuses in non-broadcast advertising. It may be that these constituencies will develop slowly because of the invisibility of much PR: it is easy to be alarmed about a page advert, but more difficult over the story on a page taken from an unseen press release without a word changed. Behind, however, the social physics of how reform movements arise, there are matters of principle raised by PR in a society which declares itself a liberal democracy with free markets and media. Public communicators in these societies should be respectful and tolerant of their audiences: they should communicate with more reason and less emotion. Their audiences should not encourage the unreasoned and the emotional. Beneficial PR is a contract between its originators and its receivers: the former should not utter false messages and the latter should inspect the reasoned persuasion before them with a sceptical but open mind. It goes beyond instrumental communication and includes Dewey's consummatory communication which 'offers an immediate enhancement of life and can be enjoyed for its own sake' (Kruckeberg and Starck 1988, p. 66). It has a communitarian element in that it recognises that individuals obtain identity and security from associative communications. It shares many features with the normative, Grunigian two-way communications model (listening, negotiating, compromising, iterative) but is more explicit about the contribution of PR to the public good. It differs in that it does not reject a role for persuasion and instead incorporates persuasion which is validated by reason. It differs also in that it does not project a solely self-generating norm. Beneficial PR exists through the exogenous forces of an accelerated pluralism sustained by adversarial democracy and market competition and, second, through the regulation of its operations by forces inside itself.

Tedlow (1997, p. 193) argues that American PR promised two benefits to business: more sales and protection from unpopularity 'which could lead to detrimental governmental or regulatory agency activity'. PR in the UK has delivered fully on the first and largely on the second. These kept promises supply much of the benefit of contemporary PR in the UK to business, especially big business. But have the promises been kept at the expense of other interests, the general body of electors and consumers? The answer is 'broadly yes but increasingly less so' (Chapters 3 and 4). The reform agenda seeks to re-balance the PR playing field more in favour of these other interests, the mass of UK citizens and consumers. At bottom, the reform of PR is about more equalitarian civic values and relationships in a democracy. In his review of the American relationship between propaganda, in which he included PR, and democracy, Sproule (1997, p. 271) describes the tension in the relationship as 'how a society aspiring to democracy may balance the right to persuade and the right of the public to free choice'.

For those in PR, a starting point for a reform agenda is to admit that the emperor has no clothes, to admit what probably a majority of UK people think: that PR is often manipulation and propaganda. Too much PR is weak propaganda in politics and boosterism in markets, delivered through a complicit media. PR people will need in future to recognise PR as manipulation, how practically to avoid it, and to understand why they face active publics criticising them. For example, they should stop offering free facilities (e.g. air travel, holidays, consumer goods) to the media and so discourage 'junket journalism'. PR people have to reflect more on what they do and its consequences. They have to pull themselves free of the tangled thicket of bad reputation in which they have fallen. PR needs reforms where reform means changes in the values and behaviour of people doing PR, whether on behalf of organisations, groups, government or themselves, towards reasoned persuasion with limited appeals to emotion and with open sourcing of messages.[4] For those who consume PR, reform means a readiness to accept with caution the possibility that PR messages could contain accurate information and reasoned conclusions. This cautious readiness is expressed in the *caveat emptor* rule. This scepticism, moreover, will benefit producers of reformed PR in the long term because of greater credibility given to their messages.

There is, also, another motivation for PR reform: it would enhance the public interest.[5] PR is a powerful form of persuasion in contemporary UK, and its communications and their effects should benefit the many, rather than the few. Who uses it and their liberty to do so cannnot be tampered with in a liberal society. But PR should encourage outcomes favoured by our society: outcomes such as reasoned, factually accurate, persuasive public debate amongst all individuals, groups and organisations wanting to speak and listen.

A reasoned persuasion?

If public debate about issues which affected large numbers of UK citizens ever conformed to Habermas's concept of the public sphere,[6] that open assembly of informed individuals in rational and disinterested discussion cannot be brought together now. The coffee houses, assembly rooms and clubs of local Georgian and Victorian England have had their day and have been replaced with mediated communications, national editions, studios, mobile phones and computers speaking across the UK. The words, the voices, the faces, the electronic messages of PR are communications from institutions and organised groups, sometimes expressive of social movements and classes behind them, and from individuals who are ambitious and/or aggrieved. The mind-set and techniques of PR offer communications with – and maybe power and influence with – politicians and public officials. The persuasive sphere has replaced the public sphere.

The persuasive sphere is the communicative aspect of the relations among groups, institutions, individuals and government about public issues and policies. These communicative relations take forms other than

PR (journalism, politics, expert debate) and they include PR in its corporate relations and public affairs aspects.[7] These communicative relations happen in civil society, and between it and government.

The persuasive sphere – the successor to the public sphere – has evolved from an interplay of societal factors: a more democratic, mass and pluralist UK society evolving out of a more elite, authoritarian bourgeois polity; the rise of mass production industries needing mass consumption and communications to sell products; a universal franchise obliging political parties to communicate with national populations; the development of communications able to reach millions of citizens and consumers. The persuasive sphere can be seen as the communicative aspect of a society based on adversarial democracy where conflicting interests are formally given equal right to debate, equal access to decision-making and where decisions are majoritarian (Mansbridge 1983). It can be seen as the site of the communicative aspect of associative democracy (Cohen and Rogers 1995), which attempts to increase the representative power of groups without undermining electorally based politics through 'the mischiefs of faction'. It can be seen as the communicative aspect of issues arising from competitive markets, such as the search for consumer sovereignty. The persuasive sphere can be associated with radical social agendas as much as conservative ones.

But the persuasive sphere, as a conceptualisation for the location of public communications, has problematic features and PR is centrally involved with the major one. This concerns the relationship between reason and persuasion. It is a problematic relationship because the influential Habermasian public sphere concept has put them in opposition and PR is always persuasive by intent, if not in consequence. The persuasive sphere concept attempts to dissolve the opposition, because any accurate empirical attempt to describe public communications on public issues and policy in a democracy today has to include PR. It is too widespread, noticeable and pervasive a feature of society to exclude. The public sphere concept cannot handle the combination of PR and democracy, for it rejects PR as pernicious for democracy because of its opposition to reason and persuasion. There is a conceptual and a historical aspect to these matters.

Any rethinking of PR must come to terms with PR's relationship to persuasion, and to reason and emotion as modes of communication in a democracy. Persuasion is integral to PR as an intention and as a desired outcome. Reason is an optional mode for achieving it. For a democracy, societally beneficial PR is reasoned persuasion. Such PR is the consequence of *choosing* to persuade by reason (supported by accurate data) rather than by emotion. Reason and emotion are alternative communicative modes of being persuasive and of achieving persuasion. PR in a democracy should proceed by more reason and less emotion. Beneficial PR in a democracy is a means of promoting the public good through a contribution to informed choice. PR as manipulation or propaganda chooses emotion and falsehood as a persuasive mode and so degrades democracy, because PR as manipulation or propaganda is communication from an authoritarian will.

For Habermas, PR is incompatible with the public sphere because it is persuasive. PR is now a more significant element of UK public communications than in the time period (eighteenth and nineteenth centuries) in which Habermas places the public sphere as a social phenomenon and in which democracy developed in the UK. He argues that the public sphere is a precondition for democracy in that it promoted accessible, rational and disinterested public debate. In the contemporary UK, PR and democracy co-exist, and this is a combination which the public sphere concept cannot accommodate. At the level of being an adequate descriptor of existing social arrangements, the public sphere concept needs amendment or transformation into the persuasive sphere.

Why should the development of persuasive mass communications, of which PR is a sub-set, be assumed to make reason rather than emotion a less utilised mode of communications? Put like that, there is an assumption that citizens of a mass democracy favour emotion rather than reason. Why put reason and persuasion into an excluded combination where the former cannot issue in the latter? The Habermasian assumption is that the citizens (and consumers) of a mass, democratic and pluralist state cannot have public debates which are reasoned, accessible to all and persuasive. This is a pessimistic presupposition and carries with it the connotation of debates in the earlier half of the twentieth century, that the involvement of common men and women in politics would lead to chaos because they were not competent to take part in government (see Chapters 5 and 6).[8]

Looked at historically, there is no evidence to favour the profound, conservative pessimism of this view. Despite their persistent, internal travails, Western liberal, democratic, market-orientated, capitalist societies, most of them with well developed PR sectors, flourish at the beginning of the twenty-first century. They are more democratic than the bourgeois representative democracies of eighteenth- and nineteenth-century Western Europe, the historical site of the public sphere concept. It is in their successors, the modern Western state, that mass persuasive communications have grown, and insofar as the public sphere puts reason and persuasion in opposition, its descriptive power about the modern Western state is limited. The citizens and consumers of these mass democracies are as capable of being persuaded by reason as any class-based elite. No doubt many or most public communicators – business and government in the case of PR – have aimed emotive, non-reasoned communications at them, no doubt these manipulative communications and propagandas have persuaded many; but it is too pessimistic a judgement to conclude that they always or mostly persuaded majorities in these democracies.

PR and the persuasive sphere

The public sphere assumes rational discourse, open to all, between disinterested individuals on matters of public interest. The persuasive sphere preserves the open access of the public sphere and asserts that persuasion should be reasoned. PR, as a set of techniques and attitudes but not as a bought service, is a low-cost gateway into the persuasive sphere. The more PR develops as a 'cottage industry' and as 'personal kit' for individuals (Chapter 3), the wider the gate is. The persuasive sphere does not, however, assume that its participants are disinterested: PR people, politicians, journalists and experts are representatives of interests and their status as participants flows from that.

Nor does the persuasive sphere assume that government is disinterested when it participates: it does so as an interested party. But its status is special and superior to other public persuaders, in that it has authority to declare its view to be the public interest and so close off discussion on a matter for that round of public debate. Before that declaration of the public interest by government, there will be a choice of views on offer represented by interests external to it (competitive groups and institutions) and internal to it (differing administrative interests and political factions). The ranking of these views as favoured policy options is the task of the highest elected political authority – the prime minister and senior ministers. It is hard to attach the word 'disinterested' to that process: if it can credibly be attached, it is at this final level of senior elected politicians.

The inability of the public sphere concept to accept the self-interested nature of public debate is a strong reason for transforming it into the persuasive sphere. The latter, however, as an actual, UK social phenomenon is far from a free and equal arena for all interests: it has been, and still is, over-occupied by what H.G. Wells called the 'monarchical and aristocratic state'[9] and by the most powerful interest in UK society – business. This over-occupation limits the quantity and quality of public debate in the persuasive sphere because alternatives are inadequately heard, respected and responded to. A fully functioning version would maximise the communicative pluralism and equality of groups and the quantity of PR would increase, with its content subject to scrutiny and amendment in the struggle for advantage. In that mature circumstance and with an internally reformed PR producing reasoned persuasion, the deformation of PR into manipulation and propaganda would cease.

Chapters 3 and 4 argue that group and value pluralism is flourishing in the UK and named the process of its development over the last 40 years as accelerated pluralism. This increases the quantity and variety of interests in the persuasive sphere that are seeking policy advantage, and with that increase comes more, varied communicative behaviour, i.e. more PR.[10] This accelerated pluralism is an external reform agent for beneficial PR: it challenges its historic, near-monopoly by business and government by creating a vigorous competition among PR messages. The judgement that this competition is beneficial to the public good rests on the Millsian assumption that out of a clash of opinions, 'true' opinion will be the residue. When these clashes of opinion are aggregated throughout a polity, the concept of adversarial democracy emerges, of which the persuasive sphere is the communicative component.

But the question then arises as to the nature of the residue of opinion left after the clash. This residue is the opinion that the majority of interested individuals, either in groups or as individuals, have formed after their consideration of persuasive communications about a matter. After a round of communications on a matter by participants in the persuasive sphere, that majoritarian opinion is the best available for making policy decisions at that time. Other rounds of communications will alter the basis and it is a matter of judgement as to how many rounds pass before policy is made. This model of the persuasive sphere in relation to policy making shows how the concept encourages a reformed PR: the more numerous and varied the participants in the persuasive sphere are in communicating competing messages, the more that pluralism will evoke another round of critical and rebutting messages in response. This process is a public dialectic scrutinising competitive messages about issues and policy in a democratic political economy. There is 'the wrangle of the market place'[11] over ideas, and over the ownership and the distribution of resources, a robust contestation about these things among interests and between interests and government. Insofar as all organisations and groups which wish to participate in the public contestation are able to do so, and do participate with reasoned persuasion, there is a crude form of communicative equality in the persuasive sphere.

Stakeholding ideas are supportive of the persuasive sphere concept, for they are a modern expression of pluralism in political economy decision-making and they imply a significant role for PR. In their Hutton (1999) version, decision-making is decentralised in economics and politics which are open, polyarchical systems. In their Plender (1997) version, the interests of finance capital are balanced against the needs of human and social capital. Stakeholding is an inclusive conception of markets and politics which encourages various outcomes: involvement by interested groups, ownership of assets with responsibilities as well as rights,[12] businesses as social institutions as well as market ones, and the formation of intermediate institutions between the state and the individuals. In this constellation of interests attempting to balance economic and social behaviours, PR is the communicative aspect of their relationships. Where it is informed, openly sourced, reasoned PR, it can provide the expertise which Lippmann (1922) argued aided effective decision-making. Sir Bernard Ingham, former Press Secretary to Mrs Thatcher, alludes (1999) to this role of expertise provision with a suggestion[13] that PR would benefit from 'a continuing independent analysis of our arguments'.

The concern over genetically modified (GM) food is an example of PR working in the persuasive sphere. Some 80 groups are under the umbrella of the National Food Alliance (NFA), working out of the London offices of the Child Poverty Action Group. The NFA is the organisational expression of food consumerism which started in the mid-1970s and of the activism which was further encouraged by the BSE crisis. The food processing industry is also active and spends some £300 million on promotion. The four large supermarkets employ a lobbyist who sits in the House of Lords.[14] Consumerists and industry both use PR heavily, as does the Health Education Council: active media campaigns; lobbying civil servants, Ministers and MPs; Early Day Motions in Parliament; information campaigns direct to the public are evidence. Over time, the following outcomes have resulted: food safety as a public concern; legislation for the Food Safety Agency;[15] more informative food labelling; increased public awareness about GM food.

These activists draw up action plans which read like standard PR campaigns applied to the individual. The plans empower what Gabriel and Lang (1995) have named 'the consumer as rebel'. Elkington and Hailes (1998) urge the Citizen 2000 to draw up a plan 'to help you use people power to shape the future you want' (p. 385). The points include: 'use your social networks'; 'talk about the issues in the shops, on the bus or train'; 'get people interested'; 'write letters'; 'start petitions'; 'write to your MP, government departments'; 'get actively involved in your community'; 'celebrate local traditions'; 'be a conscious consumer'; 'think about the social, ethical, environmental and fair trade issues associated with each product or service you buy'; 'see if you can change your lifestyle to make it easier to live your values'; 'engage the young'; 'do it yourself'; 'don't just wait for the rest of the world to sort out problems'; 'vote, vote, vote'. These actions are PR as 'personal kit' and a blueprint of participation in the persuasive sphere.

A problematic consequence of this style of public campaigning is how small a role Parliament plays in it. This consequence can be generalised into a statement about the institution. It is arguable that the rise of the consumer/citizen dealing individually and in groups with executive government via the media and via lobbying – all of which involves PR – reduces the role of Parliament. Interest and pressure group activity in a mass democracy with a mass media and lobbying capability has its major fields of operation in the studio and in Whitehall. It is ironic that it is Peter Mandelson, MP for Hartlepool and New Labour's founding PR man, who observed as Minister without Portfolio that 'the era of representative government is coming to an end'. Franklin (1998, p. 4) argues that this media- and lobbying-based process of mediation between government and electorate are 'at the expense of parliament'.

Before looking at the internal reform of PR, it is useful to relate the reform question to what Marxists call base/superstructure questions:

those issues about sources of social power and how those sources determine – or do not determine – individual and group behaviour. PR does
not generate in and of itself the effectiveness of achieved goals: rather its
effectiveness is sourced in the power of its users. Historically, PR has been
mostly used by powerful interests as a communicative technique, and it
was the precedent power of those interests which gives their PR its effectiveness. PR is a set of attitudes and techniques for communications about
political economy matters, a passive, technical consequence of causative
behaviour outside itself. It is power-neutral until invested with power by
users who are social actors with more or less of that attribute. Whatever
transformative capacity these interests have to achieve their goals will give
their PR its communicative effectiveness. PR gives them a voice and a
visible role but is not of itself a source of effectiveness. It is the neutral
channel which communicates their power or lack of it in the struggle of
interests. The need to communicate is created by the more intense
competition between interests associated with accelerated pluralism and
its communicative expression, the persuasive sphere. How interests,
groups and organisations prosper or weaken in that competition is determined by their resources: PR lets us hear and see that there is competition. A major goal of the PR reformer is to seek changes to the cast of
social actors who use PR: greater use of PR by resource-poor or otherwise
excluded interests is a significant social reform.

Internal reforms

Accelerated pluralism is the causal agent of more PR, more scrutinised PR
and therefore more beneficial PR. It is the structural approach to reforming PR.[16] The second approach is reform internal to PR, and is focused on
individuals and their practices, on how they produce PR for use by the
media and by public policy decision-makers. If the structural approach
relates PR and the political economy, the internal approach relates PR
and ethics. Many discrete initiatives can be grouped under this approach
and the unifying feature is that they affect the practice and behaviour of
PR people. Whether the source of these initiatives is internal or external
to PR is not crucial, but the judgement is that most will be externally stimulated. More important is the relationship between the two approaches:
the internal weakly facilitates structural reform. The relationship is exem-
plified in the case of lobbying regulation which while 'never likely to
restructure interest intermediation, it may in some contexts ... play a sup-
porting role to democratic life' (Greenwood and Thomas 1998). Internal
PR reforms make PR's contribution to the persuasive sphere more societally beneficial because reform makes PR more ethical in a democratic
society.

The PR which flows from this internal reform should have the following characteristics: known source, clear intent, reasoned argument, factual

accuracy, and positive but limited emotional appeal. It is dialogic, respectful of its audiences, open to challenge, ready to amend and willing to reply. Insofar as it does not share these features, it is manipulative and at worst propagandistic.[17] Beneficial PR would move away from Jensen's (1997) characterisation of hemispheric communications by PR people (as well as by lawyers and advertisers) 'who express messages that speak only to half the landscape'. 'Like the shining moon, they present only the bright side and leave the dark side hid' (p. 68). Internal reform will move PR into the 'light' more.

Jensen lists 'ethical obligations' (p. 70) which hemispheric communicators should lay on themselves because 'the public should not have to grapple constantly with misleading and fraudulent claims'. The list includes:

> the avoidance of unsubstantiated claims and distortions, of weakening the opportunity for consumers to choose rationally and of excessively stimulating the grossest levels of emotional appeals to vanity, power, fear and self-indulgence. Needs, not unbridled desires, should be targeted. Superlatives, exaggerations, embellishments, vagueness, tastelessness, puffery, and inappropriate use of testimonials should be avoided.

PR people as hemispheric communicators can 'hardly be expected to spend their resources presenting self-destructing messages – to commit suicide. But in fulfilling their mission they have definite ethical obligations' (p. 70).

Models of ethical PR are found in McElreath (1997), Spicer (1997, pp. 270–95), and in Seib and Fitzpatrick (1995). The latter open with the statement that the moral purpose of PR is social harmony, while in Pearson (1989) there is a methodology for monitoring ethical communications. The codes of professional behaviour of the IPR, the PRSA and the IABC are widely published. More generally, Pratkanis and Aronson (1992) have written, *inter alia*, a handbook for those 'who want to be effective communicators in ways that are honest and above-board' (p. xiii).

There is a well established (since 1962) regulatory regime, policed by the Advertising Standards Authority (ASA) for non-broadcast advertising, including sales promotion and direct mail and a parallel system for broadcast advertising regulated by the Independent Television Commission (ITC). It is an active system with the ASA handling 6,500 complaints in 1980 and 12,000 in 1996; and the ITC 7,800 in 1998. The goal is advertising which is 'legal, decent, honest, truthful'. The same aim should be set for PR.[18] Movement towards that goal for PR will be helped when the marketing part of PR work (MPR) is seen as commercial communications. After advertising, it is the largest component. Advertising and MPR should be perceived as being in the same category of communications, regulated to exhibit the same characteristics. To put much of PR into the same category as advertising is to dissolve some conceptual barriers to reform.

It cannot be beyond the wit of the overall UK media system, including its PR and journalism sub-systems, to produce more PR which is 'legal, decent, honest, truthful'. It is not defensible that an advert on page 2 is censured when it claims that magnetic jewellery is therapeutic, while a story on page 4 freely makes the same claim based on an un-revealed or unchecked press release. The regulation of print and broadcast adverts can influence the extent and direction of the PR reform debate[19] by highlighting similar experiences. The ASA, a state-backed industry body set up when there was a threat of legislation, is concerned with the largest volume of commercial communications (print advertising and sales promotion) in the UK[20] and much of PR is commercial communications. The ASA should be encouraged by government to explore whether it can extend its regulatory regime to PR. A related reform instrument is PR audits by plc's. There is a bridgehead to such reports in the form of the social reports, sometimes sections of annual reports and accounts, which are becoming a more noticeable big business activity.[21] These are reports to a company's stakeholders on its social and community – and therefore political – impacts and a PR report would be easy to add because PR is often the communicative aspect of social and communities programmes.

A reformed PR will make a strengthened contribution to a more equitable UK. But to lay the realisation of this onto the idealism of PR people alone is utopian; realisation will have to rely on an array of initiatives: on better professional education and development; on individual codes of conduct actively enforced; on practice changes in related areas (e.g. the media and politcs); on government encouragement; on statutory and voluntary regulation; and, finally, on a self-interested judgement by PR people that the auditing by others of their contributions to markets and to politics will be a future feature of their work. Perhaps that judgement has been made in part: the IPR has launched a Best Practice Campaign.[22]

Educators and citizens

PR, ethics and reform are three words rarely heard on the lips of PR teachers and trainers. The combination of PR and ethics has been spoken of more frequently since the mid-1990s because business ethics is moving up the higher education curriculum. Representative groups such as The Public Relations Educators' Forum should put those three words together on their agenda and start a debate on whether they accept the case for reform. Outside of PR courses, there is the question for secondary education about media literacy, and whether it should be taught as skills of recognition, interpretation and evaluation in curricula for teenage personal development. The Americans Stauber and Rampton (1995, pp. 15–16) argue that 'society would be best served ... if people were trained in the skills necessary to recognise manipulative uses of rhetoric', for PR 'often loses its ability to mislead and manipulate' when people are educated about it. These sentiments catch much of modern media in their reach and make media literacy a useful life-skill for productive participation in a media-saturated society. As a life-skill, media literacy can be viewed as a component in citizenship, the self-conscious, informed and active participation of people in public decision-making. Jon White, a leading PR academic, has suggested public education in 'social literacy' to inform people about interest group methods.[23] In this way, the following linkages are established: awareness and education about PR is part of media literacy which is an element of citizenship. It is timely to make these linkages explicit when there are calls for citizenship lessons in state schools by the Crick Committee.[24] Moreover, if PR is linked to citizenship, it could be expressed as a 'right' that people have, in the same way that they have a 'right' to legal advice in law centres. This opens up the possibility of one-stop PR shops in the high street, open as citizens' advice bureaus on communications.[25]

West (1963, pp. 119–23) notes that regulation of PR started in the early 1920s with in-house rules of conduct drawn up by the first UK PR firm, Editorial Services. He has little faith in a code of ethics by the IPR: 'Some of the best and most prosperous PROs are outside the Institute'. West wrote when the IPR was drawing up its code and the doubts remain, but in the regulatory and auditing climate of the 2000s, it is very unlikely that the IPR will cease to seek improvements to its code of conduct. The task for reformers is to ask whether the code beneficially influences the behaviour of PR people.

The concept of 'publishing' PR material should be introduced where this means that a PR production (e.g. media releases, brochures, videos) has been 'posted' physically or electronically into the public domain. PR publishers should be required to keep copies of these productions for at least three months, and intermediate media which use them (e.g. media releases used by journalists) should keep them in an archive for the same period. This will enable source material to be checked in cases of dispute.

Are the media sufficiently concerned about their use of PR material? Media managers and editors appear in many cases to rely on journalists following best professional practice: it is a matter for the individual journalist to be aware of their sources and to indicate publicly where data and opinion, other than their own, come from.[26] This is too passive a policy, suggesting low levels of concern about PR sourcing by media organisations. A stronger response is an explicit policy and set of practices about how to incorporate persuasive PR material in a journalism which claims independence, about the proportions of material permitted, when and how audiences are alerted to its presence, about how this incorporation process is monitored by an internal editorial ombudsman, and the publication of an annual report.

Elements of a voluntary regulation system have been tried before: Stauber and Rampton (1995, p. 18) report that at the end of the nineteenth century 'the paid reading notices of advertisers' (PR copy supplied by advertisers) was indicated by a star or dagger in newspapers, but it was a minority practice which fell away. The equivalent contemporary practice is to flag up copy as 'advertorial' when it is a soft sell in journalistic form and when it is next to advertisements. It is not clear, however, that the 'advertorial' badge is always put up: it should be an editorial precept to have it there. More of an identification problem is short, down-page stories, often in business, fashion, home improvement, or entertainment sections, which are the copy of a press release amended by a few words. The dagger or star device could be revived for these 'puffs', or they could be grouped together as a discrete 'best of the press releases' section.

There should be more investigative journalism as a corrective to the temptation to use PR material. A marketised media would be encouraged to investigate by a journalism research institute producing journalistic versions of official reports. It would counter the great flows of PR releases to the media with counter flows of first drafts of critical stories available to news rooms wanting to do their own follow-ups. This is a contemporary version of Walter Lippmann's suggestion in 1919, for 'an official bureau to broker disputes about the accuracy of news coverage' (Sproule 1997, p. 19). Lippmann (1919) talked of 'political observatories', independent of government, which would digest official reports into a media-friendly form. He proposed these bodies because there was not enough scrutiny by Congress of executive government.

Those media organisations concerned about PR-isation should play a more active role in the PR reform process. They should be as sceptical about PR produced by private sources as they are rightfully questioning about government PR, a point made by Curran and Seaton (1988, p. 236). They should, more particularly, help less powerful, resource-poor groups in society produce beneficial PR. The media should encourage 'outsider' pressure groups and voluntary organisations to make contact with the media, an observation made by Goldenberg (1975) in her study of resource-poor groups. They should train these groups in how to produce PR as reasoned persuasion. Stauber and Tumber (p. 30) list the qualities which influence the credibility of sources with journalists: size of groups, their location, expert knowledge, finance – and news management skills. Intervention by media organisations will increase the last of these, and will also be a distinct contribution towards developing the persuasive sphere. It will also be enlightened self-interest for many of these groups are news sources.

Regulation creeps in

A process of drift towards the regulation of PR has set in. This is in addition to the indirect regulation which is imposed on lobbying via parliamentary rules and on financial PR via legislation and codes to stop sensitive information abuse. For example, agencies wanting to join the PRCA have to meet minimum management standards by external certification. The drift is most observable in lobbying where, as a result of the 'sleaze' years from the late 1980s to the mid-1990s, commercial lobbyists set up in 1994 the Association of Professional Political Consultants (APPC), which has a regulatory code for lobbying firm staff.[27] In 1999, there was a call for 'lobbyists from pressure groups and professional services companies like management consultancies and investment banks to be regulated to the same standards of lobbying agency staff'.[28] Sir Bernard Ingham, the Press Secretary to Prime Minister Thatcher, has called for the statutory regulation of lobbyists.[29] It is reported[30] that members of the Scottish Parliament will not be allowed to do any paid work with lobbying firms, a freedom Westminster MPs have.

Parliament is involved also in a 1993 proposal by Clive Soley MP for an Independent Press Authority which would, inter alia, seek to protect the editorial autonomy of journalists. This body would be appointed by the Home Secretary and report annually to Parliament. Manipulative PR – through drip feeding information as a reward or sanction, through free gifts, trips and lunches, through pressure from owners and editors – can be a severe constraint on journalists. It is also possible to design a wider remit for a statutory body such as an Independent Press Authority to reduce manipulations. A state registration scheme for PR people would impose minimum standards.[31]

Lord McNally, a senior PR figure, has made another Parliament-centred proposal: a cross-party Parliamentary group on PR after the example of the advertising industry. 'Too often, PR seems to be on the back foot in its relations with Parliament. Instead, it should be on a mission to explain,' he observes.[32] Such a group could be a force for putting reform issues on the agenda.

A reform agenda

This is a list, not an integrated programme for reform. Its point is to illustrate that, in a spontaneous and disaggregated way and by a wide-range of sources, there has already been thought given to the reform of PR in markets, politics and the media. It is, however, still rare to find those words combined. Moreover, the individual points do not cohere into a whole and are sometimes in contradiction. Some are more fanciful, further from a probable reform agenda, than others. Some suggestions were not framed with PR in mind but can be extended to include it. Sources and/or references are given where known.

- Newspapers, journals and magazines to indicate on the page when a story has been wholly or principally sourced from PR outlets (Chapter 4, pp. 44–6; Chapter 9, pp. 122–5);
- Print media and broadcasters to keep PR releases used to generate editorial for three months;
- All media releases put out by public bodies, companies and registered charities to be kept and/or posted on the internet by them for three months;
- Media companies to publish a PR audit in their annual report and accounts, reporting on contact between their journalists and PR people; proportions of editorial sourced from PR, and their policy for ensuring how such material is journalistically treated before publication;
- Media companies to train 'outsider' pressure groups and voluntary bodies on how to produce beneficial PR and so be better news sources;
- PR awareness to be part of a 'social literacy' programme (Jon White), media literacy or civics curriculum in secondary schools;
- Media education, starting in primary schools, 'to ensure children are given the means to develop critical viewing skills ...' (Broadcasting Standards Commission);
- PR trade bodies – IPR, PRCA, APPC – to agree a unified code of conduct, written into staff contracts (*PR Week et al.*);
- A management standard for PR agencies, externally assessed and certificated (PRCA);
- Codes of PR conduct to explicitly ban the giving of free facilities and gifts to journalists;
- Public information campaigns by the industry's representative bodies on benefits of beneficial PR and aimed at individual citizens and consumers;
- Research into the need for 'one stop PR shops' along the lines of law centres;
- Journalists' professional bodies to examine the impact of journalists training PR people (Chapter 9, pp. 125–6);
- A changed focus in PR studies and research, away from organisational needs and towards effects on individuals, groups and society;
- MPs to be paid only their Parliamentary salaries and to represent outside interests without remuneration (Chapter 8);
- MPs to face criminal charges if they do not declare outside interests (Chapter 8);
- Put government PR special advisers on the same professional contracts as civil service information officers (Franklin (1998) in Chapter 8);
- Put government PR special advisers on separate, explicitly political contracts (Chapter 8, p. 109–10);
- All government press spokespeople to have a clause in their personal contracts on open information policy (Chapter 8, p. 109–10);

- Broadcast the briefings by the Prime Minister's Press Secretary (Franklin (1998) and others);
- Publish retrospectively each week the meetings' diaries of ministers and of senior civil servants with dates and interlocutors (Chapter 8, pp. 114–17);
- Amend the various conduct codes for lobbyists to promote publishing the meetings' diaries of their principals with ministers and civil servants (Chapter 8, pp. 114–17);
- Cross-party Parliamentary committee on PR (Lord McNally);
- An Oflob, an official body to regulate lobbying by PR people, management consultants, lawyers and charities (IPR to Neill Committee, July 1999[33]);
- An OfPR, an official regulatory regime complete with Office for the Regulation of Public Relations, comparable to the advertising industry (Moloney 1998);
- Time limits on government involvement in public information campaigns before referenda, and spending limits on the contesting groups;
- The Advertising Standards Authority to explore the extension of its code and adjudication service to PR (government proposal);
- Sir Bernard Ingham says (1999) that PR 'would benefit from the continuing independent analysis of the validity' of the cases it presents;
- An Independent Press Authority to re-balance the relationships of journalists with government PR people and media owners (Clive Soley MP in Franklin (1998)).
- Establish a journalists' register of interests along the lines of the Parliamentary register for MPs and Lords.

Notes

1 'It's a PR job'

1 Many prefer to avoid saying or writing 'PR' and choose 'public relations' instead, fearing to encourage what they consider to be negative connotations. 'PR' is preferred here, because that is the more common usage and because a debate should be had in the language of its participants.

2 Anthony Holden wrote a book critical of the Prince of Wales. In *The Observer* (1.11.98 Review, p. 1) he writes of the reaction: 'HRH's propaganda machine denounced my book as a "tissue of lies" . . .'.

3 *The Observer* (17.1.99 p. 17, 'Look who's coming to the rescue of Augusto') reported that the friends of General Pinochet had hired Bell Pottinger to represent his interests for a week for £200,000.

4 The first four are, following medieval political economy, the Crown and Nobles, the Church, the Commons, and, following Macaulay, the press.

5 See p. 166 of *The Whole Woman* (1999) by Greer where she quotes the financier George Soros as noting that advertising and marketing now shape values and tastes instead of reflecting them.

6 The essence of pluralism as a descriptor and as a norm is that there are many entities rather than one in the field, and that many is better than one. As a political perspective, pluralism in its several variants has been seen as an alternative to corporatist and Marxist conceptions of the political economy. As regards values and ideas, the essential feature of pluralism of them, particularly relevant here, is their 'immcommeasurability' feature as developed by Isaiah Berlin.

7 Could we say 'memetic' instead of 'transmission belt'? Susan Blackmore (1999) argues that ideas which spread far over populations do so because they are copyable, capable of imitation. Does public relations pick out these 'memes'? Are PR people spotters and spreaders of 'memes'?

8 Examples are media acknowledgement of PR sources; the extension of the regulatory concept of 'honest, decent and truthful' from advertising to PR, and PR awareness as a component of civic education.

9 See Chapter 11 for a discussion of the relationship of PR to the public space concept.

2 The PR industry from top to bottom

1 *The Tablet* 16.1.99, p. 70, reports that the press officer for the Church of England takes a proprietorial attitude towards his subject: the Church 'owns' its public image and so, like a patent, it can only be written about in an approved manner.

2 Sister Frances Meigh gave an interview to *The Guardian* G2 section, 24.9.96, p. 2.
3 There is even a hierarchy of spin doctors: 'spin nurse' has been heard on BBC Radio 4.
4 Nicholas Jones (1995) and (1997), and Andy McSmith (1997).
5 Paul Richards (1998).
6 The 1963 estimates are from West (1963), pp. 8–9.
7 Source is David Michie (1998), p. 12. Calculated by adding the PR companies' and the in-house departments' sub-totals.
8 Compare the US turnover, estimated at $10 billion as 'a conservative estimate' by Stauber and Rampton (1995).
9 Sources: The 48,000 figure is from *Public Relations: Journal of the IPR* (1993) 11(3), p. 3, with the comment working 'in some way' and the estimate that 6,000 are eligible for IPR membership. The latest turnover figure is from Michie (1998). Gray and Hobsbawn (1996) quote a £1 billion turnover and a workforce of 22,000.
10 *Marketing* published a guide (29.5.1997, p. 111) which reported that the 'top' 135 PR agencies employed 5,311 people.
11 The PR attitude is alive and well among some university staff. The author received a letter from a university colleague with the opening sentence: 'You very kindly wrote and contributed a very pleasant article for the proceedings of . . . which was greatly appreciated by us all'.
12 Source is *Research Plus*, summer 1998, p. 18. Five years earlier, the percentage was about the same: see the President's lecture by Bob Worcester, MORI chairman, to the IPR on 28.10.92.
13 *The Guardian* writes: '. . . and she was recommended for a PR post . . .'.
14 The low reputation is not confined to the UK; it is also a feature of the US literature, a search through which will quickly uncover comments such as those in a letter from Richard Cole, PR teacher from East Lansing, Michigan, USA, in *Public Relations Quarterly*, Spring 1981, Vol. 34, no. 1: 'Likely never before has public relations been more universally maligned.'
15 As the *New Machiavelli* (1997).
16 By Phil Harris and Andrew Lock (1996).
17 For a review of hired lobbyists, see Moloney (1996).
18 By White and Mazur (1995).
19 A survey carried out by the author in spring 1998. The numbers are small because the PR Educators' Forum has only 43 correspondents in 16 universities and colleges.
20 Webster (1995, p. 101): argued in relation to the public sphere concept.
21 *Viewing the Century – Noam Chomsky*, BBC Radio 3, 5.45 p.m., 21.6.98.
22 The *Creative Industries* mapping document published by the Department of Culture, Media and Sport in November 1998 estimated net revenue at £4 billion, having excluded media space costs. It gave employment to 96,000 people with 12,700 in agencies. PR does not have a separate entry in the document and is described as a related industry to advertising. It is not clear whether PR people are included in the advertising workforce total. Creative industries are defined to include music, architecture, software, arts and antiques, as well as radio and TV.
23 The second edition, published by Penguin, 1981, has some updating.
24 Grant writes (p. 32): 'If the First World War gave propaganda a bad name, advertising already had one. Long regarded as the purview of quacks and swindlers, it was becoming respectable only slowly, as the industry's attempts to curb abuses, set standards, and organise itself in a profession began to take effect.'

25 McQuail (1987, p. 293) says about PR and advertising that the 'relevant mode is mainly that of "display-attention"...'.

26 The *Creative Industries* mapping document (see note 22 in this chapter) estimates the TV and radio industry to have a revenue of £6.4 billion and to employ 63,500 people. It does not have an entry for the print media.

27 The effect of more media space to fill is described in an article by Brian MacArthur (*The Times*, 11.9.98, p. 40) about the PR tactics to maximise coverage of the Demos report on modernising the monarchy: 'A journalist quickly learns sharp lessons about the modern media industry when he becomes poacher (journalist) turned gamekeeper (PR person) and Hames (report co-author) is now a sadder and wiser man. One of these lessons, now that there are so many local and national radio and TV stations and newspapers have grown so big, is the insatiable appetite of modern news editors. They need to fill all those hours with talk or all those empty editorial pages with new articles – and a controversial subject such as the Royal Family is manna from a news editor's heaven.' In the launch day of the story, Hames gave nearly 50 interviews; spoke to audiences in Canada, Australia and New Zealand, and had previously written three articles.

28 *The Media and the PR Industry: a partnership or a marriage of convenience* (1991) London: Two-Ten Communications.

29 For an exploration of the relationship, see the regional case study by Holly Williams, a final year multi-media journalism student, 1998, at Bournemouth University, entitled 'Enemies and Allies'.

30 *The Guardian* (31.10.98, p. 26) reports that 10% of jobs – 350 jobs – on the Yorkshire Post group of newspapers are to go following a takeover. An NUJ official said 'we can see more coming as Candover looks for a return on the high price it paid, and then again if and when the papers are put up for sale'.

3 Profession of the decade – Part one

1 Three authors at least have done so since the beginning of the 1960s: West (1963), Baistow (1985), Carty (1992).

2 The sale was to an ad agency, Abbot Mead Vickers, when Freud, the great-grandson of Sigmund and son of former Liberal MP Clement, was aged 30. He started the business when he was 21. Source: *The Observer Review*, 6.9.98, p. 5.

3 'Any magazine that relies on having a big star on the cover every month and whose news stand sales depend to some extent on the appeal of that star, have already sold the pass to PRs . . . But nowadays PRs are terrifyingly efficient. They have taught all celebs never to give interviews except when they are plugging something.' Lynn Barber, 'Barbergate', *The Observer Life*, 8.11.98, pp. 16–23.

4 *The Observer*, 1.11.98 published a guide to the 300 most powerful people in the UK. Max Clifford was placed at 275.

5 *The Guardian*, 8.9.99, p. 7, 'Murder accused recruits publicist' reports that lawyers for a farmer charged of murdering an intruder have retained Max Clifford, 'the PR fixer'.

6 Note the support that Barry Horne, the hunger striker who supported animal rights, received from the Animals Betrayed Coalition. See *The Guardian*, 12.12.98, p. 8, for one example of an extensive use of the media by his supporters to get a Royal Commission on animals used for experimentation.

7 Edmund Burke, *Reflections On The Revolution in France*, first published in 1790. See 1969 Penguin edition, p. 135.

8   A fuller summary of the Lewis listing is: The media will be more multi-channel and the PR person 'must feel as comfortable on the Internet as in reading the pages of a broadsheet or tabloid newspaper'. Issues will 'move faster' between countries and between media. This media fragmentation will become more pronounced. Second, with this fragmentation 'so the opportunity grows for single-issue pressure groups to communicate immediately and powerfully directly with their audiences'. These groups are 'well organised, understand the new media extremely well and are able to appeal over the heads of conventional media to the public'.

There will be, third, the emergence of Tomorrow's Company, a stakeholding organisation which 'puts communications at the heart of competitiveness and business success. Increasingly companies will be expected to explain their actions to their stakeholders and to build sustainable relationships with all of them. As public relations practitioners, this presents for us not just a challenge but an enormous opportunity to put ourselves at the centre of strategic decision-making.'

Fourth, Tomorrow's Companies face 'a much greater demand for organisations to explain their policies and practices to their publics. Recent examples show the danger of 'serious reversal' if this is not done. 'The future of public relations is in understanding this key relationship between an organisation's publics and how accountability should be delivered.'

There is, also, globalisation making, fifth, for change and in the face of this, a 'wave' of mergers. He writes that: 'No organisation, whether domestically based or not, can, in the future, see its own market as an island and globalisation will be about understanding how shifts in geo-global political movements can affect business judgements.' Environmental anxiety is moving to the top of the policy-making agenda (e.g. global warming and pollution). PR people 'will need to understand how this mood will influence the attitudes and opinions of governments and consumers'.

Seventh is the 'youth effect', because young people are taking on 'responsibilities at a time in their lives which would not have seemed possible a generation ago'. The attitudes and opinions of the generation born in the 1970s and 1980s 'will shape the twenty-first century'.

Eighth, legal, accountancy and management firms could be 'entering our business and making a significant success'.

Ninth, PR is an unregulated industry and 'we run the constant risk of transgressing standards which the Institute and others seek to set but, also, the risk of having regulation imposed upon us'. The industry should be in the forefront of the regulatory debate 'in order that we can set the terms for the discussion and eventual decisions that will be made'. Tenth, there is growing demand for PR. 'We are living in, and benefitting from, a growth period in public relations.'

9   The literature on voluntary groups is replete with distinctions between interest, sectional, pressure, cause and promotional groups. As Alderman (1984) has pointed out, making these distinctions has turned into an academic speciality all of its own. This section of the text concentrates on pressure and cause groups where the object of association is more ideological than material, and where membership is drawn from diverse occupational backgrounds. The distinction hoped for is that between a business group or a trade union, on the one hand, and an environmental or racial equality group, on the other.

10 Wring details the public relations strategy of Herbert Morrison, the 1930s

Labour leader of the London County Council, with support from the unions and with professional PR people at County Hall.

11   See Grant (1995) Chapter 1 for a discussion about the connection of social movements to voluntary groups and their proliferation. Note p. 13: 'A count of the primary and secondary groups in Britain . . . would almost certainly run into tens of thousands.' See p. 2 for business represented by over 1,800 trade associations.

12   *The Directory of British Associations* (1998) records 6,800 entries compared with 6,000 in 1969.

13   A married couple, the Bramleys who went missing with their two foster daughters for 17 weeks, were reported to be in contact with Max Clifford just before they came out of hiding. See *The Observer*, 17.1.99, p. 6, 'Dramatic end to runaway saga'.

14   As on the BBC Radio 4 *Today* programme 30.1.99 when presenter Anna Ford and the planning director of Birmingham Chambers of Commerce agreed that the 'eco warriors' had won the 'PR battle' over the North Midlands toll motorway.

15   Business supporters are well aware of activists' groups 'which have mastered the media . . .': business is urged not to pay 'danegeld' to 'corporate responsibility revivalists'. See Halfon (1998).

16   See *The Times*, 22.3.99, p. 46, 'Swampy joins forces with lawyers and insurers'.

17   In between the very resource-rich and -poor groups are bodies like the Christchurch Chamber of Trade and Industry in Dorset. Its mission statement says the Chamber will 'represent members' views to the relevant local and national bodies, both statutory and non-statutory'.

18   Information from a telephone interveiw, 19.1.99, with Julie Walsh, Director of the Community Organisations' Forum, Tower Hamlets. This is the umbrella body linking local groups with London, regional and national bodies, especially those with regeneration funds. It does PR itself: a monthly newsletter, lobbying and media relations.

19   Information from a telephone interview with Andrew Fellows of the National Association of Councils for Voluntary Services, 27.1.99.

20   Information from a telephone interview with Adam Gaines, Director of Public Affairs for the National Council for Voluntary Organisations, 4.2.99.

21   Taken from the advertisement by the British Trust for Conservation Volunteers, *The Guardian* media section, 14.12.98, p. 20. The work is, *inter alia*, about 'well-targeted communications strategies', 'secure high profile and focused' publicity, 'managing campaigns and events', 'overseeing' a website, and 'co-ordinating internal communications'.

22   The increase in pressure group activity has been criticised (e.g. Brittan (1995), Olson (1982)) on the grounds that it unduly influences public policy when government controls a large proportion of national income, leading to ills such as pluralist stagnation, pork barrel politics and making the UK 'ungovernable'. Insofar as PR strengthens group activity, these authors, often from a public choice theory stance, will disapprove of it.

23   The Foreword is by Robert S. Lynd.

24   The chairman of Rolls Royce threatened to take the company's manufacturing out of the UK and switch it to the USA if the UK government introduced too many EU labour market and social welfare reforms, according to the *Guardian*, 25.11.98, p. 3. *The Observer*, 29.11.98, p. 9, reported that UK business was concerned about the trade consequences of extraditing General Pinochet to Spain for trial on human rights matters.

25 PR agencies reinforce the business orientation of PR studies. Harrison Cowley, a regional network of PR firms, offers student awards (December 1998) '. . . a complete launch programme of [a] new wine – targeted exclusively at UK wine drinkers – which will achieve national heavyweight coverage'.

26 The author remembers that the Labour government's 1964 national plan was distributed publicly in booklet form.

4 Profession of the decade – Part two

1 There is a distinction to be drawn between media outlets and their ownership, and the possible positive and negative correlations between them, i.e. there can be fewer owners of more outlets and more owners of fewer outlets. Most PR people would favour more outlets over less, and would be more indifferent to more owners over less. More outlets increase the opportunities for favoured audiences to receive persuasive messages.

2 See *The Observer* Business section 15.11.98, p. 15, for a report.

3 A later and current version of the 'tabloid' and 'broadsheet' split. Introduced perhaps to narrow the distinction that had grown up between 'sensationalist' and 'quality' press. Markets blur distinctions so that they can grow.

4 See, for example, the working paper of Sue Lewis: the number of journalists on Yorkshire papers is dropping while PR people are increasing. 'An evaluation of the importance of public relations sources to daily newspaper business editors in Yorkshire' was given at the Public Relations Educators' Forum, Leeds Metropolitan University, 3–4 September 1998.

5 About the USA, Dowie wrote in the introduction to Stauber and Rampton (1995) that 40% of all 'news' flows 'virtually unedited from the public relations offices, prompting a prominent PR exec [sic] to boast that "the best PR ends up looking like news"'.

6 See *The Guardian* Media section, 30.8.99, pp. 8–9. Also *The Observer* Media section 15.11.98, p. 10 reports on this growth. It summed up the task of making the magazine readable to consumers: 'the sexing of the J-cloth' and 'extolling the virtues of Kleenex toilet tissue'.

7 A trend spotted by Max Clifford: he earns his living from such work. See 'Privacy on parade', *The Guardian* Saturday Review 14.11.98, p. 2. This article could be read as the 'testament of a professional publicist'.

8 *The Sunday Times* 15.11.98, p. 7, reports 'Oxford signs Rigg in don "star wars"' on the appointment of Dame Diana, who was Emma Peel in *The Avengers*, as professor of theatre studies. Either this story was written because the news pages were empty or the following comment in the story is correct: 'Universities appoint famous people because it encourages students to apply.'

9 The quotations are from 'Privacy on parade' ibid (see note 6). Max Clifford is ubiquitous in this period. Two days beforehand, *The Guardian* G2 section carried the article 'How to give good interview [sic]' pp. 2–3. Part of it was with Max Clifford on how he would advise Monica Lewinsky to conduct herself in an interview. The writer quotes him as saying: ' "I would tell her to break down at a crucial time during the interview." That's a bit shockingly cynical, isn't it? "Look, this is a PR strategy, it is not a question of morals".'

10 See *The Guardian*, 'Celebrity nobodies', 23.6.98, p. 18.

11 See *Marketing* 26.11.98, pp. 16–17. For an American admission to living in the complaint culture, see 'Last of the student whine', *Financial Times* Weekend, 12.12.98, p. III.

12 For a journalist's view of 'trash TV', PR opportunities for self-promotion and disillusionment, see 'Tricky Nicky', *The Guardian* media section, 11.1.99, p. 4.

13   If Tannen wanted a time line for radio as public argument, she could have traced back to the 'radio priest' Fr. Charles Caughlin of the 1930s in the USA. He was a major influence in the early development of talk radio. His latest biographer (Warren, 1996) describes his broadcasting as anti-semitic, anti-communist, anti-international finance and pro-fascist.

14   Examples taken from Corcom '99 conference of the International Association of Business Communicators, London, 23–24.2.99.

15   See *PR Week*, 2.10.98, p. 7.

16   Business television shares with websites the challenge of constantly updating material. See *PR Week*, 18.6.99, p. 13.

17   Author experience in the early 1970s. A sign of limited editorial freedom is a disclaimer about the views expressed being those of individuals and not of the organisation. For those working on employee communications, the aggravation lies in checking all copy with senior management. Harrison notes (1995, p. 119) that relinquishing control by managers may make them 'uncomfortable, but it encourages openness and aims closer to the participative style of management'.

18   Examples taken from *PR Week* 9.7.99, pp. 13–4, 'Creating a breed of company converts'. *PR Week* 6.11.98 reports, p. 1, that it is presenting its fourth 'Communicating Business Strategy' with the theme of 'Your Staff as Brand Evangelists'.

19   Business and organisational studies generally take a more relaxed attitude towards persuasion. See Chapter 2 'The gentle art of persuasion: influencing others' in Hargie et al. (1999). The association by the Grunigian paradigm between 'bad' PR and persuasion may have its roots in the association between PR and propaganda, and the perception that persuasion has a linking role between the two. Another explanation for a negative association is the preference of academics for cognitive constructions of the world, rather than affective ones involving phenomena which they categorise as emotive, such as persuasion. Hargie et al. are followed in their distinction (p. 23) between 'persuasion' and 'influence': the persuador is a conscious actor; the influencer is not.

20   See Murphy (1991) for more on mixed motive PR.

5 The balance sheet

1   The huckster origins of PR can be traced to the American circus owner B.P. Barnum and other contemporaries at the end of the nineteenth century. It was said of these publicists by a contemporary journalist that they were 'the only group of men proud of being called liars'. Source: a review by S. Rampton of Ewen's (1996) book *PR! A social history of spin*, published on the internet by the Centre for Media and Democracy which describes itself as a 'nonprofit, public interest organisation dedicated to investigative reporting on the public relations industry'. The 'liar' comment should be read in conjunction with the views of Max Clifford on PR quoted in Chapter 1. Goldman (1948, endnote 2) notes 28 entries in the *American Thesaurus of Slang*. They include 'advertisementor', 'aide-de-press', 'flesh peddler', 'pufflicity man', 'space grabber', and 'tooter'.

2   Jensen goes on (p. 69): 'Furthermore, in certain circumstances, [message] receivers expect these hemispheric messages, and are on their guard. Their critical capabilities are aroused when they know what to expect ... But when audience's [sic] do not expect half-messages ... serious ethical problems are present.' Lisa Jardine of Queen Mary and Westfield College, London makes the same first point (*The Observer*, 20.9.98, p. 28) as Jensen: 'Those who buy

into pop culture are extremely shrewd about its effect on them ... In our media-savvy society, each of us makes a decision on whether to "buy in" ... or stay out and be "different".'

3   Cialdini, however, does not reference public relations in his index and an inspection of the text did not reveal many examples of compliance involving PR. His principles for gaining compliance: consistency, reciprocation, social proof, authority, liking, scarcity, and the self-interest of the compliant.

4   See Seitel (1995, p. 6) for how American PR leaders counted 472 in 1975. Experienced PR people more or less avoid any conversation about definitions. Those who are happy with the term 'PR' can be called 'PR loyalist'.

5   Prof. Benno Signitzer from Vienna University made this typology in a lecture at Bournemouth University during a sabbatical term in 1991. It was written up in a lecture guide entitled 'Theoretical approaches that can help understand Public Relations'.

6   The ability of PR to take new titles to itself and benefit from any connotative advantage in them is quite marked. Contract publishing that was, is now becoming consumer magazine publishing. See *Campaign*, 12.2.99, p. 18, 'John Brown enters unfamiliar territory with Waitrose tie-up'.

7   PR people are active on the internet, watching to defend their organisations against 'cyber-activists'. An example is McDonalds in response to the London Greenpeace supporters who were on trial for libel in what is known as the McLibel trial. See *PR Week*, 12.3.99, pp. 19–20.

8   This discussion is from the PR producers' viewpoint. Looked at from the PR consumers'/audiences' point of view, it can be restated as the perception: reality relationship. Where the perceptions of PR consumers/audiences about PR messages are in line with organisational and group reality as perceived by consumers/audiences, PR is seen an 'honest broker'; where perceptions about PR messages are out of line, PR consumers/audiences will note whether PR producers are bringing their communications further into or out of line with consumer/audience perceptions.

9   Brebner wrote as a former public servant of the British Transport Commission and of the London Passenger Transport Board. His examples are mostly from the public sector. He was published by a voluntary sector body on behalf of The Institute of Public Administration, a provenance reflecting an early definition of PR which emphasised government/citizen relations. See Chapter 9. His argument on the specialist or non-specialist nature of PR is confused: he seems to present it as 'the one specialist skill' which deals with 'the evils of specialisation' (Brebner 1949, p. 10).

10 But no more than half of its emphasis. There can be no reform of PR without considering its consumers, those who are compliant to some degree. More work needs to be done on the effects of PR on its consumers.

11 'The Public Relations Sector' by BDO Stoy Hayward (1994).

12 This has been put in a more contentious way by Geoff Nightingale (1989, p. 16), president of Synergenics Inc, the management consulting division of the American PR firm Burson Marstellar, in a privately published collection of his quotations: 'We are living in an overcommunicated society. And the only possible answer to the overcommunicated society is the oversimplified society.'

13 Goldenberg (1975), in her study of resource poor groups in the Boston metropolitan area, did not list PR as a resource for accessing the policy-making process. If a similar study was done today, it is argued that such groups would be found using it.

14 Examples include the Beirut hostages who had support groups working for them in the UK; Irish people wrongly jailed for alleged terrorism offences;

various academics alleging victimisation by their institutions; humanitarian aid workers raising awareness and funds for disasters; the parents of the murdered black teenager Stephen Lawrence. These groups can also be at the receiving end of PR campaigns against them. See *The Observer*, 21.2.99, p. 15, 'Lawrences face police backlash' via criticisms of their lawyers. See also *The Guardian*, 20.1.99, p. 1, ' "Our boys are innocent" ' for PR activity in favour of the five youths suspected of the murder.

15   Gandy (1982) was the first to publish on this concept.

16   'Principal' means here the most important usage in terms of vital tasks and is not a volume indicator. As regards volume, marketing public relations is probably the principal usage.

17   Bernays (1947) wrote, to the dismay of his colleagues, about the 'Engineering of consent'. It lacked, in their view, the discretion of knowing when to say less.

18   Schnattschneider (1975, p. 31) noted the 'pro-business or upper-class bias'of the American pressure group system.

19   Quoted on p. 131 of Ewen, as cited in Beale (1936) p. 546 and Cochran and Miller (1942) p. 333.

20   The Laswell reference refers to his entry on propaganda in the *Encylopedia of Social Sciences*.

21   Tye (1998, p. 169) notes in his biography of Bernays that ' "Propaganda" was a word Bernays seldom used in a pejorative sense'.

22   See the interview in Olasky (1987, p. 81): 'We cannot have chaos . . . and that is where public relations counsellors can prove their effectiveness, by making the public believe that human gods are watching over us for our own benefit.'

23   See Tye's (1998) biography of Bernays.

24   See the Reith Lectures by Edward Said in 1993 on the role of intellectuals in society. *The Independent*, 24.6.1993, p. 24, reproduces a version of the first one.

25   Lee was an expert on railway affairs and wrote technical articles about their tariffs. His expertise outside of PR was one of his attractions to his industrial clients. After working for Rockefeller, he became knowledgeable about what we would now call welfare capitalism. He lectured at the LSE, London, on that subject and on railways, apparently (see Hiebert 1966, p. 59). See Tye (1998) for the breadth of Bernays' output.

26   Concepts are renamed over time: note that the sociobiology of the 1970s has become the evolutionary psychology of the millennium. See *The Times Higher*, 12.3.99, p. 18, 'Human nature totally explained' for a statement of this argument.

27   See Stauber and Rampton (1995), pp. 21–4.

28   Unlike Bernays and Lee, Grunig is not an operational PR man, but a teacher and researcher.

29   This negative connotation given to persuasion in PR, and therefore its association with propaganda and manipulation, is rejected in Chapter 4.

30   This Utrecht lecture is the shortest and clearest statement by Grunig of his and Hunt's typology.

31   Habermas' translator notes, in his introduction, that the German word *Offentlichkeit* can be rendered in three ways: (the) public, public sphere, publicity.

32   In *Communication World*, Feb/Mar 1999, pp. 13–21. It is the newsletter of the International Business Communicators' Association.

6 PR as manipulation and propaganda

1   L'Etang has nominated among others the documentary film-maker John Grierson; Sir Charles Higham, an enthusiast for managing public opinion; Alan Campbell-Johnson, Lord Mountbatten's Press Secretary in India 1947–8 and President of the IPR in 1956–7; J.H. Brebner who worked for the Post Office, for the Ministry of Information and for the nationalised transport industries, and who wrote the first UK book on PR; S.C. Leslie, a PR man at the Gas, Coke and Light Co. in the 1930s, who later became a civil servant and who called for a Ministry of Public Enlightenment; Sir Stephen Tallents, secretary of the Empire Marketing Board; A.P. Ryan who managed the 'Mr. Therm' campaign and was later Assistant Controller of Public Relations at the BBC in the 1930s. See her 1999 paper on Grierson's influence on PR. Gillman (1978) lists a host of other names, perhaps not so prominent in the main.

2   See L'Etang's article in *Public Relations Review* (1998) for the sensitivity about associating PR with propaganda: she starts with an apology for so doing.

3   Grant (1994) in her review of domestic publicity by government in the period 1918–39 uses the terms interchangeably.

4   They used the phrase (p. 4) in reaction to the rising government spending on advertising and the Government Information Service.

5   A poignant example of active persuasion by PR was the 1999 DTI leaflet inserted in newspapers entitled 'Killed in Her Bed', about carbon monoxide poisoning by domestic heating systems.

6   Figures supplied by the COI on 30.9.99 for the majority of government departments, but excluding the Metropolitan Police, the Health Education Authority, Scottish Office, Northern Ireland Office and National Savings.

7   The government's proposals for the regulation of referendum spending are signs of sensitivity about public information campaigns. Government withdrawal from public campaigning at a fixed period before the vote and spending limits for the contesting parties are suggested.

8   This frequency was pointed out by David Blunkett, Secretary of State for Education and Employment, on the BBC Radio 4 *Today* news programme after 8 a.m. on 16.9.98. When asked by John Humphreys whether this was propaganda, he replied 'no' and noted that the programmes often used storylines for passing information.

9   Grant gives this example and notes that 'prestige advertising' was the term used for it. Bernays used it in the USA: he promoted the lorry manufacturer Mack by promoting the development of an inter-state highway system.

10   The source of attribution of PR people to individual organisations is from either L'Etang or Gillman. The latter was an IPR president and BOAC public relations chief. He notes that in 1809 the Treasury, which was porte-parole for foreign policy, asked the War, Foreign Affairs and Admiralty departments to read the papers each morning and send on a summary or 'a hint of the line which it wished should be taken'.

11   The early history of PR in the UK is under-researched. L'Etang has made the most notable published contribution. The factual description given here draws heavily on her work.

12   Williams' count of propagandists and PR people in January 1944 is Ministry of Information in the UK, 2,719; civil ministries, 661; armed forces ministries, 1016.

13   There is a circularity here. Basil Clarke was a journalist turned PR man who worked for the Health Ministry. Earlier he worked in Dublin explaining British government policy at the time of the Irish War of Independence. See Gillman for the short reference.

14   He concludes, however, on a congratulatory note. His last paragraph includes the following: 'the vast majority of PR activity has always been innocuous and at best a force for enlightenment.'

15   Adonis and Pollard (1997) note, in their analysis of class in the contemporary UK, that the elite wants to eliminate the term 'class' from debate.

16   This campaign produced the memorable, PR-friendly phrase that nuclear power would produce electricity 'too cheap to meter'.

17   L'Etang (1999) reports that in the 1920s and 1930s, the trade union The National Association of Local Government Officers used PR nationally and at branch level to bolster their professsional role as agents for delivering state services to the public.

18   Senior PR employees are well paid, earning over £100,000 p.a., but they (4%) are at the top of a long ladder with most (70%) under £50,000. Source: 1998 Membership Survey of the IPR. The owners of PR agencies sell their businesses for millions, this was especially true in the 1980s, or for little. In that regard, PR people cannot 'buck' the market.

19   McNair (1996) in L'Etang and Pieczka, p. 36.

20   Tedlow concludes about American academics (1979, p. 205) that 'The public relations of public relations among intellectuals has deteriorated steadily since the days of the watchdog activities of the Institute for Propaganda Analysis [est. 1937].' Tye (1998, p. 297) still notes coyness by academics in front of PR: Harvard gave him a grant for his biography of Bernays 'while most academic institutions and foundations shied away from a book in public relations'.

21   Tim Traverse-Healy (1988) *Public Relations and Propaganda – Values compared*, p. 5.

22   The UK exceptions are L'Etang and the author.

23   Jowett and O'Donnell say in the introduction (p. ix) that they do not cover advertising 'although presented as the most prevalent form of propaganda in the US'. On p. 266, they write: 'The economy dictates the flow of propaganda relative to the sale and consumption of goods.' This could be read as an implicit reference to PR for marketing purposes.

24   O'Shaughnessy notes (1999) that 'while all propaganda is necessarily biased, much bias is not all propagandist'.

25   Grant quotes (p. 12) the following, *inter alia*, as concerned about gullibility of the masses: J.S. Mill, L.T. Hobhouse, Jose Ortega y Gasset, Everett Dean Martin, N. Angell, H. Henderson.

26   There was no problem in this matter for Sir Bernard Ingham when he was the Prime Minister's Press Secretary during the Falklands War. He wrote in *PR Week*, 7.5.99, p. 3 about the Kosovo war that 'I have tried over the airwaves to ridicule journalists' pompous concern over whether they are being manipulated by propaganda. Of course, they are being manipulated by propaganda.' During the Kosovo conflict, Serbian TV broadcasting was usually called propaganda by BBC journalists: it is hard to remember instances of their calling UK broadcasting by the same term.

27   This writer owns up to a chapter in the book edited by Philip Kitchen.

28   See p. 15 of Gregory (1996). See also p. 16: 'To understand how public relations programmes and campaigns are planned and managed, it is first essential to understand the role of public relations in business.'

29   The introduction offers a precise statement of voluntary sector attitudes towards PR: 'Public relations is seen by many people as meaning slick commercial techniques, used by people who do not care about the subject ... Selling a cause "like a packet of cornflakes" is regarded with great distaste by campaigners.'

30 See Moss and Warnaby (1997) pp. 9–10, for a schema of the four types, progressing from propaganda to symmetrical.

7 Communicative equality and markets

1 The methodology employed in this book is a combination of the inductive and the critical theory approaches. It is inductive, recording in an accumulative way the opinions of the relevant literature, a succession of examples of PR in practice, demographics about it as an industry, reactions from the field by PR producers and consumers, and comments by observers to substantiate the case of pervasiveness and low reputation. It borrows from critical theory in that the application of analytical reasoning to the social phenomena under discussion leads to conclusions consistent with the concepts employed by the reasoning and consistent with the empirical data. An example would be that the usually accepted definition of an MP's role in representative democracy in the UK (an MP uses his judgement of the public interest and/or his constituency interest to determine his behaviour in Parliament and not of his personal, material interest) would lead to the reasonable conclusion in the light of the known data about the cash-for-questions episode in the early 1990s that MPs are acting in a way inconsistent with representative democracy by taking cash in envelopes from outside interests. Stepping out of 'reasoned' discourse, the 'inconsistent' conclusion could become 'morally wrong' or 'morally unacceptable' if the discourse became ethically based. The combination of opinions in the literature, data from the field plus reasoned analysis and occasional, flagged ethical judgements (especially in the last chapter) is the methodology of this book.

2 The consumer as: chooser, communicator, explorer, identity-seeker, hedonist or artist, victim, rebel, activist, citizen.

3 See *The Observer*, 3.1.99, business section p. 7, 'The euro begins stroll up the high street'.

4 Marketing PR does have enough history, though, to include Bernays who worked for Procter and Gamble for more than 30 years, as well as American Tobacco, New Jersey Telephone, Dodge Brothers Automobiles and Filene's Department Store. The source is an internet *Museum Of Public Relations* at http://www.prmuseum.com/1915-1922.html as gateway.

5 *PR Week*, 21.8.98, pp. 11–18, In-house survey. Based on '229 organisations throughout the UK'.

6 PR communication by one business with another is done under the title of business-to-business PR. PR which is not principally concerned with goods and services but with the corporate aspects of organisations (e.g. relations with government or investors) is known as corporate PR (CPR). This sector employs most of the remaining 30% of PR people.

7 See the variety of communications channels at work in the 'lifestyle' sections of newspapers and in 'style' magazines where ads, product/price/sales point information, feature articles, photographs and competitions co-exist – sometimes in the same edition.

8 Kotler in his 9th edition (1997) of *Marketing Management* notes the change of relative usage in the US (p. 672): 'As the power of mass advertising weakens, marketing managers are turning more to MPR. In a survey of 286 U.S. marketing managers, three quarters reported that their companies were using MPR.' The *Business Ratio Plus* 1997 (14th) edition on advertising from ICC Business Publications, Hampton, London reports (p. 71) 'some shift away

from "traditional" advertising towards the use of direct marketing techniques'. This benefits PR.

9   See the *Financial Times*, 23.11.98, p. 10, 'Celebrity endorsement proves recipe for success'. It gives examples of positive and negative endorsement. A reason given for its potency is association of the viewer/buyer with the 'famous' via the endorsed item. BBC2 carried 'Delia's How To Cook' in October/November 1998.

10   Media studies writers would treat these events as 'pseudo-events' and as frivolous examples of making news and agenda setting.' See Curran and Seaton (1988, 3rd edn.) *Power Without Responsibility* London, Routledge, pp. 232–6.

11   *PR Week* (2.10.98, p. 13) reports that 'There is no doubt that conducting a suvey is an excellent way to generate publicity for a client' and that the polling organisation NOP has 'over 200 PR agencies as regular customers'.

12   One should muse before the attraction of the ironic wrapped up in banal expression. The film *The Producers* contained the lyric 'Springtime for Hitler' with the couplet 'Don't be stupid, be a smarty, come and join the Nazi Party'.

13   The caption to the associated photograph reads: 'Bournemouth, once a somnolent town synonymous with bath-chairs, is riding a PR wave and reinvented (sic) itself as BoMo.'

14   High culture goods also uses MPR. *The Times Higher* (9.10.98, p. 16) described competitions such as the Booker prize for best novel as those 'blending writing, money and public relations'. At whatever cultural level, much of PR is 'froth' defined as obvious pandering to customer/client interests and vanity in a trivial way. Witness a *PR Week* section (9.10.98, p. 10) on 'Christmas Gifts and Incentives': 'Avon ... matches make-up to journalists'. Once, alcohol was enough.

15   Quoted from *The Cause Related Marketing Guidelines*, published by Business in the Community, 1998.

16   Quoted from *The Game Plan: Cause Related Marketing Qualitative Consumer Research*, published by Business in the Community, 1997.

17   ibid

18   The author recalls the debate happening in the late 1960s when he listened to PR colleagues telling him that PR directors in the boardroom were sure to outnumber marketing ones in a short time.

19   Bell is suspicious 'of academics in my real PR world' (p. 29). 'Could it be that there is a correlation between PR as an insecure, immature industry unable to agree a universal definition, and the emergence of the academic as a cloak of respectability?'

20   The literature tends to elide marketing into marketing communications, but it is hard to argue that the former's market research, product design, testing and development, and production aspects are integrating with PR.

21   Not only in cinema is PR old established. Read the *Financial Times* Weekend section, 2.1.99, p. iii for an interview with Eleanor Lambert, the 95-year-old American fashion PR who started work in 1930 and is now known as the Empress of Seventh Avenue. Why does she still do PR? 'I still have ideas, I suppose.'

22   The Conservative adminstrations practised their belief in market communications. Expenditure by Government on advertising in 1992 was £53 million. Source: Deacon and Golding (1994, p. 4).

23   Word-of-mouth between consumers in retail markets is the largest source of non-mediated communications.

24 See *The Guardian*, 19.2.99, p. 6, for the ad. The story was also carried editorially: see *The Daily Telegraph* p. 12 the next day.
25 See Sinclair (1987, pp. 20–2) for a discussion on the consequences of abolishing the distinction between information and persuasion in advertising which is relevant to the cognate activity of MPR.
26 For the latter two, they should turn to pp. 90–3 and p. 88 of Chonko (1995).
27 Guidance on doing City PR is contained in *Through the thicket* (1995, 2nd ed.), produced by the Financial Communications Committee, set up by the IPR, the PRCA and the Investor Relations Society.
28 See Michie (1998, pp. 25–44): 'Nowhere is the PR industry dirtier than in pockets of the City, where the censuring of major PR firms ... for mishandling price-sensitive information should not distract attention from the fact that their real offence was getting caught.'

8 PR, electoral politics and lobbying

1 See Boorstin (1961) *The Image, or, What happened to the American Dream*, Chapter 1 for their origins: he involves journalists and politicans in their development as well as PR people.
2 One title for this skill transfer into politics is Machiavellian marketing, a movement tracked by Harris and Lock (1996). See also Harris et al. (1999).
3 That Harold Wilson found PR 'degrading' is in a letter of Malcolm Muggeridge to *The Times* of 27.6.61. In the letter, Muggeridge refers to his own description of PR as organised lying. From West (1963, p. 97).
4 See Norris et al. (1999, p. 9) where they set out their model of the process and effects of political communications in election campaigns. See also index where there are no entries for public relations, marketing or spin doctors, nor any incidental references in the text where propaganda is referred to. This absence is in line with many other political, cultural and media studies texts.
5 Dick Morris, the Republican political consultant who helped President Clinton develop policies which distinguished his administration from the Republican leadership and the Democratic Congressional leadership, and used polling to find what those policies were, could be a candidate for celebrity status. Freidenberg does not list PR in the index yet he claims Bernays as 'the first true forerunner of the contemporary political consultant', and notes him as 'the first modern public relations expert' (p. 16).
6 So far the species 'astroturf lobbier' has not been spotted: they develop in the field support for policy or person where none existed beforehand.
7 See *PR Week*, 26.3.99, p. 11, 'Should political candidates hire their own PR agencies?'
8 See *The Economist*, 17.7.99, p. 29, 'Televising Parliament Zero Rated'.
9 William Harston, *The Independent*, Friday Review, 3.7.1998, p. 7, dates the earliest use of spin in its modern political sense to late 1986. There is a class system for spinning in the UK: spin nurse has been spotted.
10 But not all spin doctors are in politics and those who are not tend to avoid publicity. See Hollingsworth (1997) on Sir Tim Bell.
11 Source is TV Channel Four News, 7 p.m., 6.7.1998.
12 He quotes (p. 13) Charlie Whelan with 'You have to be economical with the truth sometimes, although you should never lie, but it's very difficult', and (p. 15) Ed Balls, special advisor to the Chancellor of the Exchequer, with 'our job is to explain, sell, justify, package'.
13 The status of government press officers is a political issue. See *The Times*,

18.8.99, p. 2, 'Blair PR unit condemned', for a Tory attack on the alleged centralisation in Downing Street of the government information service through setting up a central 'rapid rebuttal unit'. An editorial in the same edition says: 'The provision of information unsullied by spin doctors is essential to oil the wheels of public debate.' The same article claims that the New Labour government has spent £4 million on special advisers, twice the amount of the previous Tory administration. The Press Secretary to Mrs Thatcher, Sir Bernard Ingham, reports that in its first year, New Labour dismissed 25 of the 44 senior information officers. See *PR Week*, 6.8.99, p. 8.

14   See *Confessions of a Spin Doctor*, Channel Four, 25.9.99, 7–8 p.m., for a view into the over-emotional, manipulative world of some political press officers.

15   The BBC2 TV programme Correspondent (31.10.98, 7.15 p.m.) examined the White House press corps, the most contested site in the world for government/media relations. The internet gives the opportunity of control to third parties. That may be good for liberal democracy.

16   The 'outsider'/'insider' distinction is Grant's (1989).

17   The Transport and General Workers Union is using the lobbying firm APCO to publicise their 'Don't Fly Lufthansa' campaign after 270 workers were sacked. The firm will campaign in Germany and in Brussels. See *PR Week*, 23.7.99, p. 4, Public Sector column. An advertisement for the campaign was in the directory for the Labour Party Conference, 1999.

18   See Moloney (1996).

19   See Moloney (1996) pp. 8–11, for activity levels; see *PR Week*, 26.2.99, p. 11 'Lobbyists turn to the local experts'.

20   See *The Daily Telegraph*, 20.2.99, p. 22, 'GM foods: we stand firm' by Tony Blair.

21   West finishes his book with: 'When people care so little for any cause that they leave the business or the argument to the experts, our society will be ripe for rule by an oligarchy of PROs and Professor Rollo Swavely will hold the chair of Image Building at MacMillan College, Oxford.'

22   See Moloney (1996), pp. 2–8, 79–82.

23   See Moloney (1996), pp. 36–64.

24   See Shaw (1996). The advice includes: have a 'fear and loathing' relationship with officials, forge coalitions, use the media for results rather than coverage, and organise events. The book is a social movement equivalent of a DIY book on PR for business.

25   In the US, loyalists are fewer. By 1987, only six of the top US agencies used 'public relations' in their titles and only 75 of the Fortune 500 companies did so. Source: the paper 'Tracing the parallel evolution of public affairs and public relations: An examination of practice, scholarship and teaching' at The Fifth International Public Relations Research Symposium, Lake Bled, Slovenia, 1998.

26   Irish PR people are reported to be against a register in the Irish Parliament requiring them and political journalists to declare their interests. See *PR Week*, 19.2.99, p. 7, 'Irish lobbyist register criticised by institute'.

27   Meeting frequencies is important political information. A Parliamentary Question about meetings between the biotechnology industry and the UK government on genetic modification in food got the reply that 100 were held between May 1997 and Spring 1999. Source is BBC Radio 4 *Today* programme, 16.6.99, 7.45 a.m.

28   See *PR Week* 9.7.99, p. 2 for both suggestions.

29   David Hencke in *The Guardian*, 14.8.98, p. 15, estimates 65 public bodies.

9 PR, journalism and the media

1 See *PR Week*, 2.7.99, p. 8, 'Gannett's Newsquest acquisition threatens regional democracy' for an American media group, '. . . attracted by the profitability of the consolidating regional press', bidding for a UK regional newspaper group with an eye to its websites, internet auctions and electronic directories. The American vice-chairman is quoted as saying: 'We like the way they create product, initiating new products and what they are doing with the internet.'

2 The phrase is from the Henley Centre for Consumer Change. For a commentary on the connections, see *The Observer*, 7.2.99, p. 26, 'Hoddle's blood. Better than sex for selling papers'.

3 Grant notes (pp. 33–4) that Pick was a solicitor and statistician and got his job in charge of publicity only because he complained about its quality, and that Stephen Tallents who was one of the most influential publicists of the inter-war years was a career civil servant with no experience in PR.

4 Could the phenomenon be seen differently from the media's viewpoint? Is there a journalisation of PR going on? The thought is occasioned by Mathew Annis, a third year undergraduate journalism student at Bournemouth.

5 See Franklin (1997), p. 4.

6 See *The Guardian* Editor section, 17.9.99, pp. 12–13, 'News at a price'.

7 Reported in *PR Week*, 23.10.98, p. 15.

8 Thanks to Philip MacGregor for these observations on working practice.

9 A justification for journalists' attitudes towards PR is compressed into Baistow's title for his chapter on PR: 'The Fifth Estate makes news'.

10 See the *Guardian*, 10.7.99, p. 20, 'Put the brakes on freebies', and *PR Week*, 13.8.99, p. 6, 'Freebies and the personal finance sector shouldn't mix'.

11 See *Management Today*, Jan. 1999, pp. 29–32.

12 A good example is the journalist who became managing director of the PR firm Text 100. See the *Guardian*, 15.8.98, Jobs p. 16: interesting quote on 'changing sides'.

13 The memory of Valerie Cowley, who was a national newspaper journalist. The memory also of the author, who worked on the regional press.

14 Notes from the session by Professor Peter Golding at the Media and Democracy seminar, Loughborough University, 6 January 1998.

15 Others have followed: Kizzi Nkwoocha is known as 'the black Max'. See the *Guardian* The Week section, 14.3.98, p. 5.

16 Ekow Eshun writes in *The Guardian*, 'Celebrity nobodies', 23.6.98, p. 18.

17 Reported by Drs. Rachel Gibson and Stephen Ward at the Media and Democracy seminar, see note 14.

10 Inside PR

1 See Franklin (1997) pp. 25–35 for the variations in journalists' images.

2 'PR has become respectable, especially in the City . . . where merchant banks insist on public companies appointing a PR consultant as part of the advisory team, during a takeover battle . . .', reported Airdre Taylor of Taylor Bennett, a head-hunting firm, in the London *Evening Standard*, 28.2.98, p. 39. Also read Michie (1998) Part one for a self-assured rebuttal about low status.

3 Sennett (1998) in *The Corrosion of Character* wrote about Rose who went into New York advertising in middle age; found that 30 was old; middle age was rejected; networking was all and that 'The trick is, let nothing stick to you'.

4 Miller (1999) did a US survey of 51 novels and 67 film portrayals of PR people going back to the 1930s.

5   Valerie Cowley notes that PRs can handle the reputation of their principles in two ways: as manipulative 'fixers' or as tending 'gardeners'.
6   See Dowling (1994) for multiple reputations.
7   See Kruckeberg and Starck (1988) p. 20: 'Organisations want to survive and prosper. Adverse public opinion – especially in a free and democratic society – can threaten such survival and prosperity, while positive public opinion can help assure survival and prosperity.'
8   PR benefits from some of its association with Royalty. Read the *Sun* 6.1.99, Sun Woman section, p. 2, about the engagement of Prince Edward and Sophie Rhys-Jones for a temporary cessation of hostility: 'At last the waiting is over for the Royal match made in PR heaven'; there is, however, the counter-balancing 'But there was a time when we wondered if the PR dream wasn't simply a smokescreen of convenience'.
9   There is some awareness that lawyers could do lobbying. See 'Lawyer Lobby-ists in Brussels' in *Newsletter of the ECPR Standing Group on European Level Interest Representation,* January 1999, vol. 5, no. 1, p. 23 for the view that American style lawyer/lobbyists are appearing in Brussels. Available from Robert Gordon University, Scotland.
10 Reich lists them seventh in a primary list of eleven and before a secondary list of twenty six. This counting is trivial, maybe revealing but is satisfying to PR people. They are ahead of management consultants, marketing, advertising people and journalists as well as university professors. Later (p. 229) he argues that their formal education has four aspects: abstraction, system thinking, experimentation and collaboration.
11 BBC TV News, evening of 8.1.99, for example. But did the organisers – and the media – note that MPs were not in session?
12 See *The Guardian* 4.2.99, p. 5, 'Badger cull may be widened to slow TB'.
13 A *PR Week* survey (21.8.98, pp. 11–18) of in-house departments found that 55% of respondents say that their budget is derived from marketing resources and that media relations is the largest single spend in the overall budget at 16%, with corporate and financial PR at 8% each.
14 Dr. Raymond Boyle, who studied police and media relations in Strathclyde, gave the example of a media campaign warning an area in advance of extra policing to combat car theft and this warning having a crime reduction effect in itself. He was talking at the PREF conference, Leeds Metro University, 3–5 September 1998.
15 *The Times* 18.1.99, p. 5, 'Police search kept low-key' reported that the police did not 'want to push them [the Bramleys] into a corner'.
16 See *PR Week* editions of 27.3.97, p. 9, 'Investing in PR talent' and of 26.3.99, p. 15 'Modern Values'.
17 Becoming the story was the proximate cause of the downfall of the Chancellor of the Exchequer's spin doctor Charlie Whelan in January 1999. See *The Times*, 15.1.99, p. 38, 'Pitfalls of the PR superstar' for a judgement about how public prominence could affect Sophie Rhys-Jones, wife of Prince Edward.
18 If it can be imagined that newsworthy people need the PR equivalent of a per-sonal fitness plan, read *The Independent* Review, 9.2.99, p. 14, 'Crisis? What Crisis?'
19 *The Times*, 28.1.99, p. 16, 'Brussels spin doctors told truth must often be hidden' reported that an internal advice note for EU media spokespeople asked for 'hypocrisy' in dealing with the press: 'It is necessary to learn how to control aspects of information ... which could give rise to bad interpretation.'
20 It comes up frequently in interviews and in short lists of qualifications for top

jobs. See *PR Week*, 8.1.99, p. 24, for the profile of a communications director of a Whitehall department.

21 See *PR Week* Top 150, 26.4.98, p. 59. The agencies had a total of 4,281 staff.

22 See the London *Evening Standard*, 8.1.99 for an article by Simon Mills dismissing PR women as having a 'nice telephone manner' and the ability to 'organise a decent party'.

23 According to the 1998 IPR membership survey: done in April; mailed to 5,500 members and attracted a 20% response rate.

24 The Open University's public relations department changed its name to communications because the change 'reflects the importance of the University communicating with its external as well as internal audiences. The team felt that Communications more accurately describes what and how they do that'. See *Open House*, January 1999, no. 358, p. 4. See *PR Week*, 29.1.99, p. 28, 'New top dog at Cohn and Wolfe' for a similar view and the comment that 'PR as a term carrries too much baggage'.

25 The re-balancing is also semantic: 'vocational education' is now under competition in the UK from 'professional education'. In the USA, this latter term is more accepted and is a descriptor for one approach to the PR curriculum on campus: the balance of control should be with PR people. See Kruckeberg (1998).

26 The ground for this bridging research has already been laid by Goldenberg (1975), Ericson *et al.* (1989) and Schlesinger and Tumber (1994) in their 'externalist' studies of media sources. The dominant conceptual focus has been the media and effects outwards: a new one could be the PR activities of organisations/groups and effects on the media and beyond.

27 The title is *Age of Propaganda* and the sub-title *The Everyday Use and Abuse of Persuasion*. However, the index carries no references to persuasion or public relations. Page 9 states that 'Not all persuasion is propaganda'.

28 Sources are the IPR's annual reports and accounts.

29 See *PR Week*, 1.1.99, p. 9: 'I'm in public relations and I'm proud of it' as an example of this approach with the emphasis on creativity as the distinguishing feature of the industry. It is not clear how this PR loyalist approach regards a booklet entitled 'The Quick and Dirty Guide to PR', published by the Local Government group of the IPR and sponsored by Northcliffe Newspapers.

30 Unacceptable they may be but used they are: journalists admitted to manipulation by Greenpeace over Brent Spar, but still used their PR material.

31 If PR was reasoned persuasion, it would be interesting to see the effect on the volume of PR material put out by PR people.

11 A beneficial PR

1 Boorstin (1961, pp. 34–5) lists the following as characteristics of propaganda: information intentionally biased to an audience which has a 'willingness to be inflamed' and 'our desire to be aroused'; the substitution of opinion for facts; purposeful lies; leading an audience to believe that truth is simpler, more intelligible than it is; an oversimplification of experience.

2 This redistributive role for PR would seem to cover or fall between two 'contrasting presuppositions' about PR made by Grunig and Grunig (1992), p. 8: PR maintains a system of social privilege or PR leads to social reform.

3 Hiebert (1966) ends his biography of Ivy Lee (p. 317) with the hope that believers in 'a free and open society will in time devise controls of public relations without destroying its essential usefulness'. Pimlott (1951) implied

controls. In the UK today, Simon Lewis, the Queen's Communication Secretary, has warned of the possibility of regulation (see Chapter 2).

4   Ivy Lee drew up a four point plan for the 'publicity bureau' of the Electric Railway Association. The first was the known sourcing of all PR material. See Hiebert 1966, p. 89. Known sourcing applies to people as well as paper and the internet. MPs should know the PR connections of colleagues when they sit on the Commons Agriculture Select Committee. *The Observer* 11.7.99, p. 3, reports that Peter Luff MP, its chairman, apologised for not telling other members he was paid £10,000 for advice to Bell Pottinger who lists Monsanto as a client.

5   PR codes of conduct recognise the public interest. See PRCA's *Aims and Activities* document (1996), p. 5, 'Professional Charter', section 2 headed 'Conduct Towards The Public, The Media and Other Professionals'.

6   The public sphere of Habermas accords in part with the civil association concept of Oakeshott (1975): a relationship of equals, a self-sufficient relationship, not for a purpose. Oakeshott distinguished this from enterprise association: voluntary agreement among individuals to associate in the pursuit of a common purpose.

7   The forms do not include advertising and the aspects do not include marketing PR. The persuasive sphere is not concerned with commercial communications as instrumentalities but it could be concerned with them as issues and as policy in the political economy.

8   Abercrombie *et al.* (1980) offer a more optimistic view about a populous democracy: that the interests of dominant groups in liberal democracies are widely rejected by less powerful groups; that the latter have resistant culture and organisations.

9   See Jonathan Freedland (1989, p. 231) for a case for 'empowered individuals and communities'.

10 If the concept of memetics is considered – see Dawkins and *The Selfish Gene* – the proposition that 'more pluralism leads to more PR' becomes 'more PR leads to more pluralism'. Is PR a replicator of ideas over generations about the political economy? Is it an efficient and effective one?

11 Heath uses this phrase in 'A Rhetorical Perspective of PR' (1992), borrowing it from the American scholar of rhetoric Kenneth Burke (1945/1969).

12 See Haslett (1994) for a discussion on current capitalism and morality which ends with an implied stakeholding model: equal access to necessities and opportunities; to productivity and freedom.

13 See *PR Week*, 24.9.99, p. 3. He also notes, elliptically, that 'the advertising industry has the Advertising Standards Authority'.

14 Lady Thornton who had previously worked for the Co-operative Wholesale Society as public affairs and policy adviser for twelve years. See *PR Week*, 15.1.99, p. 7.

15 A claim made by Prof. Tim Lang on the Food Programme, BBC Radio 4, 27.3.99, 11 a.m. The programme is the source of the other claims and data about food activism. For more on food activism as a challenge to public policy-making, see *The Guardian* G2 section, p. 2, 7.6.99. The article is illustrated by a good example of PR pseudo-event.

16 Is the case for the reform of PR and its acceptance or rejection by PR people itself a case study about the role of reasoned persuasion? I am indebted to Richard Reader for the observation.

17 At the time of the Kosovo war from March 1999, journalists and commentators juxtaposed references to propaganda and PR as in phrases such as 'Nato propaganda about bombing civilians was a bad PR operation'.

18 The active regulation of advertising and the lack in PR raises the possibility of using PR to publish statements that were banned in advertisements. See 20 below. And also see *PR Week*, 3.9.99, p. 15: 'The death knell is beginning to toll across Europe for TV advertising aimed at kids, and PR people are coming up with more innovative methods of marketing to the under-12s'. Toy makers 'will have to think more laterally about getting their messages across, relying more on clever PR.'

19 The Advertising Standards Authority criticised ads in a draft report (see *The Guardian*, 1.3.99, p. 5, 'Monsanto ads condemned') published by Monsanto about genetically modified food as 'confusing, misleading, unproven and wrong'. The ads were complained of by The Green Party, GeneWatch, the Soil Association and the Royal Society for the Protection of Birds. Four complaints were upheld and nine rejected. See *The Guardian*, 6.11.99, p. 9, 'Monsanto GM food ads found to mislead'. TV advertising is regulated by The Independent Television Commission (ITC) which in spring 1999 ran a TV ad campaign under the slogan 'We're here to ITC they don't get away with it'.

20 The advertising industry body, the Advertising Association, is aware that flouting its rules is a form of promotion. See its briefing note 'Advertising and self-regulation' by Andrew Brown, June 1995 for the p. 4 section 'Deliberately breaking the rules to achieve PR'. It is 'an area currently concerning the business'.

21 *The Observer* work section 27.6.99, p. 16, reports in 'Canny companies come clean' that a survey of 98 of the FTSE 100 companies by Pensions and Investment Research Consultants found that 79 report in some way on social matters, though only 14 produce dedicated reports.

22 See *PR Week*, 18.6.99, pp. 8–9, 'Setting business guidelines for PR'. The aim is to 'encourage the public relations industry to examine its own and related disciplines to improve the quality of in-house and consultancy practice'.

23 The suggestion was part of his response to the question 'If propaganda and public relations can be used to cause social harm, how can society, the general public and individuals be protected from their misuse?' He listed seven points based on awareness, education and codes of conduct. See Traverse-Healy (1988) p. 17.

24 See the *Independent*, 23.9.98, p. 9.

25 See Moloney in *PR Week*, 13.6.96, p. 6, 'Why this cause célèbre has done PR a favour', and an undergraduate third year dissertation by Robin Baker of Bournemouth University on the subject.

26 Thanks to Ian Mayes, Readers' Editor of *The Guardian* for views (21.4.99).

27 The APPC calls for its code to be incorporated into staff contracts and handbooks. See *PR Week*, 8.1.99, p. 4, 'APPC members to face shake up on code guidelines'.

28 See *PR Week*, 2.4.99, p. 2, 'PRCA calls for further lobbyist regulation'. The call came from the chairman of the PRCA public affairs committee.

29 ibid, p. 7.

30 *The Independent*, 30.5.99, p. 9, 'Lobbyist gifts are banned for Scots'.

31 Broached by Traverse-Healy (1988), p. 18.

32 See *PR Week*, 8.1.99, p. 9, 'We must not sell ourselves short to Parliament'.

33 See *PR Week*, 23.7.99, p. 1, 'IPR head calls for regulatory body for all lobbyists'.

Bibliography

Abercrombie, N., Hill, S. and Turner, B. (1980) *The Dominant Ideology Thesis*, London: George Allen & Unwin.

Adonis, A. and Pollard, S. (1997) *A Class Act*, London: Hamish Hamilton.

Alderman, G. (1984) *Pressure Groups and Government in Great Britain*, London: Longman.

Alvesson, M. and Willmot, H. (1992) *Critical Management Studies*, London: Sage.

Aronoff, C. and Baskin, O. (1983) *Public Relations: The profession and the practice*, St. Paul, Minn: West Publishing.

Baistow, T. (1985) *Fourth-Rate Estate: Anatomy of Fleet Street*, London: Comedia.

Baker, R.S. (1906) 'Railroads on trial', *McClure's Magazine*, 26 March, pp. 535–49.

Banks, S. (1995) *Multicultural Public Relations*, London: Sage.

Barnard, C. (1968, 2nd edn.) *The Functions of the Executive*, Massachusetts: Harvard University Press.

Barney, R. and Black, J. (1994) 'Ethics and professional persuasive communications', *Public Relations Review*, 20, 3, pp. 233–48.

BDO Stoy Hayward (1994) *The Public Relations Sector*, London: Department of Trade and Industry.

Beale, H. (1936) *Are American Teachers Free?*, New York: Octagon Books.

Bell, Q. (1991) *The PR Business*, London: Kogan Page.

Bernays, E. (1923) *Crystallizing Public Opinion*, New York: Boni & Liveright.

—— (1928) *Propaganda*, New York: Liveright.

—— (1947) 'Engineering of consent', *Annals of the American Academy of Political and Social Science*, 250 (March), pp. 113–20.

Black, S. (1962, 1st edn.) *Practical Public Relations*, London: Pitman.

—— (1973) *The Institute of Public Relations 1938–73: The first twenty five years*, London: The IPR.

—— (1989) *Introduction To Public Relations*, London: Mondino Press.

Blackmore, S. (1999) *Meme Machine*, Oxford: OUP.

Blumler, J. and Gurevitch, M. (1981) 'Politicians and the press: An essay in role relationships', in D. Nimmo and K. Sanders (eds.) *Handbook of Political Communication*, London: Sage.

Blyskal, J. and Blyskal, M. (1985) *PR: How the Public Relations Industry Writes the News*, New York: William Marrow.

Boorstin, D (1961) *The Image, or, What happened to the American Dream*, London: Weidenfeld and Nicholson.

Brady, R. (1943) *Business as a System of Power*, New York: Columbia University Press.

Brebner, J. (1949) *Public Relations and Publicity*, London: National Council of Social Science.

Brittan, S. (1995) *Capitalism with a Human Face*, London: Edward Elgar.

Bryant, B. (1996) *Twyford Down*, London: E & FN Spon.

Burke, K. (1969) *A Grammar of Motives*, Berkeley: University of California Press. (Original edition published 1945)

Caporaso, J. and Levine, D. (1992) *Theories of Political Economy*, Cambridge, CUP.

Carey, A. (1995) *Taking The Risk Out of Democracy*, Sydney: UNSW Press. (Ed. Lowrey, A)

Carty, F. (1992) *Farewell to Hype*, Dublin: Able Press.

Chonko, L., (1995) *Ethical Decision Making in Marketing*, London: Sage.

Cialdini, R. (1993) *Influence: The psychology of persuasion*, (2nd edn.) New York: Quill William Morrow.

Cochran, T.C. and Miller, W. (1942) The Age of Enterprise: A social history of industrial America, New York: Macmillan.

Cohen, J. and Rogers, J. (1995) *Associations and Democracy*, London: Verso.

Cohen, S. and Young, J. (eds.) (1973) *The Manufacture of News*, London: Constable.

Coogan, T. (1993) *De Valera*, London: Arrow Books.

Creeden, P. (1991) 'Public relations and "women's work": Toward a feminist analysis of public relations role', *Public Relations Research Annual*, Grunig, L. and Grunig, J. (eds.) New Jersey: Lawrence Erlbaum Associates, vol. 3, pp. 67–84.

Curran, J. and Seaton, J. (1988, 3rd edn.) *Power without Responsibility: Press and broadcasting in Britain*, London: Routledge.

Cutlip, S., Center, A. and Broom, G. (2000) *Effective Public Relations*, (8th edn.) London: Prentice Hall International.

Dahl, R. (1961) *Who Governs*, New Haven: Yale University Press.

—— (1971) *Polyarchy: Participation and opposition*, New Haven: Yale University Press.

—— (1982) *Dilemmas of Pluralist Democracy*, New Haven: Yale University Press.

—— (1989) *Democracy and its Critics*, New Haven: Yale University Press.

Dartnell's Public Relations Handbook (1996; 4th edn.), Chicago: Dartnell.

Daymon, C. (1998) 'Culture formation during industry transformation: life in a new British television station', in conference proceedings (September) of *British Academy of Management*, University of Nottingham.

—— (2000) 'Leadership and emerging cultural patterns in a new television station', *Studies in Cultures, Organisations and Societies*, vol. 6, forthcoming autumn edition.

Deacon, D. and Golding, P. (1994) *Taxation and Representation: The media, political communication and the poll tax*, London: John Libbey.

Dilenschneider, R. (1999) 'The year ahead', *Communication World*, vol. 16, no. 3, pp. 13–21, San Francisco: IABC.

Directory of British Associations (1998) Beckenham, London: CBD Research.

Dolphin, R. (1999) *The Fundamentals of Corporate Communications*, Oxford: Butterworth-Heinemann.

Dowling, G. (1994) *Corporate Reputations*, London: Longman.

Dozier, D. and Ehling, W. (1992) 'Evaluation of public relations programs', in J. Grunig (ed.) *Excellence in Public Relations and Communicative Management*, Hove: Lawrence Erlbaum.

Elkington, J. and Hailes, J. (1998) *Manual 2000 Life Choices For the Future You Want*, London, Hodder & Stoughton.

Encyclopedia of the Social Sciences (1933) New York: Macmillan.

Ericson, R., Baranek, P. and Chan, J. (1989) *Negotiating Control: A study of news sources*, Milton Keynes: Open University Press.

Ewen, P. (1996) *PR! A Social History of Spin*, New York: Basic Books.

Ewles, L. and Simnett, I. (1985) *Promoting Health*, Chichester: John Wiley.

Fallows, J. (1996) *Breaking the News: How the media undermine American democracy*, New York: Random House.

Fill, C. (1999) *Marketing Communications*, (2nd edn.) Hemel Hempstead: Prentice Hall.

Finer, S. (1958) *Anonymous Empire: A study of the lobby in Great Britain*, London: Pall Mall.

Franklin, B. (1994) *Packaging Politics: Political communications in Britain's media democracy*, London: Edward Arnold.

—— (1997) *Newszak and The News Media*, London: Edward Arnold.

—— (1998) *Tough on Soundbites, Tough on the Causes of Soundbites*, London: Catalyst Trust.

Freedland, J. (1998) *Bring Home The Revolution*, London: Fourth Estate.

Freidenberg, R. (1997) *Communication Consultants in Political Campaigns*, Connecticut: Praeger.

Gabriel, Y. and Lang, T. (1995) *The Unmanageable Consumer*, London: Sage.

Gandy, O. (1982) *Beyond Agenda Setting: Information subsidies and public policy*, Norwood, USA: Ablex.

Gillman, F. (1978) 'Public relations in the United Kingdom prior to 1948', *Journal of the International Public Relations Association*, April, vol. 2, 1, pp. 43–50.

Glasgow University Media Group (1982) *Really Bad News*, London: Writers and Readers Publishing Co-operative.

Goldenberg, E. (1975) *Making the Papers*, Massachusetts: Lexington Books.

Goldman, E. (1948) *Two-Way Street: The emergence of the public relations counsel*, Boston: Bellman.

Grant, M. (1994) *Propaganda and the Role of the State in Inter-War Years*, Oxford: OUP.

Grant, W. (1989) *Pressure Groups, Politics and Democracy*, London: Philip Allan.

Grant, W. (1995) *Pressure Groups, Politics and Democracy in Britain*, (2nd edn.) Hemel Hempstead: Harvester Wheatsheaf.

Gray, R. and Hobsbawn, J. (1996) *Cosmopolitan Guide to Working in PR and Advertising*, London: Penguin.

Greenwood, J. and Thomas, C. (1998) 'Regulating lobbying in the Western World', *Parliamentary Affairs*, vol. 51, no. 4, pp. 487–500.

Greer, G. (1999) *The Whole Woman*, London: Anchor.

Gregory, A. (1996) *Planning and Managing a Public Relations Campaign*, London: IPR/Kogan Page.

Grunig, J. (1989) 'Presuppositions as framework for PR theory', C. Botan and V. Hazleton (eds.) *Public Relations Theory*, Hove: Lawrence Erlbaum.

—— (1992a) 'Communication, public relations, and effective organisations: An overview of the book', in Grunig, J. (ed.) *Excellence in Public Relations and Communication Management*, Hove: Lawrence Erlbaum, pp. 1–28.

—— (ed.) (1992b) *Excellence in Public Relations and Communications Management*, Hove: Lawrence Erlbaum Associates.

—— (1992c) *Public Relations as a two-way symmetrical process*, Culemborg, Holland: Phaedon. (Speech to the School of Journalism and Communications, Utrecht)

Grunig, J. and Grunig, L. (1992) 'Models of public relations and communications', in J. Grunig (ed.) *Excellence in Public Relations and Communicative Management*, Hove: Lawrence Erlbaum.

Grunig, J. and Hunt, T. (1984) *Managing Public Relations*, New York: Holt, Rinehart & Winston.

Grunig, J. and White, J. (1992) 'The effects of worldviews on public relations', in J. Grunig (ed.) *Excellence in Public Relations and Communication Management*, Hove: Lawrence Erlbaum.

Grunig, L. (1995) 'Empowering women and culturally diverse employees', in D. Dozier *et al. Manager's Guide to Excellence in Public Relations and Communication Management*, Hove: Lawrence Erlbaum.

Habermas, J. (1989) *The Structural Transformation of the Public Sphere*, MIT Press: Massachusetts. (Original German edition 1962.)

Halfon, R. (1998) *Corporate Irresponsibility: Is business appeasing anti-business activities?*, London: Adam Smith Institute.

Haralambos, M. (1985) *Sociology*, (2nd edn.) Slough: University Tutorial Press.

Hargie, O., Dickson, D. and Tourish, D. (1999) *Communication in Management*, Aldershot: Gower.

Harris, P. and Lock, A. (1996) 'Machiavellian Marketing: The development of political marketing in the UK', *Journal of Marketing Management*, vol. 12, 4, pp. 313–28.

Harris, P., Moss, D. and Vetter, N. (1999) 'Machiavelli's legacy to public affairs: A modern tale of servants and princes in UK organisations', *Journal of Communication Management*, vol. 3, no. 3, pp. 201–17.

Harris, T. (1991) *The Marketer's Guide to Public Relations*, New York: John Wiley.

Harrison, S. (1994) 'Codes of practice and ethics in the UK communications industry', *Business Ethics*, vol. 3, 2, pp. 109–16.

—— (1995) *Public Relations: An introduction*, London: Routledge.

—— (1996) 'Teaching the truth', a paper at *Public Relations Educators' Forum*, St. Mark and St. John College, Plymouth, March 24–26. (Harrison is at Leeds Metropolitan University.)

—— (1998) 'The Local Government Agenda: News from the town hall', in Franklin, B. and Murphy, D. (eds.) *Making The Local News*, London: Routledge.

—— (ed.) (1999) *Disasters and the Media*, Basingstoke: Macmillan Business.

Hart, N. (1987) *Effective Public Relations: Applying public relations in business and industry*, Maidenhead: McGraw-Hill.

Haslett, D. (1994) *Capitalism with Morality*, Oxford: Oxford University Press.

Hawthorn, J. (ed.) (1987) *Propaganda, Persuasion and Polemic*, London: Edward Arnold.

Haywood, R. (1990) *All About Public Relations: How to build business success on good communications*, (2nd edn.) Maidenhead: McGraw-Hill.

Heath R. (1992) 'The Wrangle in the Marketplace: A rhetorical perspective of public relations', in E. Toth and R. Heath, *Rhetorical and Critical Approaches to Public Relations*, New Jersey: Lawrence Erlbaum.

Herman, E. and Chomsky, N. (1988) *Manufacturing Consent*, New York: Pantheon Books.

Hiebert, R. (1966) *Courtier to the Crowd*, Ames, Io: Iowa State University Press.

Holbrook, T. (1996) *Do Campaigns Matter?*, London: Sage.

Hollingsworth, M. (1997) *The Ultimate Spin Doctor: The life and times of Tim Bell*, London: Hodder & Stoughton.

Holtz, S. (1998) *Public Relations on the Net*, New York: American Management Association.

Holub, R. (1991) *Jürgen Habermas: Critic in the public sphere*, London: Routledge.

Humphrys, J. (1999) *Devil's Advocate*, London: Hutchinson.

Hutton, W. (1999) *The Stakeholding Society*, Cambridge: Polity Press.

IPR (1998) *Handbook*, IPR: London.

IPR (1998) *Managing Communication in a Changing World*, IPR: London.

James, B. and Moloney, K. (1995) *Towards A Classification of Environmental Groups*, working paper: Bournemouth University.

Jefkins, F. (1988) *Public Relations Techniques*, London: Heinemann Professional Publishing.

Jensen, J. (1997) *Ethical Issues in the Communication Process*, New Jersey: Lawrence Erlbaum.

Jones, N. (1995) *Soundbites and Spindoctors*, London: Cassells.

—— (1997) *How The General Election Was Won and Lost*, London: Indigo.

—— (1999) *Sultans of Spin*, London: Victor Gollancz.

Jordan, G. (1998) 'Towards regulation in the UK: From "general good sense" to "formalised rules" ', *Parliamentary Affairs*, vol. 51, no. 4, pp. 524–38.

Jowett, G. and O'Donnell, V. (1992) *Propaganda and Persuasion*, London: Sage.

Keen, C. and Greenall, J. (1987) *Public Relations Management in Colleges, Polytechnics and Universities*, Banbury: HEIST Publications.

Kemp, G. 'Public relations in marketing', in W. Howard (ed.) (1988) *The Practice of Public Relations*, (3rd edn.) London: Heinemann, pp. 125–36.

Kitchen, P. (ed.) (1997) *Public Relations: Principles and practice*, London: International Thomson Business Press.

Kitchen, P. and Papasolomou, I. (1997) 'The emergence of marketing PR', in P. Kitchen (ed.) *Public Relations: Principles and Practice*, London: International Thomson Business Press, pp. 239–71.

Kotler, P. (1997) *Marketing Management*, (9th edn.) New Jersey: Prentice Hall.

Kotler, P. and Mindak, W. (1978) 'Marketing and Public Relations', *Journal of Marketing*, 42, October, pp. 13–20.

Korten, D. (1995) *When Corporations Rule The World*, New York: Kunarian Press.

Kruckeberg D. (1998) 'The Future of PR Education: Some Recommendations', *Public Relations Review*, vol. 24, 2, pp. 235–47.

Kruckeberg, D. and Starck, K. (1988) *Public Relations and Community*, Westport, Conn: Praeger.

Kumar, K. (1993) 'Civil Society: an inquiry into the usefulness of an historical term', *British Journal of Sociology*, vol. 44, no. 3, September 1993.

Langer, J. (1998) *Tabloid Television: Popular journalism and the 'other' news*, London: Routledge.

Labour Market Trends, London: Central Statistical Office.

Le Bon, G. (1896) *The Crowd: A study of the popular mind*, London: Macmillan.

L'Etang, J. (1996) 'Public relations as diplomacy', in J. L'Etang and M. Pieczka (eds.) *Critical Perspectives in Public Relations*, London: International Thomson Business Press.

—— (1998) 'The development of British public relations in the twentieth century', for the *IAMCR Conference*, Glasgow. Later published as 'State propaganda and bureaucratic intelligence: The creation of public relations in the 20th century', *Public Relations Review*, 24(4) Winter 1998, pp. 413–41, Maryland: JAI Press.

—— (1999) 'Grierson's influence on the formation and emergent values of the public relations industry in Britain', at *Breaking the Boundaries* conference, Stirling University, 28–31 January 1999.

Lindblom, C. (1997) *Politics and Markets*, New York: Basic Books.

Lippmann, W. (1919) 'Liberty and news', *Atlantic Monthly*, December, pp. 779–87.

—— (1922) *Public Opinion*, London: George Allen & Unwin.

Mallinson, W. (1996) *Public Lies and Public Truths*, London: Cassell.

Mansbridge, J. (1983) *Beyond Adversary Democracy*, London: University of Chicago Press.

Marchand, R. (1998) *Creating the Corporate Soul: The rise of public relations and corporate imagery in American big business*, Berkeley: University of California Press.

Martin, J. (1992) *Cultures in Organisations: Three perspectives*, New York: OUP.

McAlpine, A. (1997) *The New Machiavelli*, London: Aurum Press.

McElreath, M. (1997) *Managing Systematic and Ethical Public Relations Campaigns*, (2nd edn.) London: Brown & Benchmark.

McIntosh, D. and McIntosh, A. (1985) *A Basic PR Guide for Charities*, London: The Directory of Social Change.

McNair, B. (1995) *An Introduction to Political Communication*, London: Routledge.

—— (1996) 'Performance in politics and the politics of performance' in J. L'Etang and M. Pieczka (eds.) *Critical Perspectives in Public Relations*, London: International Thomson Business Press, pp. 35–54.

McQuail, D. (1987) *Mass Communication Theory*, London: Sage.

McSmith, A. (1997) *Faces of Labour: The inside story*, London: Verso.

Mattelart, A. and Mattelart, M. (1998) *Theories of Communication*, London: Sage.

Michie, D. (1998) *The Invisible Persuaders*, London: Transworld Publishers.

Miller, C. (1987) *Lobbying Government*, Oxford: Blackwell.

Miller, G. (1989) 'Persuasion and public relations: Two "Ps" in a pod', in G. Botan and V. Hazleton (eds.) *Public Relations Theory*, Hillsdale: Lawrence Erlbaum Associates, pp. 45–66.

Miller, K (1999) 'Public relations in film and fiction: 1930s to 1995', *Journal of Public Relations Research*, 11, 1, pp. 3–28.

Moloney, K. (1996) *Lobbyists for Hire*, Aldershot: Dartmouth Press.

—— (1997) 'Teaching public relations in UK universities: Teaching about a practice with an unpleasant odour attached', *Working Papers in Public Relations Research, no 1*, Bournemouth University. ISBN 1-85899-026-2

—— (1998) 'It's a PR job: A question of reputation and its consequences for teaching, researching and doing PR', *Working Paper in Public Relations Research no. 2*, Bournemouth University. ISBN 1-85899-071-8

—— (1999) 'Publicists – distribution workers in the pleasure economy of the film industry', in J. Bignell (ed.) *Writing and Cinema*, Harlow: Longman.

—— (2000) 'Nicco and Charlie: two political servants', in P. Harris et al. (eds) *Machiavelli, Marketing and Management*, London: Routledge, pp. 164–75.

Moloney, K. and Noble, P. (1999) 'Where are they now: a survey of six years of PR graduates', at the International Association of Business Communicators annual conference, London, 23 February. (Available from Bournemouth University.)

Moore, S. (1996) *Introduction to Public Relations*, London, Cassell.

Moss, D. and Warnaby, G. (1997) 'The role of public relations in organisations', in

P. Kitchen (ed.) *Public Relations Principles and Practice*, London: International Thomson Business Press.

Murphy, P. (1991) 'The limits to symmetry: A game theory to symmetric and asymmetric public relations', in L. Grunig and J. Grunig (eds.) *Public Relations Research Annual*, vol. 3, Hillside, New Jersey: Lawrence Erlbaum.

Nelson, J. (1992) *Sultans of Sleaze: Public relations and the media*, Monroe, Maine: Common Courage Press.

Nightingale, G. (1989) *Nightingales*, The Hague: Burson marstellar BV.

Nolan (1995) *First Report of the Committee on Standards in Public Life*, London, HMSO, Cm 2850–1.

Norris, P., Curtice, J., Sanders, D., Scammell, M. and Semetko, H. (1999) *On Message: Communicating the campaign*, London: Sage.

Oakeshott, M. (1975) *On Human Conduct*, London: Clarendon.

Olasky, M. (1987) *Corporate Public Relations: A new historical perspective*, Hove: Lawrence Erlbaum.

Olson, M. (1982) *The Rise and Decline of Nation*, New Haven: Yale University Press.

O'Shaughnessy, N. (1996) 'Social propaganda and social marketing', *European Journal of Marketing*, vol. 30, 10–11, pp. 62–75.

—— (1999) paper on political marketing as a hybrid concept, for Political Marketing conference, 15–16 Sept, Bournemouth University.

Packard, V. (1981) *The Hidden Persuaders*, (2nd edn. 1st edn.: 1957) London: Penguin.

Pearson, R. (1989) 'Beyond ethical relativism in public relations', in J. Grunig and L. Grunig (eds.) *Public Relations Research Annual*, vol. 1, pp. 67–86, Hillsdale, NJ: Lawrence Erlbaum.

Pilling, R. (1998) 'The changing role of the local journalist', in B. Franklin and D. Murphy (eds.) *Making The Local News*, London: Routledge.

Pimlott, J. (1951) *Public Relations and American Democracy*, Princeton: Princeton University Press.

Plender, J. (1997) *A Stake in the Future*, London: Nicholas Brealey.

Pratkanis, A. and Aronson, E. (1992) *Age of Propaganda*, New York: Freeman.

The Quick and Dirty Guide to PR (1998) London: Institute of Public Relations.

Rees, L. (1992) *Selling Politics*, London: BBC Books.

Reich, R. (1991) *The Work of Nations*, New York: Knopf.

Richards, P. (1998) *Be Your Own Spin Doctor*, Harrogate: Take That.

Robins, K., Webster, F. and Pickering, M. 'Propaganda, information and social control', in J. Hawthorn (ed.) (1987) *Propaganda, Persuasion and Polemic*, London: Edward Arnold.

Rosenbaum, M. (1997) *From Soapbox to Soundbite: Party political campaigning in Britain since 1945*, London: Macmillan.

Scammell, M. (1995) *Designer Politics: How elections are won*, London: Macmillan.

Schlesinger, P. and Tumber, H. (1994) *Reporting Crime: The media politics of criminal justice*, Oxford: Clarendon Press.

Schnattschneider, E. (1975, reissued) *The Semisovereign People*, Hinsdale, Illinois: The Dryden Press.

Seib, P. and Fitzpatrick, K. (1995) *Public Relations Ethics*, Fort Worth: Harcourt Brace.

Seitel, F. (1995) *The Practice of PR*, (6th edn.) New Jersey: Prentice Hall.

Sennett, R. (1998) *The Corrosion of Character*, New York: Norton.

Shaw, R. (1996) *The Activist's Handbook*, London: University of California Press.

Sighele, S. (1898) *Psychology of Sects*, Paris: Giard and Briere. (Reprinted in translation 1975, New York: Arno Press.)

Silver, R. (ed.) (1985) *Health Services Public Relations*, London: King Edward's Hospital.

Sinclair, J. (1987) *Images Incorporated*, London: Croom Helm.

Smith, T. and Young, A. (1996) *The Fixers: Crisis management in British politics*, Aldershot: Dartmouth Press.

Smythe, J., Dorward, C. and Reback, J. (1992) *Corporate Reputation: Managing the new strategic asset*, London: Century Business.

Sperber, N. and Lerbinger, D. (1982) *Managers' Public Relations Handbook*, Reading, Ma: Addison Wesley.

Spicer, C. (1997) *Organisational Public Relations: A political perspective*, Mahwah: Lawrence Erlbaum.

Sproule, J. (1997) *Propaganda and Democracy*, Cambridge: CUP.

Stauber, J. and Rampton, S. (1995) *Toxic Sludge is Good for You*, Maine: Common Courage Press.

Susskind, L. and Field, P. (1996) *Dealing With An Angry Public: The mutual gains approach to resolving disputes*, New York: The Free Press.

Tannen, D. (1998) *The Argument Culture: Changing the way we argue and debate*, London: Virago.

Tarrow, S. (1994) *Power in Movement*, Cambridge: CUP.

Tedlow, R. (1974) *Keeping the Corporate Image*, Connecticut: JAI Press.

Thorson, E. and Moore, J. (1996) *Integrated Communication: Synergy of persuasive voices*, New Jersey: Lawrence Erlbaum.

Trotter, W. (1916) *Instincts of the Herd in Peace and War*, London: Macmillan.

Traverse-Healy, T. (1988) *Public Relations And Propaganda – Values Compared*, Gold Paper No 6, Geneva: International Public Relations Association.

Tutt, B. (1999) 'Political marketing, partisan politics and the televising of the House of Commons', at political marketing conference, Bournemouth University, 15–16 September.

Tye, L. (1998) *The Father of Spin: Edward L. Bernays and the birth of public relations*, New York: Crown.

Useem, M. (1984) *The Inner Circle*, New York: Oxford University Press.

van Riel, C. (1995) *Principles of Corporate Communication*, London: Prentice Hall

Vogel, D. (1996) *Kindred Strangers: The uneasy relationship between politics and business in America*, New Jersey: Princeton University Press.

Wallas, G. (1908) *Human Nature in Politics*, London: Constable.

Ward, S. (1992) *Getting the Message Across*, London: Journeyman.

Warren, D. (1996) *Charles Caughlin, the Father of Hate Radio*, New York: Free Press.

Webster, F. (1995) *Theories of the Information Society*, London: Routledge.

Wernick, A. (1991) *Promotional Culture*, London: Sage.

West, P. (1985) *Educational Public Relations*, London: Sage.

West, R. (1963) *PR The Fifth Estate*, London: Mayflower Books.

White, J. (1991) *How to Understand and Manage Public Relations*, London: Business Books.

White, J. and Mazur, L. (1995) *Strategic Communications Management*, Wokingham: Addison-Wesley Publishing, and London: Economist Intelligence Unit.

Williams, F. (1946) *Press, Parliament and People*, London: Heinemann.

Wragg, D. (1987) *Public Relations for Sales and Marketing Communications*, London: Kogan Page.

Wright, D. (1993) 'Enforcement Dilemma: Voluntary nature of public relations codes', *Public Relations Review*, vol. 19, 1, pp. 13–20.

Wring, D. (1997) 'Reconciling marketing with political science', *Journal of Marketing Management*, vol. 13, 7, pp. 651–63.

—— (1998) 'A "spin" off the old wheel: The Machiavellian role of Morrison and Mandelson as political communicators', in *Proceedings of the Machiavelli at 500 Conference*, 18–19 May 1998: Centre for Corporate and Public Affairs, Manchester Metropolitan University'.

Index